CLAIMING POWER IN
DOCTOR–PATIENT TALK

LOCATING DIALECT IN DISCOURSE
The Language of Honest Men and Bonnie Lasses in Ayr
Ronald K.S. Macaulay

ENGLISH IN ITS SOCIAL CONTEXTS
Essays in Historical Sociolinguistics
Edited by Tim W. Machan and Charles T. Scott

COHERENCE IN PSYCHOTIC DISCOURSE
Branca Telles Ribeiro

SOCIOLINGUISTIC PERSPECTIVES ON REGISTER
Edited by Douglas Biber and Edward Finegan

GENDER AND CONVERSATIONAL INTERACTION
Edited by Deborah Tannen

THERAPEUTIC WAYS WITH WORDS
Kathleen Warden Ferrara

SOCIOLINGUISTIC PERSPECTIVES
Papers on Language in Society, 1959–1994
Charles Ferguson
Edited by Thom Huebner

THE LINGUISTIC INDIVIDUAL
Self-Expression in Language and Linguistics
Barbara Johnstone

THE DISCOURSE OF CLASSIFIED ADVERTISING
Exploring the Nature of Linguistic Simplicity
Paul Bruthiaux

QUEERLY PHRASED
Language, Gender, and Sexuality
Edited by Anna Livia and Kira Hall

CLAIMING POWER IN DOCTOR–PATIENT TALK
Nancy Ainsworth-Vaughn

CLAIMING POWER IN DOCTOR–PATIENT TALK

NANCY AINSWORTH–VAUGHN

New York   Oxford
OXFORD UNIVERSITY PRESS
1998

Oxford University Press

Oxford   New York
Athens   Auckland   Bangkok   Bogota   Bombay
Buenos Aires   Calcutta   Cape Town   Dar es Salaam
Delhi   Florence   Hong Kong   Istanbul   Karachi
Kuala Lumpur   Madras   Madrid   Melbourne
Mexico City   Nairobi   Paris   Singapore
Taipei   Tokyo   Toronto   Warsaw

and associated companies in
Berlin   Ibadan

Published by Oxford University Press, Inc.
198 Madison Avenue, New York, New York 10016

Oxford is a registered trademark of Oxford University Press

Library of Congress Cataloging-in-Publication Data
Ainsworth-Vaughn, Nancy.
Claiming power in doctor–patient talk / Nancy Ainsworth-Vaughn.
p.   cm. — (Oxford studies in sociolinguistics)
Includes bibliographical references and index.
ISBN 0-19-509606-1; ISBN 0-19-509607-X (pbk.)
1. Physician and patient.   2. Oral communication.
3. Interpersonal relations.   I. Title.   II. Series.
R727.3.A37   1998
610.69'6—dc21   97-36258

9 8 7 6 5 4 3 2 1

Printed in the United States of America
on acid-free paper

For Dale

ACKNOWLEDGMENTS

For crucial early encouragement to do this research, I thank Howard Brody, Barb Given, Maureen O'Higgins, Lou Snow, and Marie Swanson. Candace West also provided important encouragement at an early stage, in the form of a lengthy critique of the first version of chapter 3. For encouragement as the work developed, my deepest debt is to Deborah Tannen, Kathleen Ferrara, and Thomas Huff. Their interest, advice, and ideas were invaluable.

Critiquing a manuscript is quite a task. Deborah Tannen, Kathleen Ferrara, Madeleine Mathiot, Robert Arnold, Mary Talbot, Thomas Huff, and Steven Sutherlin read the entire manuscript, and parts of it were read by Howard Brody. I benefited enormously from the comments of these scholars. In preparing the book for publication, I appreciated the highly professional work and courteous personal attention of the editorial and production staff at Oxford University Press, especially Cynthia Read and Cynthia Garver.

Beginning in 1991, this research was supported in part by a faculty research grant from the Cancer Center at Michigan State University, an All University Research Initiation Grant from the MSU Foundation, and research leave granted by the Department of English at Michigan State University. I am deeply grateful for this support. Without it, I estimate, the research and writing would have taken twice as long to complete.

Perceptive and assiduous research assistance came from Beth Christensen, Mary Ann Crawford, Aza Economides, Anne Hope, Mary Jo Mercer, and Pam Warner. In this regard, I owe special debts to Elda Keaton and Mary Zdrojkowski. Elda, my friend for more than 20 years, devoted her fine mind and many precious hours to producing superb fine-grained transcriptions. Mary was a wonderful research assistant and a staunch friend. Other friends and family who provided much-appreciated support include (listed alphabetically, since no hierarchy is implied) Jenny Banks, Marjorie Cruse, Cathy Davidson, Noël Houck, Grace Iverson, David Johnson, Alison Mackey, Beth and Tim Mazzola, Jeannette Opalski, Myrna Simms, Brad and Mike Strait, Robin Vaughn-Strait, Linda Wagner-Martin, and the three Sherwood clans: Etheridge, Schumacher, and Smalley.

My deepest gratitude goes to my husband, Dale Vaughn. While I was immersed in this project, Dale's unfaltering love nourished every part of my life. Thank you, Dale, for the joy of exploring the north woods of Michigan and the reefs of Bonaire and Palau, and thank you for the wit and cheer that makes our everyday life so much fun. You were the counterbalance to all the effort and frustration of writing; you restored my sanity and my strength; and without you, both the book and I would be impoverished.

Finally, my profound thanks go to the patients and physicians who agreed to be audiotaped. Many of them, including some cancer patients who did not live to see this book be published, agreed to participate in the study because they wanted someone else to benefit from reading about their experiences. I hope that this book will carry out that wish.

SERIES FOREWORD

Sociolinguistics is the study of language in use. With a special focus on the relationships between language and society, sociolinguistics addresses the forms and functions of variation across social groups and across the range of communicative situations in which speakers and writers deploy their verbal repertoires. In short, sociolinguistics examines discourse as it is constructed and co-constructed, shaped and reshaped, in the interactions of everyday life and as it reflects and creates the social, mental, and sometimes even the physical realities of that life.

Some linguists examine the structure of sentences independent of who is speaking or writing and to whom, independent of what precedes and what follows in the discourse, and independent of the setting, topic, and purpose of the discourse. By contrast, sociolinguists and discourse analysts investigate linguistic expression embedded in its social and situational contexts. Among observers who are *not* professional linguists, interest likewise focuses on language in discourse—for it is discourse that mirrors the patterns of social structure and strategic enterprise that engage the attention of so many people.

Oxford Studies in Sociolinguistics offers a platform for studies of language use in communities around the globe. The series invites synchronic or diachronic treatments of social dialects and registers, of oral, written, or signed discourse. It welcomes studies that are descriptive or theoretical, interpretive or analytical. While its volumes usually report original research, an occasional one synthesizes or interprets existing knowledge. The series aims for a style that is accessible beyond linguists to other humanists and social scientists, and some volumes may appeal to educated readers keenly interested in the language of human affairs—for example, the discourse of lawyers engaging clients and one another with specialist registers or, as in the volume at hand, of doctors and patients talking about the challenges of treating cancer and other illnesses. By providing a forum for innovative studies of language in use, Oxford Studies in Sociolinguistics aims to influence the agenda for linguistic research in the twenty-first century and provide an array of provocative analyses to help launch that agenda.

In *Claiming Power in Doctor–Patient Talk*, Nancy Ainsworth-Vaughn analyzes more than one hundred healthcare encounters, paying particular attention to the role of questions, story telling, and control of topics in talk between doctors and patients. Coupling quantitative and qualitative research techniques, this book is more than an analytical foray or a scholarly treatise. Combining insights from sociolinguistics, anthropology, and sociology, and exhibiting a sensitivity informed by personal experience with challenges like those facing the patients in her study, Professor Ainsworth-Vaughn has written an admirable applied sociolinguistics treatise. In addition to characterizing her rich data, explaining her analytical tools, and offering insightful analyses that invite reconsideration of important theoretical questions in discourse analysis, she concludes her book with suggestions especially for physicians—suggestions intended to bring about a better and more therapeutic balance of power in talk between patients and physicians.

We are pleased to have this combined empirical, practical, and theoretical analysis of *Claiming Power in Doctor–Patient Talk* as the latest contribution to Oxford Studies in Sociolinguistics.

Edward Finegan

CONTENTS

PART IV: IMPLICATIONS FOR PRACTICE

CLAIMING POWER IN DOCTOR–PATIENT TALK

Introduction

In this book, I provide new information about talk in the medical encounter, analyzed in an unusual way.

This is the first study to analyze in detail the ways patients claim power through talk; previous studies have focused on doctors' claims to power. No other study has given an overview of the many ways power is claimed in medical talk. This is the first study with equal numbers of female and male physicians in the data; female physicians were very much in the minority in other studies. No other book on medical discourse has included substantial numbers of cancer patients and oncologists or considered the impact of a cancer diagnosis.

This is one of the few studies based on sequential encounters of doctor–patient pairs rather than encounters isolated from their interactional history. And it is one of the few (about 25% of the total) studies of private practice rather than clinics.

In short, the people studied and the settings they were in are unusual in the literature.

The analytical focus is also new. Several of the speech activities I describe have never previously been examined in medical encounters (e.g., topic transitions, rhetorical questions, and storytelling in diagnosis).

For medical settings, my methodology is unusual. There are few book-length studies that apply ethnographic discourse analysis to medical talk. Most other books have used ethnography, with little analysis of discourse; analysis of talk, with little ethnography; or approaches including neither one, such as essays, sociohistorical accounts, or entirely quantitative studies.

In discourse theory, I offer new definitions for major speech activities (topic transitions, rhetorical questions, and diagnosis). The chapters on storytelling break new ground in examining the role of sociocognitive content and identity in an extended speech activity.

Throughout the book, patients' use of power in medical encounters is reconceptualized—perhaps I should say "conceptualized," as patients and power-fulness are topics seldom linked heretofore.

And finally, this is the first book to provide extended analysis of physicians' cooperative discourse. The book provides models of appropriate, constructive use of power by physicians.

The book is written in an accessible style. In order to speak to audiences be-yond sociolinguistics and discourse analysis, I avoid academic jargon wherever possible without sacrificing accuracy or substance.

Most of the book will be of equal interest and accessibility to both academic and nonacademic audiences. However, some parts may be of more interest to one group than to the other. For instance, chapter 1 is about theory and methodology. Language scholars may choose to look closely at all of chapter 1. Physicians and medical educators may prefer to skim the central part of the chapter (where issues of discourse theory are argued) and focus instead on the beginning, where I set out my general theoretical tenets, and the end, where I give details about the en-counters I studied.

Although my interest in discourse theory is obvious, the theoretical issues in which I am interested are those that are consequential in the nonacademic world. In this book, I use theory and consequences to contextualize one another. The result is a book that is more interesting—though simultaneously less comfortable—to read than a book that stays completely within the usual parameters of either theory or application.

My decision to write for a dual audience grew out of personal experiences in medical settings. Like the patients and doctors I describe in this book, I have inte-grated my lifeworld—including my profession—with my medical experiences. I begin this introduction with the story of those personal experiences.

A Medical Journey

Although I have taught and done research in applied linguistics since 1973—and in discourse analysis since 1979—it was not until the late 1980s that my profes-sional interest in doctor–patient talk began to be realized.

My interest began earlier, with my mother's final illness. In 1982, my mother was diagnosed with lymphoma, a cancer of the blood system. I was the only family member nearby. We went from physician to physician. Once an oncologist was chosen, we went from appointment to appointment, test to test. During the 15 months my mother lived after diagnosis, she was in and out of the hospital fairly often, so we also frequently dealt with hospital staff.

We were fortunate in finding a physician who was able to communicate with us in a way that gave us hope and made us feel human, but he was neither the first nor the last physician we met, and many times our talks with physicians left us feeling battered and despondent. It did not occur to me then that I might study this "cross-cultural" communication.

What did occur to me at the time was that my mother and I were fortunate to have a physician in the family, my older brother. In spite of the distance between his specialty and oncology, and the thousand-plus miles that separated us, he was able to answer many of our questions in detail, answers we either could not or did not elicit from our own physicians. The fact that we spent a great deal of time on the phone to him dramatized for me the limitations of a typical brief medical encounter. This point is all the more telling in view of the fact that my mother's physician never cut short her medical encounters and even gave her copies of articles about lymphoma and its treatment.

Early in 1986, I was diagnosed with breast cancer. My own odyssey through medical settings began. My daughter, who was beginning medical school at the time, joined my brother in providing information to me; again that information was given outside medical settings.

Within medical settings, as I negotiated the meaning of tests, research, various possible treatments, and my responses to treatment, I often thought, "This discourse should be recorded." My wish then was that analysis of the discourse could eventually lead to a reduction of some of its difficulties. After the cancer went into remission, my interest in medical discourse grew into two research projects in which I collected data on other patients (especially cancer patients), in order to provide much-needed new information on this important institutional setting.

Because I have firsthand reasons for understanding the importance of talk in the medical encounter, I have tried to write in a way that clearly describes discourse processes to those who do not have background in language study. No doubt some textual density regarding linguistic and sociolinguistic concepts remains, and this is appropriate given the dual nature of the book's audience.

Although I tried to avoid unnecessary academic jargon, I have not abandoned scientific documentation. Sentence by sentence, academic claims should be documented. This is done by including, in parentheses, the names of researchers who published on the topic and the years in which their work was published. With a researcher's name and a date, readers who want to pursue the issue can use the bibliography at the end of the book to locate the publication.

My experiences with testing and treatment throughout the history of this illness provided me with insight into experiences patients may have in medical events. However, I did not use data on my own experiences in any of the following analyses. This book is about data I gathered from 1988 to 1995, on other patients.

As the preceding autobiography suggests, my understanding of these medical events is that of a member of three social groups directly involved in their construction: as the primary support person for my mother; as a cancer patient myself; and as a patient with the usual assortment of allergies, flus, and other ailments that lead to medical care. In addition, I gained insight from my talks with the physicians in my family and other medical providers.

In 1987, I began asking my own physicians for permission to record my encounters with them, and to my surprise they readily gave permission. I have read transcripts of those audiotapes but have not analyzed them, and they are not quoted in this book. These tapes did raise issues, and the fact that they were so easily obtained encouraged me to take the next step in gathering data.

As I read the literature on medical discourse, I noticed that researchers often found patients to be passive. In fact, patients were usually characterized this way. I wondered how the dynamic interaction between doctor and patient might create passivity or activity on the patient's part.

The particular circumstances of the encounters that were studied were important. Most research on medical encounters in the United States has been conducted in free or low-cost clinics. Those medical settings are very different from private practice, where long-term relationships between provider and patient are common.

A search of the literature on medical discourse found only one study of sequential interactions between physicians and patients in private practice—Silverman's (1987) analysis of British medical encounters. Silverman did find differences between encounters in private practice and those in the National Health Service:

> Although these private patients do not challenge the clinical judgments of the doctor, many claim the kind of extensive rights over the agenda of the consultation which are rarely claimed or granted in the NHS clinics observed in this study. (1987:111)

In the United States, one finding of Roter, Hall, and Katz (1988:109) suggests a similar contrast between free and for-fee encounters: Clinic patients asked fewer questions than private-practice patients, even though the clinic visits were twice as long as the private-practice visits.

In this book, I offer data on private-practice encounters in the United States. There is a great need for study of the entire spectrum of medical encounters; this book begins to fill that need, focusing not only on an understudied setting but also on understudied ways in which patients claim power.

As I analyzed medical discourse, I always returned to questions about power. My research, then, is about power-claiming speech activities in long-term relationships between patients and their physicians in private practice.

Power in Medical/Social Talk: A Complex Negotiation

How do patients and doctors try to claim power in the medical encounter? How do they try to share power? Every chapter in this book describes ways of claiming and sharing power over talk itself and over the definitions of self that emerge from talk.

Studies in various cultures have shown beyond doubt that medical encounters often are highly asymmetrical interviews which primarily consist of doctors asking questions and patients answering (e.g., West 1984b [United States]; Hein and Wodak 1987 [Austria]; Weijts et al. 1992 [Netherlands]). In the encounters I studied, questions are indeed an important speech activity. However, in my data a great deal more than just "Q and A" takes place. Instead, I found a wide range of speech activities and overall patterns of talking and listening. Patients were more active in claiming power and doctors were more willing to share power than was the case in most of the previous literature.

In studies of medical encounters in free and low-cost clinics, the researcher usually records one encounter between each physician and patient. The physician and patient usually do not know one another and often do not expect to have a continuing relationship. It is not so surprising, in that context, that these studies have suggested that doctors virtually always dominate encounters while patients are passive and powerless, and that encounters consist primarily of questions by physicians and answers by patients.

My study gathered quite different data. Since 1988 I have been recording sequential encounters between each physician-patient pair, in a private-practice setting. This book is based on 101 such encounters, involving 40 patients and 13 physicians. Some sequences of encounters began with a first meeting between doctor and patient, but many sequences were encounters between people who had been in a doctor–patient relationship for several years. These doctor–patient pairs had the opportunity to develop the intimacy of people who have carried out numerous private conversations on important personal topics. The intimacy that can be created by doctor–patient conversations is usually one-sided—because patients reveal more than physicians do—but it is nevertheless profound.

These encounters were not all alike. I found a great deal of variety in the discourse, with some highly asymmetrical encounters and some encounters where power was notably shared between physician and patient. I do not suggest that these patients claim or realize as much power in encounters as doctors claim or realize. I do, however, show in detail how *both* patients and doctors claimed power. Often patients claimed power in ways previously unexamined in the literature on medical encounters.

A close examination of a variety of encounters, including those where patients successfully claim power, can help defeat the tendency to overgeneralize patients' passivity to the point of stereotyping or creating a self-fulfilling prophecy. Physicians in training can learn to recognize and support patients' appropriate attempts to shape their own destiny.

To place this and other research in perspective, I turn now to a critique of the way medical encounters have usually been studied.

Sequences and Definitions

If we are to have thorough analyses of any event, we need a variety of descriptive approaches. But in describing medical talk, there has been little theoretical/methodological variety. In the great majority of studies of the medical encounter, talk has been coded into categories and then analyzed statistically. In such approaches, the words spoken are treated as inconsequential: The words are assumed to be transparent windows through which we view the underlying function of the utterance (e.g., question, command, warning). The words themselves are discarded after coding has taken place.

However, there is a growing body of work that focuses on talk itself (e.g., West 1984b; Lock and Gordon 1988; Maynard 1991; Fisher and Todd 1993). This work can be called "discourse analysis."[1]

Discourse analysts (of all persuasions—see chapter 1) study the details of language in the encounter. In discourse analysis we attend to the words themselves, and also to their timing, their loudness, their subtle connections to past and subsequent discourse. Everything that makes up the texture of talk is assumed to be consequential. These details of talk constitute significant meaning in speech activities rather than being dismissible windows on meaning. In this book the question is not, "What is the function of this utterance? Once I decide that, I can code it." Instead the question is, "What is it about the details of this talk that leads us to infer a particular kind of claim to power? Once I know that, I can show *how* power is claimed and ratified."

In discourse analysis, evidence consists of the details of talk in context. For this reason, examples are liberally used throughout the book and especially in the chapters on stories. Coding studies, by contrast, seldom provide examples of the actual texture of talk.

Another problem with coding studies is that they are either/or approaches. Each utterance is coded as having only one meaning or one function. For example, in a coding study, either the utterance is a question or it is something else. The reality is, however, that a sentence usually has more than one function; the utterance might be a question, and a warning, and a request for assistance. Multiple possible functions and messages for each utterance are the norm in language, as we examine in detail in chapter 5 and also see in chapters 6 and 7.

Besides multiple functions—an utterance is simultaneously a question and a warning—language also has ambiguity: An utterance can offer the possibility of being one or the other. A speaker often phrases an utterance in such a way that it may or may not be taken as having a certain function. The lay term for this is "strategic ambiguity."

Coding cannot capture the multifunctionality and ambiguity with which speakers negotiate, leaving open multiple possible interpretations; and negotiation is central to medical encounters.

The problems with coding imply another general concern with research on the medical encounter. Greater attention is needed to definitions for speech activities. For instance, "question" is a central concept. Researchers often simply say that they counted questions, as if everyone knows what a question is. But there are significantly different ways of defining a question (chapters 4 and 5).

In any quantitative study of speech activities (such as questions or commands), the definition of a speech activity can determine the results of a study. How many questions you count depends on what you are considering to be a question. In discourse study, definitions must be seen as problematic.

Definitions, in discourse study, are a problem because every utterance is perceived within a context, and it is the complete configuration of words in the relevant context (not words alone) that is assessed for meaning. Clearly, we cannot build all relevant contexts into each definition of a speech activity—the description would never end, as we situated a sentence within a conversation within a relationship within a history within a location, with all the contexts changing constantly over time.

However, we need a definition in order to do a quantitative study; without a definition, how can we know what is being counted? The choice should be a complex definition with as many relevant discourse factors as possible included, and clear statements about how doubtful cases were treated. We are just beginning to articulate such definitions.

I term my approach to defining discourse phenomena the "theory of accumulating support." In identifying a discourse act, such as a question, my fellow analysts and I examined talk in context. In some cases there were a variety of ways in which a hearer could interpret an utterance. How do hearers (and analysts) decide which interpretations have the most likelihood? I suggest that hearers and analysts attend to both the nature and the number of contextual features supporting an interpretation.

Some contextual features are more important than others: "Did you . . ." is a syntactic signal with great salience for the identification of a possible question. But no interpretation can be made until all the relevant contextual features are assessed. Perhaps other features of the context will show "Did you" to be the start of a rhetorical question. Often features pile up in support of one interpretation; hence the notion of "accumulating" support.

Definitions are not the only factor that varies among studies of medical encounters. Using fundamentally the same definition, two quantitative studies of questions (West 1984b; Ainsworth-Vaughn 1994b and chapter 4, this volume) reported very different results. West found patients asking 9% of all questions, whereas the patients I describe in chapter 4 asked 39% of all questions. Because our definitions agreed, other factors, such as setting, diagnosis, and possibly gender, must have made a significant difference.

Finally, I suggest that we need to open our analytical perspectives in a search for meaning in theoretical approaches other than our own. Both qualitative and quantitative approaches, and the theoretical variants within these general approaches, provide important ways of understanding medical discourse.

To summarize: The texture of medical talk is important, and there is much to learn about it. We need to reexamine medical encounters with attention to our definitions, to the local situation (setting, diagnosis, gender), and to the complex, multilayered nature of talk. We also need to review our conceptions of power and the way it is enacted in discourse, and throughout analysis we need to acknowledge the creative tension between differing analytical approaches. This book addresses all these needs.

The primary audience of this book is twofold—discourse analysts and medical practitioners—but other readers will find it accessible in style and rich in real-life examples of talk between patients and doctors. I am concerned with both theory (of discourse) and practice (implications for patients and doctors in training), and therefore I include both sociolinguistic theory and straightforward remarks about applications.

In language classes, these chapters can be used to illustrate generalized discourse phenomena, such as co-construction or the way narratives constitute other speech activities. In medical education, the book will go far to dispel stereotypes of patients as passive and incompetent, and doctors as all-powerful and always domineering. Medical students will find many models for sharing power with patients. Of course, there are also some examples of physicians undercutting patients' power-claiming strategies, but this book primarily focuses on cooperative power-claiming by both patient and physician, with emerging joint control of the encounter.

Plan of the Book

Part I introduces theories and methods for studying medical talk. In chapter 1, I discuss theoretical issues and qualitative and quantitative methods (I use both in this book) and describe my data and methodology. Chapter 2, based on the first six minutes of a medical encounter between an oncologist and a patient with breast cancer, uses both qualitative and quantitative descriptions to provide an overview of speech activities in a medical encounter. In chapter 2, instead of focusing on one speech activity (as I do in chapters 3 through 7), I show how several major speech activities and discourse features are used to claim both power over the discourse and also power over future actions, such as treatment. Chapter 2 is an attempt to suggest the limitations of all studies that focus on only one speech activity as an index to power.

Part II consists of quantitative studies of questions and topic transitions. All readers will be interested in the overall findings, but some details of these two quantitative studies may be of more interest to sociolinguists and discourse analysts than to medical professionals or other readers.

In chapter 3, I describe and quantify male and female physicians' claims to power through different kinds of topic transitions. The way the topic is changed varies with the gender of the physician.

Chapter 4 records my quantitative study of questions. Patients asked almost 40% of the questions—a dramatic contrast to the small percentages other researchers found. Why the difference? I discuss methodology, definitions, and contextual features as possible sources of disparity. At the end of the chapter, I use an extended transcript to qualify my own analysis (and all quantitative analyses): Questioning in this transcript can be seen as either appropriate or inappropriate use of power.

Part III takes up the moment-by-moment construction of the emerging encounter. Chapter 5 continues the study of questions begun in the previous quantitative chapter but changes methodologies. In chapter 5, a qualitative look at rhetorical questions finds ambiguity in their meaning. As I define them, some rhetorical questions offer listeners a choice: They can be treated as serious or nonserious, rhetorical or real. Like so many other discourse acts, they serve multiple social and medical purposes.

Ambiguity of rhetorical questions is a central resource for patients because it allows them to be deferent and active at the same time. With ambiguous statements, patients can make suggestions about diagnosis or treatment without appearing to make suggestions. Thus, they leave intact the physician's roles of diagnostician and prescriber of treatment.

In chapters 6 and 7, I describe localized stories in medical talk. This storytelling occurs not only at the edges (first and last minutes) of the medical encounter but also in the process of diagnosis. I am not speaking of "the patient's story" (H. Brody 1987; Charon 1989), which is an overview of a patient's illness within its life context. Instead I am drawing attention to the way patient and physician jointly construct medical discourse through specific, concrete discourse moves. Everyday conversational practices such as storytelling are at the heart of this co-construction (chapter 6).

Labovian, habitual, and hypothetical narratives are used to construct a diagnosis (chapter 7). When the narratives are evaluated, as they usually are, they become stories. Until now this role for localized narratives and stories in diagnosis has gone unnoticed. Besides constructing the diagnosis, stories can be used to define selves (chapters 6 and 7).

In chapter 8, I turn to implications for practitioners. I draw together the ways in which patients laid claim to power in my data and discuss what physicians can do to support patients' activity in their own behalf.

I hope that it will become clear that, though I examine patients and doctors who cooperate as therapeutic partners, I recognize the difficulties of communication in encounters and the need to examine physicians' domination of encounters. I suggest that we must examine all kinds of encounters. We must study not "the" medical encounter but, rather, many types of encounters.

Patients' and physicians' power-claiming talk is crucial to the makeup of all medical encounters. We are these patients and physicians. When we become aware of our own and others' ways of claiming power, we can change those ways of talking as ethics and context demand.

It may seem obvious that patients need to know about available power-claiming discourse strategies. Medical ethicists (H. Brody 1992) believe that physicians also need to know about the power-claiming strategies they use, in order to own that power, and they need to know about patients' power-claiming strategies in order to support patients who are trying to gain appropriate control over their medical lives. Both patients and physicians need to look closely at newly emerging data on medical discourse. To this inquiry the present book contributes extensive, specific description of the discourse strategies patients and physicians use to construct power and identity for themselves and for one another.

I

STUDYING POWER

1

A Sense of the Moment

Theory, Methodology, Data

Writing about gendered interaction, Tannen has said, is like "stepping into a maelstrom" (1994:3). There are good reasons for the emotion generated by discussing gendered behavior: Everyone has experience with the topic. What happens between men and women matters a lot. Power is involved, and power is always a hot topic. There are many advocates for women, focused on the injustices women endure, who wish to keep those injustices at the center of the debate. Scholars from several disciplines are working on the topic, and their assumptions and vocabularies differ—which leads to considerable misunderstanding and distrust.

Almost as much emotion can be evoked by discussing doctor–patient interaction, for the same reasons: Everyone who reads this is either a doctor or a patient, or both. What happens in medical encounters matters immensely. Power of several kinds is realized in medical encounters—including, commonly, a struggle between doctor and patient. There are many advocates for patients, aware of abuses of physicians' authority, who wish to maintain a focus on those abuses. Scholars from medicine, sociology, anthropology, public health, and language study are involved, and they use quite different and sometimes incommensurable research paradigms. Again, considerable misunderstanding and distrust is generated by differences in theory and method. Hence this chapter: a description of my theoretical approach and my methods, including specifics about my data and the way it was gathered.

My research paradigm arises primarily from anthropology and linguistics, though I draw on ideas from sociology as well. Studies such as mine are much less common than studies originating in medicine, sociology, and public health. For this reason, it is especially important to discuss my methodology.

I am both a sociolinguist and an anthropologist. As a sociolinguist, I attempt to isolate, define, and count certain speech activities that are crucial in the medical encounter (questions, topic transitions, stories). These are quantitative methods, albeit simple ones. Quantitative methods are familiar to most readers: define, then count, then hypothesize as to the significance of the count. My hope as a sociolinguist is to examine quantities of topic transitions (chapter 3) and questions (chapter 4) to arrive at a rough index of their significance in the balance of power between doctor and patient. I take a relatively broad view of speech activities, gauging their overall significance. There are, however, significant differences between my quantitative methods and those in widespread use throughout the social sciences.

First, because I am working with language in sequences, statistical methods are not appropriate, though counts and percentages can be considered. Second, although I use definitions, I view them as problematic. Both of these two beliefs rest on the qualitative tenet that meaning depends on ever-changing context.

The paradox is that each speech activity is both unique and patterned. When we do quantitative work, we ignore uniqueness, in order to establish a definition that will apply across events. We need a definition in order to have accurate counts, and counting the frequency and distribution of the activity is our purpose.

However, when we do qualitative studies of discourse, we try to capture a sense of the complex, unique moment. We show the existence of choice among multiple possible meanings, and we show the relationships between choice and context. Generalizations are still made (or at least implied), but not in the same way.

Pattern is important in qualitative work, just as it is in quantitative work. Discourse sequences are patterned in the sense that all speech activities are organized. In a qualitative study, we uncover the way talk is organized into appropriate sequences. We also show how pattern—organization and meaningfulness—exists as part of the larger web of social events. An activity cannot be meaningful in itself. It must refer to context. This fact calls into question any studies based on definitions that ignore the context surrounding each utterance. If context is not considered, then the numbers produced by quantitative studies are meaningless.

Because quantitative work summarizes many encounters, and qualitative work focuses on one or a few encounters, there is tension between quantitative and qualitative methods. From a qualitative point of view, quantitative studies cannot adequately represent meaning because they cannot provide the context of every "question" or "topic transition" counted. Only examining the sequential, moment-to-moment construction of meaning in unique events adequately represents their meanings.

My position is that all studies, even qualitative ones, do ignore some context. We can find connections between any one event and all the rest of the world, but, of course, not all of the world can be discussed in the analysis. Analysts always have to choose aspects of the context that seem relevant to the speech event. I carry out quantitative studies only after an exhaustive attempt (involving multiple analysts) to develop definitions that rest on contextual features; in my view, there is no other kind of valid definition. In preparing for the following quantitative studies of questions and topic transitions, my co-analysts and I went over the data many times, testing and modifying our definitions, looking at the discourse sequences around every utterance that might be a "question" or a "topic transition" in our data. We could not report all of our extensive considerations of sequential context, but purely qualitative studies likewise cannot report all of their extensive study of sequential context.

I have just been questioning quantitative studies, saying that they need a qualitative basis. Criticism also goes in the opposite direction. Quantitative researchers often question qualitative analysis: How representative can qualitative analysis be?

In purely qualitative study of speech activities, a few stretches of discourse are analyzed in great detail. Readers have to take the word of the analyst about the representative nature of these fragments. For instance, in chapters 6 and 7, I describe storytelling by participants in medical encounters. I do not attempt to count the stories told. A quantitative researcher might object that instances of storytelling must be counted in order to show that it is important. Otherwise, we might be considering an isolated occurrence which does not deserve attention.

However, because the line between stories and simple narration of events is not always clear, numbers of stories in medical encounters cannot be quantified. The line between rhetorical questions and "true" questions (chapter 5) also is unclear, because utterances are often ambiguous in function. Because they are difficult to count, should we give up any analyses of these speech activities?

Some counts can be made, and I do count rhetorical questions in chapter 5. In fact, it was the difficulties with counting that led to my analysis of ambiguities in these common questions (the rest of the chapter).

Even when uncounted, rhetorical questions and stories are worth studying, for several reasons. First, as is the case with stories in my data, multiple analysts may find that the speech activity is common. Three research assistants found numerous narratives and stories in my data, although they could not agree in every case as to whether a given extract was a narrative or a story.

Another reason qualitative analysis is important is that an activity may be crucial to the event. For instance, storytelling, in the localized, structured form studied by discourse analysts, can sometimes be an activity central to developing a diagnosis (chapter 7). Clearly, it is important to examine how this crucial meaning—a diagnosis—is constructed in real time through sequential activities.

As well as being qualitative, the following studies are ethnographic (some would say the two terms are redundant, but in my usage they differ). In order to produce an ethnographic picture, I quote and describe speakers in detail.

An ethnography provides a sense of the moment, with all its multiple possible meanings. Individual speakers do not produce speech activities one by one, like pearls on a string. Instead, they cooperate with one another by providing opportunities for other speakers to choose from among multiple possible meanings. An ethnographic account (such as my analyses of stories and rhetorical questions) will try to describe this process. Inevitably, such accounts will include hypotheses about what speakers were doing. As I discuss later in this chapter, qualitative researchers differ about the best way to arrive at hypotheses with a high degree of validity.

These studies vary along a continuum from purely qualitative study (the chapters on stories), through a mixture of qualitative and quantitative study (the whirlpool discourse, rhetorical questions), to studies that are primarily quantitative, although based on qualitative definitions (true questions, topic transitions). Throughout the book, even in primarily quantitative studies, I provide detailed examples of the speech activities I am studying.

All methodologies have strengths and all have limitations. Quantitative analysis, even simple nonstatistical quantitative analysis such as that in chapters 3 and 4, cannot acknowledge multiple meanings and usually provides only a few examples drawn from actual talk. Qualitative analysis, focused on specific moments, can fully explicate those moments but cannot provide an overall picture. Some forms of quantitative analysis are completely incompatible with qualitative assumptions, and vice versa.

But if we provide careful definitions based on qualitative views of meaning, we can profitably use simple quantitative methods. If speakers can recognize a recurrent speech activity, we as analysts can find the bases for its recognition and then make simple counts of its frequency and distribution. These counts can and should be complementary to qualitative ethnographies.

Once we acknowledge the limitations of each method, we can recognize the strengths of each. Together these methods give a more vivid picture of medical encounters—a truer sense of the moment-to-moment construction of power—than either could provide alone.

Because qualitative research is likely to be an unfamiliar methodology to readers in medicine, and because qualitative study of language differs from qualitative research in general, some explanation of qualitative methods is in order.

Principles of Qualitative Research

This section is my own synthesis of relevant ideas from recent texts on qualitative research in general (Cameron et al. 1992; Lincoln and Guba 1985; Marshall and Rossman 1989; Strauss and Corbin 1990). The following section of the chapter narrows the focus to the way language, in particular, has been studied with qualitative methods.

Qualitative research is based on the following tenets.

Naturalistic data in sociocultural context

The events studied should be familiar to the participants, events which either would or might unremarkably have taken place regardless of the presence of the researcher. The research report must describe the context of the event in terms of setting, participants' understanding of its purposes and normal conduct, and other socially organized features of context.

Researchers' immersion in the cultural milieu

Qualitative researchers often do "participant observation," taking a role in the event. Of course, this attempt is complex and problematic, but less so, its proponents will argue, than attempting to observe without acknowledging one's role. In its best form, participant observation implies that researchers have accepted the fact that they are not invisible, that they have some sort of relationship with other participants.

Qualitative researchers are as open and honest as possible about their goals. "As possible," in my own case, means that I provided a brief description of my research project to prospective participants. The description stated that my goal was to study interaction between physicians and patients and that I would use the data as a basis for articles which might be used in training physicians. I did not specify that I was interested in questioning, storytelling, and so on. In fact, when I began the research I knew that I was interested in questioning (since it is a major topic in the literature), but I had no idea that storytelling was a central feature of medical encounters. It would have been impossible for me to inform participants of all the foci that might eventually emerge from the research.

The fact that a qualitative researcher is as open as possible with other participants allows relationships to develop on a foundation of mutual respect.

Assessing participants' views: A central purpose

Through participant observation and interviewing, the researcher attempts to discover the way participants construe events. This ethnographic principle is the reason for the use of semi- or unstructured interviews in many qualitative studies (including this one).

Acknowledgment of researcher involvement

Qualitative researchers may attempt, in their writing, to reflect on their involvement, to "locate" themselves in relation to the goals and methods of the study. They should provide any information that would help readers evaluate the conclusions reached. It might be thought that acknowledging one's own involvement implies that the researcher will not strive for balanced appraisals, but the opposite is true. This acknowledgment is a crucial part of the attempt to achieve accuracy. One of the ways this acknowledgment functions is to motivate the researcher to bring in other analysts whose views may serve as a corrective for individual interpretations (compare the following point).

Multiple analysts

Reliability of conclusions is achieved partly by using multiple analysts. Although every academic thesis is examined by others in the research community, in qualitative research special efforts are made to gather multiple perspectives as early as possible in the research. This tenet follows from the qualitative assumption that objectivity cannot be achieved by one researcher. Multiple analysts provide a crucible of debate which tests possible interpretations. In the present research, four analysts were directly involved in forming and testing criteria for quantitative analysis of questions and topic transitions. The qualitative work was circulated among other analysts (mentioned in Acknowledgments), as well as receiving anonymous review during the process of publication as both articles and this book. Other qualitative analysts also commented on transcription conventions.

Ethics of relationships with other participants

Because there are real relationships between the researcher and the other participants, the usual social requirements for real relationships are in effect. Researchers are required to treat other participants as they would treat anyone who generously expends effort or time on their behalf. Researchers must be forthcoming about information other participants need to know. Courtesy is essential; introductions, greetings, farewells, appropriately reciprocal behavior, and fulfilling commitments are examples of normal social behavior expected. However, the requirement is for reciprocity and honesty, not necessarily for full-blown friendships to develop. In one qualitative study I conducted (not part of this book), a participant asked my research assistant to be godmother to her child. In the Hispanic culture shared by participant and researcher, the godmother role invokes a lifetime commitment to involvement with the child and its family. Although the researcher accepted, she was not required, under qualitative tenets, to do so.

No absolute hypothesis to be proved or disproved

Much qualitative research is exploratory in nature. Its goal is to identify an important arena for interaction and then gather data on the interaction itself and on the surrounding context. Therefore, studies begin without hypotheses to be proved or disproved. As the study progresses, working hypotheses are developed, but the attempt is to develop reliable generalizations, not absolute hypotheses.

Extended time frames

Qualitative research takes place over a longer period of time than traditional sociolinguistic research. Researchers must plan to be at the research site regularly for long enough to develop, and check, theories supported by a variety of observations. This may take months or years. The research reported in this book began, in pilot form, in 1988; a second, larger-scale phase of gathering data took place between 1991 and 1995. The extended time frame was necessary in order to follow patients through several successive appointments with their physicians. It was not unusual for patients to see their physicians at intervals of three or six months, creating periods of up to one and one-half years for my research involvement with a patient.

Qualitative Study of Language

Differences from other qualitative work

Although *qualitative research* is the broad category into which *microethnography of language* can be placed, the two are not always identical. Outside of discourse analysis, qualitative researchers often code their data into themes and actions rather than considering the ways meaning is constructed through the details of the spoken language. This coding process and the written report about it may involve quoting participants, but details of talk are not analyzed.

To a discourse analyst,[1] such coding processes discard important data. Discourse analysts believe that language is constitutive of the event rather than being a transparent medium through which we view the event. In our discipline, any categorizing and coding (and often there is none) must be based on identifiable features of the discourse in context rather than on implicit intuitive judgments. We never set aside the structure and texture of language (Bauman and Sherzer 1989; M. Goodwin 1990; Gumperz 1982; Tannen 1989c). For this reason, microethnographers of language work from tapes and transcripts of actual discourse, repeatedly hearing and reading the data.

This is not to say that intuitive judgments have no role in discourse study. Intuition is based on implicit social knowledge and is our first guide to recognizing the nature of speech activities. For my purposes, it is essential to make this implicit knowledge explicit. Much of my effort in considering these medical encounters has been spent in articulating implicit features of discourse (cf. Erickson and Schultz 1977), an exercise in pragmatics as well as ethnography.

A spectrum of approaches to discourse

Because much of the work on medical discourse has been done within the theoretical framework of conversation analysis, it is helpful to mention some of the overlaps and areas of difference between conversation analysis and the work I am doing here.

Both methodologies are ethnographic in the sense that both attempt to discover participants' organizational strategies and points of view. Both methodologies use surrounding discourse as data in understanding some fragment of talk. A major difference lies in the fact that studies such as mine take the anthropological view that several kinds of data count as evidence for the meaning of an utterance. I accept as evidence discourse data, interviews with speakers, talk by the same speaker recorded in other situations, and the analyst's participant observation and field notes.

Many conversation analysts would accept instead only discourse data from the immediate local context. To capture this contrast, henceforward I reserve the term "ethnographic" for studies that accept participant observation and other data from beyond the immediate discourse context.[2]

The two approaches clearly share important methods. The situation is complicated by the fact that the approaches have changed over time. In general, conversation analysis originated in sociological work such as that of Sacks, Schegloff, and Jefferson (1974); ethnographic discourse analysis originated in anthropology with the work of Gumperz and Hymes (1964, 1972).

In the 1960s, ethnographic discourse analysts described participants and the social context of an event and attempted to explain the event in relation to (or as part of) sociocultural context. They were influenced by linguistic focus on the rule-governed nature of language; perhaps speech events had definable rules for their sequences. Conversation analysts, at that time, took a very different approach. They did not describe participants and social context of language events, and they insisted that events were constructed by speakers' choices rather than following fixed rules for sequence.

In the intervening years, the two approaches have come to share a number of crucial assumptions and a great many analytical techniques. Both the term "conversation analysis" and the term "discourse analysis" are now applied to a spectrum of analytical approaches, many of them overlapping.[3] My own work, which I would describe as "ethnographic discourse analysis," originates in the anthropological paradigm. However, I also take as fundamental the conversation-analysis principle that participants engage in the process of constructing unique speech activities. Like most other discourse analysts, I rely on insights from the important body of work in conversation analysis and use many detailed techniques of analysis which originated with conversation analysis.

The two schools agree that a primary object of study is "the competences that ordinary speakers use" (Heritage and Atkinson 1984:1). For Sacks this competence would be "machinery": "[I]nteractions [are] products of a machinery. We are trying to find the machinery" (1984:26–27). The machinery consists of ways discourse is structured, such as the way topics are introduced, maintained, and closed; the organization of turns at talk, including interruptions; forms of questioning and what counts as an answer; ties between stories and the preceding conversation; and other types of discourse structure. These kinds of discourse structure are of central importance to both schools.

However, as Schegloff (1991a) points out, it is difficult to separate the "machinery" (social organization and meaning) from speakers' cognitive schemata (referential meaning). For instance, topics an observer cannot link together might be linked by speakers, in a referential schema unknown to the observer. The observer might find a story disjointed or think a sudden topic change has been carried out, when in fact participants can infer cohesion based on socially shared cognitive schemata.

The theoretical issues on which researchers in these two traditions have varying views fall into three categories: the research focus, use of contextual evidence to support claims, and the role of preexisting social norms and structures.

First, the two groups differ in their primary research focus: Conversation analysts are primarily interested in describing social practices, of which language is one. Discourse analysts, as I use the term, are primarily interested in describing language in its socially situated sequences. In practice, however, these positions are not far apart.

Second, practitioners of the two traditions may differ in the types of contextual data they admit as evidence. Some conversation analysts find their evidence only in local discourse context, the preceding and following utterances. This is an attempt to ground analytical claims directly in the data, avoiding premature generalizations that might come from imposing the analyst's preconceptions upon the data. These analysts believe it possible to show that certain elements of the social surroundings were "demonstrably oriented to," at the time of speaking, by the speakers (Schegloff 1991b)—but not possible to show what else is in the speakers' awareness.

Others, both discourse analysts and conversation analysts, agree that local discourse context is a prime source of evidence for their claims but wish to go beyond the local discourse context. They regard other recorded interactions, including interviews, as a source of interpretation of specific discourse sequences and social practices (Cicourel 1982; Grimshaw 1987; Tannen and Wallat 1987; Ferrara 1994). They also accept field notes and participant observations as evidence. In fact, they prefer that the researcher be a "participant observer"—actually out "in the field," observing the interaction as it was taking place. It is this approach that I term "ethnographic."

It needs to be reiterated that a number of analysts are currently mixing the two approaches. Grimshaw (1987) accepts and uses ethnographic participant observations as evidence for analytical interpretations, and Cicourel (1982, 1987) uses his own detailed observations in two teaching hospitals along with discourse data from a series of medical encounters and an interview he conducted. But both Grimshaw and Cicourel would likely be classified as conversation analysts. M. Goodwin (1990) applied techniques from both ethnography and conversation analysis to longitudinal data on groups of adolescents. Moerman (1988) makes explicit the two theoretical approaches and argues for a convergence of the two.

The third area of disagreement relates to positivism as opposed to postmodern tenets (Cameron et al. 1992). At issue is the role of social structure as opposed to human agency. I agree with K. Davis (1988), who follows Giddens (1984) in accepting a role for both in discourse. Not everyone agrees that there is a role for social structure. The contrast is captured in subheadings from Graddol and Swann (1989): "Language Creates Social Reality," and "Language Reflects Social Reality." Some conversation analysts can accept only the first of these assertions, regarding the second as based on a positivist fallacy (i.e., the claim that social reality exists independent of the emerging discourse).

In this view, a social role does not exist independent of a person's enactment of it. It is only in that enactment that evidence is to be found about the aims of speakers. For these analysts, we cannot go beyond the enactment to the wider situation without risking the imposition of our own presuppositions on the data. So all analytical interest must be focused on the spoken discourse immediately surrounding the utterance to be described.

The following section pursues this last issue. It must be treated in detail because the anthropological position I take is the basis for my use of certain kinds of evidence drawn from context beyond the immediate discourse.

Connecting discourse with social context:
Schemata and their instantiation

It is unlikely that anyone would argue against the idea that speakers bring their histories with them into an interaction. Their experiences of past similar events and their views of others' social roles must in some way be a resource in constructing the present event. As Cicourel puts it:

> [Participants] must be capable of interpreting and summarizing their own and others' activities throughout discourse. They must, therefore, develop theories of knowledge or schemata that will guide their perceptions of a setting and the talk and actions." (1982:49; cf. Tannen and Wallat 1987).

In my view, these schemata for the conduct of talk are the bridge between the social world and the discourse event. Participants' schemata for constructing selves and events are instantiated—made concrete—in the moment-to-moment creation of medical encounters. Evidence about participants' schemata can come from the speakers themselves (in interviews) and from their behavior as observed by the ethnographer, behavior which may occur before, during, or after the event at hand. The researcher's own cultural and linguistic knowledge will inevitably be used as a resource for understanding these schemata.

Some conversation analysts would argue, however, that the researcher does not have access to any part of the speaker's knowledge unless it is displayed in the local discourse. If this is true, any comments about the larger social context would be groundless interpretation. But ethnographers would reply that a great deal of cultural or social information is never overtly acknowledged in the unfolding event, and in fact it would be a social gaffe to display such information overtly at that time. If analysis is to be based solely on local discourse context, the analyst may not mention such covert topics even if they are critical to understanding the event.

An ethnographer attempts to address the role of covert cultural and social information by bringing multiple types of data into the analysis: speakers' earlier or later behavior; their own reports of history and motive, provided in interviews; and the ethnographer's observations of the setting and participants. We look for patterns, repetition, and connections among many kinds of data.

An example of such evidence in my data appears in chapter 5. In Mr. Frisell's first recorded encounter with Dr. Finn, he used rhetorical questions to make sexual jokes. I was able to provide extensive context, apart from the immediately preceding and following discourse, for this use of rhetorical questions.

In his interview after the fact, Mr. Frisell put forward one schema as an explanation for his joking: "It's another way to break the ice." Dr. Finn saw his joking differently. She had a schema for cancer therapy in which laughter and positive attitudes are correlated with recovery from cancer, and she saw Mr. Frisell's jokes within that schema. Other schemas were used by other participants; the head nurse-manager in this practice reported that she and the other nurses felt offended when Mr. Frisell tried to tell sexual jokes because it was inappropriate in a professional setting.

These may not be the only relevant schemas. Participants may not be conscious of all their own schemas, and they may not always tell the truth about their schemas. However, their proffered schemas are part of the data. I regard as data the fact that, in my later interview with him, Mr. Frisell offered his schema when it had not been solicited. The fact that he invited Dr. Finn to go water skiing is data, although the invitation was subsequent to many of the sexual rhetorical questions I analyze. Some conversation analysts would not accept these types of data because they are not part of the local discourse context.

One can agree that analysis should be empirically grounded without agreeing that only the local discourse context provides empirical grounds. "Empirical" data is a deceptive phrase. The connotation is that of information untainted by the analysts' speculation. But all events require interpretation (e.g., through the use of frames and schemas). Analysts inevitably use their own frames and schemas, "members' knowledge" of social structure, even in considering the local discourse context. No analyst can escape interpretation; none can limit analysis to the text alone. Anthropologists will argue that bringing in data from the larger cultural and social context increases the validity of the interpretation of local events.

There is error inherent in the process of interpretation (Wilson 1989:98), and all analysis involves interpretation. Those who wish to restrict the source of empirical data to local context and those who wish to expand it to other contextual sources are taking different avenues in the attempt to reduce that inherent error.

Theoretical Approach of the Present Study

I understand language users to be authors and continual revisers of meaning, using linguistic structure as one resource for positioning themselves in the social world (Tannen 1989c, 1993a). They make choices and construct texts embodying social identities, in accord with social maxims and their understanding of the event as a genre (M. Goodwin 1990; Gumperz 1982; Hymes 1972; Polanyi 1979; ten Have 1989). Discourse is a major arena for the moment-to-moment realization of an individual's social identity as well as having transactional purposes specific to its context (e.g., medical or pedagogical).

Ethnographic discourse analysis adds ethnographic and sociolinguistic dimensions to the study of discourse as negotiated meaning (Auer and di Luzio 1992; Gumperz 1982; C. Goodwin and Goodwin 1987; M. Goodwin 1990; Tannen and Wallat 1983; Tannen 1989c, 1993b). These analyses report the ethnographer's observations of the social context of the data, attempt to specify in detail linguistic contextualization cues, and analyze representative stretches of discourse. Ethnographic discourse analysis also has illuminated the fact that participants can differ in the way they construe cues (Gumperz 1982; Tannen 1990; Tannen and Wallat 1987). For instance, a physician and a patient may live through the same encounter but emerge with differing views of what happened.

By making explicit the discourse cues physicians and patients use, I hope to aid patients and medical professionals in achieving more closely shared meanings for the interaction. Each group can come to understand how the encounter is co-

constructed moment-to-moment through speech activities. If doctors and patients can become aware of how power is claimed and ratified, they can do a better job of pursuing the goals of the event.

The Data: Settings, Participants

To gather discourse data on long-term interactions, in 1988 I launched a small-scale study of sequential medical encounters, continuing data collection until 1990. Between 1991 and 1995, I carried out a large-scale study of sequential encounters in oncology settings.

Tables 1.1 and 1.2 list the non-oncology and oncology patients who contributed tape-recorded encounters to these two studies, and table 1.3 lists physicians who participated. The analyses in this book are based primarily on the 101 encounters tape recorded in the two successive studies between 1988 and 1995. Selected participants from both studies were interviewed, and the interviews were also

Table 1.1   Participants: Non-oncology Patients

Last Name	Patient Code	Age	Doctor	Diagnosis	No. of Visits
Women					
Chejell	CJ	60[b]	Finn	Blood disorder	1
Evans[a]	EAA	21	Fouts	Vaginal yeast infection	2
Foley	FM	75	Myhill	Hemachromatosis	2
Feblen	FB	45	Myhill	Hemachromatosis	3
Judd[a]	JB	25	Floyd	Routine breast exam	1
"	"	"	Moltner	Ankle sprain	1
Kelly[a]	KE	38	Midgard	Varied (esp. bronchitis)	9
Lane[a]	LA	52	Fife	Diabetes	4
"	"	"	Mey	Diabetes	3
"	"	"	Fewning	Estrogen deficiency	3

Total women in non-oncology encounters: 7
Total physicians in women's non-oncology encounters: 9
Total non-oncology encounters with women: 29

Men					
Ager	AG	34[b]	Myhill	Low red blood cell count	2
Hicks	HEK	55[b]	Myhill	Low red blood cell count	2
Rariman	RR	15	Myhill	Low red blood cell count	2

Total men in non-oncology encounters: 3
Total physicians in men's non-oncology encounters: 1
Total non-oncology encounters with men: 6

Total non-oncology patients: 10
Total physicians in non-oncology encounters: 9[c]
Total non-oncology encounters: 35

a. Participant in initial small-scale study
b. Estimated age
c. Two physicians, Finn and Myhill, participated in both oncology and non-oncology encounters.

Table 1.2   Participants: Oncology Patients

Last Name	Patient Code	Age	Doctor	Diagnosis	No. of Visits
Women					
Earley	EA	67	Finn	Breast cancer	2
Fitton	FI	53	Finn	Breast cancer	2
Feher	FG	44	Miller	Breast cancer	1
Hake	HK	35	Finn	Lymphoma	3
Ivey	IJ	44	Miller	Lung cancer	1
"	"	"	Mrandi	"	1
Kijhell	KJ	55	Finn	Breast cancer	1
Magiff	MA	73	Feit	Breast cancer	2
Melan	ML	70	Finn	Breast cancer	3
Mesler	MS	40	Miller	Lymphoma	3
Hazen	RH	58	Miller	Breast cancer	3
Ross	RJ	63	Feit	Colon cancer	2
Tinden	TD	60	Myhill	Pre-leukemic condition	1
Wells	WL	47[a]	Munn	Lung cancer	3
Wester	WE	67	Finn	Breast cancer	2

Total women in oncology encounters:	15
Total physicians in women's oncology encounters:	6
Total women's oncology encounters:	33

Last Name	Patient Code	Age	Doctor	Diagnosis	No. of Visits
Men					
Benton	BE	48	Finn	Lymphoma	3
Brade	BR	47	Miller	Lymphoma	1
Cerona	CE	43	Finn	Lung cancer	3
Cox	CR	61	Finn	Lymphoma	3
Dunham	DW	67[a]	Miller	Lung cancer	3
Frisell	FR	38	Finn	Testicular cancer	3
Jordan	JR	62[a]	Miller	Liver cancer	2
Kuda	KD	67[a]	Feit	Throat cancer	1
Liggitt	LG	63	Munn	Lung cancer	3
Lecy	LC	27	Finn	Testicular cancer	3
Mahon	MC	86	Feit	Prostate cancer	1
Morris	MR	73	Myhill	Lung cancer	3
Mapston	MP	45[a]	Miller	Melanoma	2
Porter	PR	71	Miller	Cancer in abdomen	1
Sloworski	SW	70	Munn	Lung cancer	1

Total men in oncology encounters:	15
Total physicians in men's oncology encounters:	6
Total men's oncology encounters:	33

Total oncology patients:	30
Total physicians in oncology encounters:	6
Total oncology encounters:	66

a. Estimated

Table 1.3   Participants: Physicians

Name	Age[a]	Specialty
Women		
Fife[b]	36[c]	Internal Medicine
Feit	40	Medical Oncology/Hematology
Fewning	38[c]	Obstetrics/Gynecology
Finn	40	Medical Oncology/Infectious Diseases
Floyd[b]	43	Surgical Oncology
Fouts[b]	39	Family Practice
Fewning[b]	36	Obstetrics/Gynecology
Men		
Mey[b]	40	Internal Medicine
Munn	45	Medical Oncology/Infectious Diseases
Midgard[b]	35	Family Practice
Myhill	60	Hematology/Medical Oncology
Miller	49	Medical Oncology
Moltner[b]	34[c]	[On duty in "ready care" emergency room]

a. Ages for physicians were provided by a local physicians' referral service which maintains a data bank regarding area physicians. Ages are given as of the first taping of the physician. Physicians Fife and Fewning left the community before their ages were recorded. Dr. Moltner's real name was unknown, so that his age had to be estimated.

b. Participant in initial small-scale study

c. Estimated age

audiotaped. In the second study, I made field notes and observed the workings of the practices, as I detail below.

In this book, patients and physicians are referred to with pseudonyms. Pseudonyms for physicians begin with F when the physician is female[4] and with M when the physician is male. Pseudonyms for patients were chosen to relate to the tape code of the recording. For example, the name "Melan" was chosen to relate to the "ML" code assigned to the original tape recordings of this participant's medical encounters.

At the end of each excerpt from a transcript, I cite a coded reference to the patient, the encounter, and the location of the excerpt in the transcript of this encounter—for example {RH1, 6-36}. RH is the patient code (see tables 1.1 and 1.2). The number 1 in RH1 shows that this was the first encounter recorded with patient RH. Together, the patient code and number make up the tape code (referred to in tables 4.1, 4.3, 4.4, and 4.6).

After citing the tape code, I cite the page and line of the transcript of the encounter. In {RH1, 6-36}, the excerpt began on page 6, line 36, of the transcript of RH's first encounter.

Two patients, JB and LA, were recorded seeing two different doctors. In their tape codes, the patient code is followed by a doctor code. So LAD1 is the tape code for LA's first encounter with a doctor coded D, and JBO is the tape code for JB's encounter with a doctor coded O (because there was only one encounter between the two, there is no number in the tape code).

Small-scale study: 1988–1990

In 1988, four of my women acquaintances agreed to record their sequential inter-actions with their seven private-practice physicians; this project continued until 1990. Again, the tapes raised issues, such as the role of diagnosis, interactional history, and gender.

In the initial study, four women tape-recorded their 17 medical encounters with six physicians. Patients took tape recorders into their encounters over a pe-riod of months or years. I was not present in the physicians' offices, except in the case of Ms. Kelly's interactions with Dr. Midgard. On several occasions, I babysat for Ms. Kelly's four-year-old daughter while Ms. Kelly saw Dr. Midgard—a part of the bargain by which she agreed to do the taping. All participants were offered copies of the tapes, but only Ms. Lane accepted. She said in an interview that she did lis-ten to these tapes and that her purpose in listening was to consider the informa-tion provided by the physician.

In all these encounters, except that between Ms. Jubb and Dr. Moltner, the physician–patient relationship was expected to be ongoing, although there was considerable variation in the length of association; except for Ms. Kelly, patients had seen the physician no more than twice previously. Ms. Kelly was a patient of three years' standing when she began taping (she taped for three more years).

Large-scale study: 1991–1995

Between 1991 and 1995, I audiotaped 66 encounters between 30 patients and six physicians in three hematology–oncology practices in two midwestern communities.

The nature of the practices varied slightly. Dr. Miller was in a group practice located in the community but affiliated, somewhat tenuously, with a local univer-sity and medical school. Dr. Finn at first practiced in two locations, the university setting (where Dr. Myhill also practiced) and an office in the community (where Dr. Munn also practiced). Dr. Finn later moved her entire practice to the commu-nity location at which Munn practiced. She was recorded in both locations.

Dr. Feit's practice was located about 80 miles from the town in which the other practices were situated. She shared an office with an obstetrician in a medical build-ing next to a small community hospital, on the outskirts of an extremely large metropolitan area.

Doctors Myhill, Finn, and Miller were officially affiliated with the university medical schools; however, only Dr. Myhill taught classes. Dr. Munn and Dr. Feit were not affiliated with the university. Medical students and residents were often present in all the practices located near the university but were never present in Dr. Feit's practice, 80 miles away. The presence of medical students in encounters does not necessarily imply a strong connection between the cooperating physicians and the university. Other than having medical students present, these practices appeared to function as private-practice settings. Some influence of the university and its contemporary views of appropriate practice undoubtedly was evoked by the presence of medical student observers.

It is important to note that the influence of a university connection is just one of the influences on a physician. Dr. Finn and Dr. Miller both were officially affiliated with the local medical school. Interviews revealed that neither was given a course in doctor–patient relationships in their original medical school, elsewhere in the country. Dr. Miller, as chapter 2 shows, played traditional roles of authority and control. Dr. Finn, as chapter 6 suggests, played a less authoritarian role, sharing control over the discourse with her patients. Dr. Miller was only nine years older than Dr. Finn, so it seems unlikely that age explains the contrast. Gender may play a role (chapter 3). Personality may play a role. However this complex of factors may have functioned, the simple fact of affiliation with a university is only one of many influences upon a physician's behavior.

In the large-scale second study, I reversed the order in which I approached prospective participants. First, physicians and medical staff were recruited. Second, having secured physicians' permission, I recruited patients as they arrived at the office.

When recruiting patients, I provided the same brief description of the research that was given to medical staff. Then, after going through my statement of the nature and purposes of the research, I made it very clear that patients' participation was entirely voluntary. The following points were made:

- This research was not connected with the clinic in any way and therefore had no connection to the patients' medical treatment.
- The patient's welfare and comfort were paramount and the patient should not agree to participate if he or she felt uncomfortable with being taped.
- I already had sufficient participants and was sure I could recruit others, and therefore tapes from this patient were not essential.

Patients were then handed a consent form with the remark that if they decided to participate they could give the signed form to the nurse. Patients who did agree usually said so at that point. Those who did not simply were not heard from again. In this way, I provided a face-saving way for patients to refuse participation.

One reviewer of this manuscript wondered whether these methods of recruiting needed to be reported in such detail. They do. This was my first contact with patient participants and with these methods I avoided coercion. If patients had signed on under any hint of coercion, my study would have been damaged both ethically and in quality of data. The ethical issues are obvious. As for the issues of data quality, if patients are uncomfortable with being recorded but agree because they see little choice, they may change their discourse behavior while recording is taking place (e.g., they may become quiet and guarded).

Because most other studies of medical encounters did not discuss their recruiting methods, we cannot estimate the influence of their methods. In free and low-cost clinics, the precise ways patients are approached become even more important than in private practice because patients in subsidized clinics often have less control over their treatment than do patients in private practice. Even in today's managed-care environments, private-practice patients in general have more control than those in free and low-cost clinics.

Approximately three fourths of the patients I approached agreed to participate; of those who refused, a disproportionate number were men. Only about half of the men who were approached agreed to participate. These high rates of agreement to participate imply that the data are not skewed toward a minority of patients and physicians who are unrepresentative of other patients and physicians, except possibly in regard to male patients.

Patients who participated agreed to tape three successive visits. However, not all these were collected, because three patients died after contributing one tape and several did not return after contributing one or two tapes.

A radio microphone was worn by the physician; the receiver and tape recorder were in a nearby room, where I sat adjusting the volume when necessary to record someone speaking in a low voice. Often there were long waits for scheduled encounters to take place, and during this time I was able to observe the routines of the two offices and the interactions among nurses, physicians, patients, and other personnel, such as residents in training and medical students. In one office, I asked for something to do to help and was given nontechnical tasks such as answering phones, taking messages, and carrying orders to the laboratory down the hall. I also made field notes and interviewed ten patients and two physicians, all of whom had completed their parts in the study. These notes and interviews, and my observations, provided background for the analysis of the medical discourse recorded.

Transcription as Construction of Data

Like language itself, transcription is not a transparent lens through which we view events (Ochs 1979). Speakers design language use as part of their construction of the event. But this also holds true for the methods with which we study language; they too construct something, in this case the data. Transcription is an important example (Edwards and Lampert 1993). Transcription systems are designed to conform to theoretical tenets and to meet analytical needs; I needed to survey large numbers of transcripts, looking for the smaller stretches of analytical interest. I followed Riessman's (1993) suggestion that a large corpus of discourse data should first be transcribed in rough form to allow just this sort of survey; fine transcriptions were later made of selected portions of the discourse.

Transcription is, for the most part, in conventional spelling, rather than in respellings as is often the case in analyses of medical discourse. There are several reasons for this choice. The transcription is more readable this way, and readability is important when diverse audiences are being addressed, as is the case here. Also, English letters do not allow precise phonetic transcription because one letter may represent various sounds ("o" in *bone, done,* and *gone,* for example) and one sound may be represented by several different letters (such as differing ways of spelling the [s] or [k] sounds). Therefore, inaccuracy is inevitable with respellings.

Also, virtually all transcriptions that use respellings are inconsistent. Transcribers never respell as much as they could; "city" is never respelled "siddy," for instance. Inconsistent choices to respell usually are not overtly justified by the transcriber and thus remain theoretically unprincipled.

Even when a phonetic transcription is possible with English orthography, the phonetic and phonological phenomena transcribed may not be relevant to the structure of the discourse event. Examples would be "iz" for "is" and "liddle" for "little." Both appear in published transcriptions of medical discourse. Of course, "is" always is pronounced with a [z]. And in American English, the huge majority of speakers pronounce the middle consonant of "little" as an alveolar flap, or "d" (the Brooklyn dialect may be an exception). These pronunciations are the norm and have no social significance. In this book, respellings are never used for invariant pronunciations such as "iz" or "liddle." I do, however, use respellings to represent pronunciations that may vary in some socially significant way—for example, with level of formality. For instance, "goin'" and "'kay" (variants for "going" and "okay") are associated with casual speech, as opposed to more formal varieties of talk.

Overall, in transcribing I tried to strike a balance between detail and readability. Detail helps the reader re-create the sound of the talk, but overly detailed transcripts are hard to read. A complete list of transcription conventions used in this book, with examples, appears in the appendix. These conventions draw on Edwards and Lampert (1993) and on the systems in M. Goodwin (1990) and Tannen (1989c).

2

The Whirlpool Discourse

Many Ways of Claiming Power

In this chapter, I illustrate ideas about power and give an overview of the multiple ways in which it can be claimed by patients and physicians. I suggest that all studies of power that measure only one speech activity—including my own studies of questions and topic transitions in chapters 3 and 4—are necessarily incomplete. This does not render such studies valueless. They provide important detailed pictures of ways of claiming power and data on who claims it and how often this happens. But when such studies are seen as exhaustive, absolute indices of the power balance between physician and patient, they often wrongly suggest that patients have no power and physicians have it all. The truth is much more complex.

Attributing all power to physicians contributes to stereotyping patients as passive and even incompetent. Without denying abuses of power by physicians, we can acknowledge patients' participation in decision making. To do so, we must examine the various ways the word "power" is used and we must develop an overview of power. With an overview, we can contextualize studies of just one speech activity.

Whether qualitative or quantitative, studies of power in medical discourse have usually focused on only one speech activity. Ainsworth-Vaughn (1992b) classified topic transition activities in relation to physicians' gender; K. Davis (1988) examined stories in gynecologist–patient interaction; Fisher and Groce (1990) studied accounts given by patients to nonphysician providers in relation to gender; West

(1984a), Frankel (1979), and Ainsworth-Vaughn (1994b) did quantitative studies of questions. In each case, the assumption was that the speech activity in focus served as a rough index to the providers' and patients' power in the encounter.

This chapter, by contrast, provides a picture of several major power-claiming discourse strategies working simultaneously. I discuss definitions and analytical categories for power and then describe the ways speech activities, discourse strategies, and other actions (uncapturable in terms of discourse structure) were used by the physician and patient to construct power. The discourse features of interest include interruptions, questions, the ways structural affiliation is invoked, and topic control. To anchor the discussion, I use a transcript of the initial six minutes of a physician–patient encounter.

Contexts for the Analysis

The following discourse excerpt is from the first recorded encounter between Dr. Miller, a 49-year-old oncologist, and Ms. Hazen, a 58-year-old woman.

This encounter was chosen for fine-grained analysis because my global impression of the interaction between Dr. Miller and Ms. Hazen was that this interaction was typical of the asymmetrical power balance so often described in other studies. When I chose the encounter, I had not yet done any analysis, so the choice was not made on the basis of the findings reported here. Instead, this study was exploratory, asking and answering these questions: What power-claiming discourse features appear in a typical, asymmetrical medical encounter? Who uses them? What makes up the asymmetry?

Before I did this analysis, I recorded Dr. Miller in a total of 17 encounters during my 1991–1995 study (see table 1.2) and thus was very familiar with his style. Dr. Miller appeared to fit the often-published description of a doctor who controls his medical encounters, asking numerous questions and portraying himself as an authority. Ms. Hazen, whom I met for the first time the day of this recording, gave the impression of being a quiet, deferential person in comparison with the other patients whose discourse I studied.

At the time of this encounter, Ms. Hazen was just finishing chemotherapy for breast cancer. She held two jobs: nurse's aide in a nursing home and companion to an Alzheimer's patient.

As is common in private practice, Dr. Miller and Ms. Hazen had an interactional history of several months duration. Also implied in the term "private practice" is an element of choice. For Ms. Hazen, the element of choice did exist; when Dr. Miller left the practice, Ms. Hazen did not accept his replacement, to whom she was assigned by Dr. Miller's staff. After one visit with Miller's replacement, she changed to a physician in a different practice. These two elements of the setting— interactional continuity and choice—may have supported Ms. Hazen's inclination to negotiate for her agenda.

The oncology diagnosis also may have played a role. In my quantitative study of 40 encounters (chapter 4), oncology patients asked twice as many questions (11.57/visit) as non-oncology patients (5.75/visit). The seriousness of the medical issue may motivate patients to raise their level of participation in the encounter. That sense of urgency appears in Ms. Hazen's remarks in the present discourse.

Besides setting and diagnosis, ethnicity of the participants may have made a difference in the degree to which the patient participated in shaping the encounter. Both patient and physician were white. Roter, Hall, and Katz, in a summary of results of 38 quantitative studies of medical interaction in which ethnicity was reported, found that "non-whites received less information and less positive talk than whites" (1988:112). West (1984b) also found patterns in her data suggestive of the influence of ethnicity (e.g., more black patients than white were first-named by the physician).

In her everyday life, Ms. Hazen was herself a caregiver in medical settings. Her familiarity with that role may have influenced her toward activity in her own medical encounters. However, Ms. Hazen's jobs are not at all prestigious within medical hierarchies, so they would not provide an extensive basis for the negotiation of identity and power (bases for negotiation are discussed in detail in chapter 4).

Having provided relevant ethnographic context, I now turn to the whirlpool discourse excerpt, which itself contextualizes the subsequent discussion of the nature and uses of power.

The Whirlpool Excerpt

The excerpt that follows is a transcript of the first six minutes of a regularly scheduled appointment between Dr. Miller and Ms. Hazen. In private practice there are many more repeat encounters than initial ones. The whirlpool excerpt, a repeat encounter, is intermediate between a series of history-taking questions (typical of first encounters), in which the patient's participation is limited, and the conversational discourse of a routine, unproblematic oncology checkup, such as Mr. Frisell's checkup described in chapter 5.

Transciption symbols and conventions are described in the appendix.

Apparently there were a few unrecorded utterances before the physician turned on the radio microphone. When the tape begins, Ms. Hazen is focusing Dr. Miller's attention on pain in her chest and on a hard place at the site of her surgery. Dr. Marsh, referred to in the excerpt, was Ms. Hazen's surgeon.

```
 1  Ms. Hazen:   It ACHES right in here it just RUBBIN' it
 2                  hurts .
 3               an' that . when I . it just, y'know,
 4                  PULLS 'n .
 5               LAST night I could just feel it .
 6                  tightening right up . in my chest.
 7  (4 sec)
 8  Dr. Miller:  Did you do anything exceptionally
 9                  . heavy?
10  Ms. Hazen:   N- [no]
11  Dr. Miller:      [In] the last day or two?
```

12	Ms. Hazen:	*WELL* I'm gettin' back to work,
13		I was *off* last week ya know,
14		I was gone to my *daugh*ter's.
15	Dr. Miller:	Um hm.
16	Ms. Hazen:	'N I got back to . the *nursing* home .
17		SUNDAY night.
18	Dr. Miller:	>Yes< but did you l-lift a PATIENT? . or:
19		.
20	Ms. Hazen:	Well I, I'm *ALWAYS* lifting patients and
21		[me]
22	Dr. Miller:	[see] it
23	Ms. Hazen:	you think maybe that might be it?
24		Gettin' back to [work]?
25	Dr. Miller:	[Well] I'm wondering if .
26		[yeah]
27	Ms. Hazen:	[yeah]
28	Dr. Miller:	[[yeah]]
29	Ms. Hazen:	[[Being]] off work for a week I got off .
30		my routine of . . LIFTING and . . .
31	Dr. Miller:	I don't *know*.
32	(4 sec)	
33	Ms. Hazen:	How does *that* look today.
34	Dr. Miller:	Ah, white count is *3.7*,
35	Ms. Hazen:	Uh-huh
36	Dr. Miller:	which is a
37		*LITTLE* low,
38	Ms. Hazen:	But . that's GOOD
39		for [me though].
40	Dr. Miller:	[But but] *that's* about what you
41		run, yeah ((chuckles))
42	Ms. Hazen:	((chuckles))
43	Dr. Miller:	*Actually*, you've been considerably *lower*
44		than that.
45	Ms. Hazen:	Uh . YEAH I know.
46	(4 sec)	
47	Dr. Miller:	This is your LA:ST
48	Ms. Hazen:	yeah
49	Dr. Miller:	cycle.
50	Ms. Hazen:	I *HOPE*. ((chuckles))
51	Dr. Miller:	WELL IT'S YOUR LAST CYCLE and then we'll
52		do a reevaluation.
53	Ms. Hazen:	M-hm.
54	Dr. Miller:	So this is your last cycle of *THIS* [and]
55	Ms. Hazen:	[M-hm]
56	Dr. Miller:	there *REALLY* wasn't anything measurable
57		*before*

58		[so] I don't *expect* to find anything.
59	Ms. Hazen:	[(?)]
60	Dr. Miller:	So . y'know.
61	Ms. Hazen:	mm
62	Dr. Miller:	I *think* you can safely
63		assume that this is your last
64		*treat*ment.
65		and *you'll* be right NINETY-NINE point
66		nine-nine percent of the [time] .
67	Ms. Hazen:	[M-hm.]
68	Dr. Miller:	>So<
69	Ms. Hazen:	I'm *HOPING* that spot that was . in my
70		*right* lung, I mean my *right* breast
71		will be . . y'know, this took [*CARE*]
72	Dr. Miller:	[We'll]
73	Ms. Hazen:	of it.
74	Dr. Miller:	*WE'LL* do: *another* mammogram
75	Ms. Hazen:	Uh huh .
76	Dr. Miller:	as PART of the evaluation.
77		So we'll find *OUT*.
78		(3 sec)
79	Ms. Hazen:	m . m *HOP*ing (???)((chuckles))
80	Dr. Miller:	[C'mon up.]
81	Ms. Hazen:	[*PROBABLY*] it's the same . thing. same
82		KIND of TUMOR that was in my LEFT
83		probably.
84	(4 sec)	
85	Dr. Miller:	Did DR. MARSH uh . put a *needle* in that?
86	Ms. Hazen:	No no
87	Dr. Miller:	No, in the, in the *LUMP* in the .
88		[*right* breast?]
89	Ms. Hazen:	[Oh in-in the] *RIGHT* breast no.
90	Dr. Miller:	[[<Okay.>]]
91	Ms. Hazen:	[[because]] it just was a sus-*suspicious*
92		. [spot] .
93	Dr. Miller:	[>Yeah. <]
94		Okay *OKAY*
95	Ms. Hazen:	[And so]
96	Dr. Miller:	[It was] NOT
97		anything you could *SEE*,
98	Ms. Hazen:	Yeah.
99	Dr. Miller:	*EXCEPT* on the mammogram.
100	Ms. Hazen:	*MAMMOGRAM*.
101	Dr. Miller:	Right.
102	Ms. Hazen:	An' . *HE* said that ah . . y'know I was
103		done with HIM un-unless, y'know, *YOU*

104		had .
105	Dr. Miller:	[M-hm.]
106	Ms. Hazen:	[something] else showed up, so. (9 sec)
107		That's *SO* darn *hard* in there.
108	(5 sec)	
109	Dr. Miller:	What *DOES Dr. Marsh* think that is.
110	Ms. Hazen:	*HE* said it's *scar* tissue. . he [said]
111	Dr. Miller:	[Now]
112		*BRING* your arm down. .
113	Ms. Hazen:	*HE* said that uh . y'know he had to do so
114		much re*pair* in [there and] *he* said .
115	Dr. Miller:	[>Okay *o*kay<]
116	Ms. Hazen:	"Y-you have to under*stand* . that um .
117		*y*'know . that it's going to take a
118		*WHILE* t' . get it . y'know . .
119		heal *up*."
120	Dr. Miller:	*TAKE* a deep breath in . . and again? . .
121		NOW I need you to lay down for me.
122		(5 sec) *Well* . y'know *THEY'VE* . *LEARNED*
123		. how to do those . . *incisions* . in
124		*VERY* precise [ways].
125	Ms. Hazen:	[Uh] Uh huh .
126	Dr. Miller:	But the *WAY* they end up looking when
127		you're all done is m-MUCH different
128		[from] one person to ano[ther].
129	Ms. Hazen:	[Mm.] [*I*] see.
130		>M-hm.<
131	Dr. Miller:	*You* have more . *FIRM*ness HERE . than *I'm*
132		used to seeing,
133		but then see you've done HARD . physical
134		[labor]
135	Ms. Hazen:	[Yeah.]
136	Dr. Miller:	. and they CUT through *muscles* and
137		[things].
138	Ms. Hazen:	[Yeah] . [*oh* yeah],
139	Dr. Miller:	[and I don't]
140	Ms. Hazen:	Uh huh.
141	Dr. Miller:	I DON'T know how he had to put that
142		[*all*] back to[geth]er.
143	Ms. Hazen:	[Yeah] [yeah]
144		Well see, eh y'know that TUMOR was so *big*
145		. he [said]
146	Dr. Miller:	[Yeh.]
147	Ms. Hazen:	size of a . *base*ball, an' [he] said
148	Dr. Miller:	[Mm]
149	Ms. Hazen:	"I had to do a lot of *repair*" but

150		. see it-IT-IT *scares* me because it .
151		SEEMS like it's going right up in-in
152		*here*
153		well see it *IS*
154		right here is the end of .
155	Dr. Miller:	[>Yeh.<]
156	Ms. Hazen:	[and] *that's* gettin' quite close to
157		((nervous chuckle)) [.] my NECK up
158	Dr. Miller:	[Yeh]
159	Ms. Hazen:	there.
160	Dr. Miller:	But see that feels like MUScle .
161	Ms. Hazen:	uh huh
162	Dr. Miller:	to me,
163	Ms. Hazen:	uh huh
164	Dr. Miller:	OR scar,
165	Ms. Hazen:	uh huh, uh huh .
166	Dr. Miller:	I don't *know*
167	Ms. Hazen:	Yeh, yeh.
168		(3 sec) My KIDS [say]
169	Dr. Miller:	[Does] THIS *BOTHER YOU*
170		enough . . that if they could go in
171		and REMOVE that some time,
172		would you [want] that d[one]?
173	Ms. Hazen:	[O:h] [*I*-I] would be
174		afraid to even [have] him go *IN*
175	Dr. Miller:	[Okay]
176	Ms. Hazen:	[doctor],
177	Dr. Miller:	[okay]
178	Ms. Hazen:	because
179	Dr. Miller:	I've
180	Ms. Hazen:	[Yeh]
181	Dr. Miller:	[I'm] just *ASKING* .
182	Ms. Hazen:	Yeh
183		because [(???)]
184	Dr. Miller:	[because] *SOME* women will .
185		*SOME* women will end up with a little
186		TAG down in the arm pit .
187	Ms. Hazen:	Uh huh, uh huh
188	Dr. Miller:	Just the way the *incision's* made a[gain],
189	Ms. Hazen:	[Yeh]
190	Dr. Miller:	[okay?]
191	Ms. Hazen:	[uh huh]
192	Dr. Miller:	And if that *BOTHERS* them enough,
193		y'know wearing [BRA] straps [and that]
194	Ms. Hazen:	[Yeh] [yeh m-hm]
195	Dr. Miller:	sort of thing .

196		then I tell 'em go [back] and get it .
197	Ms. Hazen:	[Yeh]
198	Dr. Miller:	*revised* . but
199	Ms. Hazen:	because it
200	Dr. Miller:	IF IT *DOESN'T*
201		*BOTHER* you .
202	Ms. Hazen:	M-hm
203	Dr. Miller:	I would tell you to
204		leave it [alone] .
205	Ms. Hazen:	[yeah] uh huh (3 sec)
206		*I know my KIDS WAS WONDERING if* .
207		*you* thought I should ah . be advised
208		to have a . >let me . um stand for
209		that< . to ah have . get a *whirl*pool
210		. hot tub or a *whirl*pool .
211		to *massage* that.
212	Dr. Miller:	(2 sec) >:Oh<.
213		>Take a deep breath in. (2 sec) Again.<
214		(4 sec) *WE'LL LOOK* AT THE *WHOLE PICTURE*.
215	Ms. Hazen:	Ah hah . >okay<
216	Dr. Miller:	Okay?
217	Ms. Hazen:	Okay.
218	Dr. Miller:	Like . whether or not we think you need
219		any *radia* [*tion*] . to this *side*?
220	Ms. Hazen:	[Mm.]
221		M-hm.
222	Dr. Miller:	BECAUSE it was a big tumor.
223	Ms. Hazen:	Yeah .
224	Dr. Miller:	Aah we'll look at . if we THINK you've
225		had enough of the [*chemo*],
226	Ms. Hazen:	[M-hm]
227	Dr. Miller:	which I'm pretty sure [we] already
228	Ms. Hazen	[Yeah.]
229	Dr. Miller:	[know] the *answer* to THAT,
230	Ms. Hazen:	[M-hm]
231	Dr. Miller:	but we'll lo- think that *through*,
232		and then *I THINK* if this is CAUSING you
233		dis*COM*fort . .
234		we should maybe have PHYSICAL therapy or
235		somebody e [*VAL*]uate you to *SEE* . if a
236	Ms. Hazen:	[Yeah.]
237	Dr. Miller:	WHIRLPOOL treatment or a DEEP HEAT
238		treatment
239	Ms. Hazen:	yeah
240	Dr. Miller:	or something [would]
241	Ms. Hazen:	[ah]

```
242  Dr. Miller:    help that. .
243                 MY GUESS IS that you have more
244                   MUSculature there,
245                 because you do so much [. lifting].
246  Ms. Hazen:                      [Yeah lifting]
247  Dr. Miller:    Okay?
248  Ms. Hazen:     Because I DO do a lot
```

{RH1, 6–36}

Having put this transcript on the table, I would like to consider Ms. Hazen's and Dr. Miller's ways of claiming power through talk. First, however, I need to establish definitions and analytical categories for power.

Kinds of Power

What is "power"?

Berger and Luckmann (1966) and Honneth (1991) review philosophical and social-theory analyses of the nature of power. A recurrent theme in these analyses is the definition of power as implementing one's agenda. In this approach, power is ethically neutral. Inevitably, in every decision, the preferences of one or more of the participants are enacted. I agree with this description of power. However, an anonymous reviewer of this chapter (in an earlier article form) objected to the idea that power is ethically neutral. The reviewer cited Burbules (1986) as a major proponent of the opposing view.

Burbules's definition of power is worth considering, in part because it is close to the popular understanding of power. Most people use the word "power" to mean domination, as Burbules does, and we generally avoid saying, or even thinking, that we are claiming power.

In Burbules's (1986) view, power is always domination, and domination involves a conflict of interest. If there is no conflict of interest, power is not realized. Thus, Burbules does not see parents as exercising power when they protect young children from danger against the children's will. It is in the interests of a child to be protected. Burbules is looking at the outcome; children are saved from harm when they are restrained from playing in the street, therefore the action is in their best interest, therefore power is not used. To move to the medical realm, we can imagine a physician acting to put a comatose patient on a respirator to save the patient's life; the patient is unable to act in her own interest, so the physician does so; for Burbules this is not a use of power.

There are several difficulties with this position. First, if we look at the process, not the outcome, it seems appropriate to label the parent's physical restraint as *power*. Second, the social/ethical situation is seldom so clear as in the examples of the child and the comatose patient. In medicine, patients may disagree with physicians about what is in their best interests. Even in the example of the comatose patient, these disagreements may arise; the patient's family may believe that the patient has no hope of regaining meaningful life and should be allowed to die. This raises the point that judgments of probable outcomes have a lot to do with judgments of best interests, and probable outcomes can be just as difficult to assess as best interests. If it is difficult, sometimes impossible, to know what someone's best interests are, a definition of power that rests on this knowledge is a shaky one.

In putting the comatose patient on a respirator, the physician may or may not have exercised power, as Burbules sees it, depending on our judgment of best interests. In my view, the physician did exercise power, power whose source lay in the physician's socially legitimated ability to make a medical decision and carry it out, power which is not defined by its outcome and which is in itself ethically neutral. Whether or not this action was ethically wrong, it was powerful.

Power as process

In the encounters I studied, decisions were negotiated between physicians and patients. Both put forward their views of probable outcomes and best interests. It is often difficult to say whose agenda prevailed in the end because participants modified their proposals on the basis of what they were hearing during the negotiation. This is illustrated in the whirlpool discourse; Ms. Hazen and Dr. Miller both propose actions (surgery, hydrotherapy). In the face of Ms. Hazen's rejection of surgery, and Dr. Miller's hesitance about hydrotherapy, the other participant in each case reiterated the proposal and then dropped it. Perhaps they were convinced, and their agendas then changed. Perhaps not. We might find some of the answer in an immediately subsequent interview, but even this would capture the negotiation only partially, because participants tend to remember the meaning that was finally agreed on—not every step of the negotiation along the way.

So both speakers were involved in making decisions in this encounter. If power resides in making a decision about what will happen, then both Dr. Miller and Ms. Hazen exercised power in the encounter. As Tannen points out, "It is misleading . . . to reify power as if there is one source of it and somebody has it and someone else doesn't" (1987:5). Power is constructed moment-to-moment during interaction, with all participants being involved, in turn, as either its claimers or its ratifiers.

The bases and discourse realization of power

My focus here is primarily on the process of constructing power. This focus involves, first, the bases for the power negotiation (H. Brody 1992; K. Davis 1988), and second, the discourse means for claiming control (Frankel 1979; Lakoff 1990; Fairclough 1989; K. Davis 1988; West 1984b; Ainsworth-Vaughn 1992a, 1992b, 1994a, 1994b). Control may be claimed over the emerging discourse or over future action (e.g., plans for treatment).

K. Davis (1988, following Giddens 1976, 1984) recognizes both "agency" (action of individuals) and "structure" (membership in social institutions) as bases for claiming power. Discourse moves are part of agency. *Structural power* in medical encounters is that arising from the speaker's affiliation with the social institution of medicine (e.g., physicians' socially legitimated right to prescribe drugs). The physician has a virtual monopoly on this basis for negotiation.

We can also speak about *charismatic power*, influence based on personal characteristics, such as kindness or decisiveness; *social power*, influence based upon social prestige; and *Aesculapian power*, ability to heal based on medical knowledge (these categories are from H. Brody [1992]). Both physicians and patients have access to these kinds of power, but physicians usually have much greater Aesculapian power than patients, and their social status is often quite high, as a result of the structural and social bases for power they enjoy. Participants' personal, social, and professional histories are brought into the event and serve as bases for the power negotiation that takes place there.

Besides categorizing by the bases on which power is claimed, we can discuss power in terms of the ways it is constructed in interaction. Power is constructed partially through actions that control the emerging discourse: participants' successful claims to speaker rights.

Speaker rights are related to identity. Theory in discourse study suggests that language users are engaged in constructing texts that embody their own and others' social identities, in accord with social maxims (Polanyi 1979) and their understanding of the event as a genre (Gumperz 1982; Hymes 1972; Scotton 1983; ten Have 1989; Wilson 1989). So talk is a major site for the moment-to-moment construction of an individual's social identity, as well as having goals specific to its context (e.g., medical or pedagogical goals). Identity is constructed in part by successful claims to speaker rights—the right to take a turn, to hold the floor an appropriate length of time, to initiate and pursue a topic, to finish a point. Most of this book is about the way identity and power are constructed, moment to moment, through talk in the medical encounter.

A third category of power involves control over plans, decisions, and physical actions. A patient may exercise power by physically tearing up a prescription on the way out of the clinic door. Tearing up the prescription, or choosing not to return for another appointment, would be nonverbal actions. But control over plans for treatment—future action—is a crucial form of power in the language of medical encounters. Like all the other types of power, control over action is available to both patient and provider, though not necessarily with equal ease of access for both. In the whirlpool discourse, as we will see, Ms. Hazen tried to exert control over plans for her treatment (i.e., future action).

Gender and power

Constructing gender in interaction involves relating actions to "normative conceptions of attitudes and activities that are appropriate for particular sex categories" (West 1993:59). These norms for gendered behavior are intimately tied up with rights to power, and talk is governed by gender/power norms just as other social activities are (Graddol and Swann 1989). For example, most studies find that men talk more than women, using up a scarce resource (time) and controlling topic (James and Drakich 1993). In the whirlpool discourse, Dr. Miller does talk more than Ms. Hazen does (and this was his pattern in general).

Study of gender and language is spread across many disciplines and methodologies are controversial. Most researchers agree that women and men grow up with two differing sets of norms for behavior; the ideal woman is culturally depicted as cooperative (seeking solidarity) whereas the ideal man is culturally depicted as competitive (seeking power) (M. Goodwin 1990; Tannen 1993b). Obviously, these norms pull women and men in different directions regarding interruptions, control of topic, and other ways of claiming power in conversation.

This "two cultures" hypothesis must be qualified. In Thorne's (1993) study of a fifth-grade class, more than half of the boys did not display the gender ideals. Still, the ones who did were the popular, influential boys. Here we see both the influence of gender ideals (the boys who exemplified them were popular) and the limits of that influence (other boys felt free to develop alternative ways of being masculine).

Tannen (1990, 1993c), popularly regarded as the source of the two-cultures hypothesis, actually suggests a more complex view of gender and discourse. For Tannen, gendered discourse, in which participants try to approach the cultural norms of cooperation and competition, is a reality. However, a discourse move can simultaneously realize power and solidarity. For example, a patient may address a woman doctor by her first name both because he feels friendly toward her (solidarity) and because he feels superior to her (power).

The literature on gender in medical interactions is reviewed in West (1993), Fisher and Groce (1990), and in chapter 3. In the whirlpool discourse, it may be that Ms. Hazen is deferent, and Dr. Miller is authoritarian, in part because of their orientation toward gender norms. Chapters 3 and 4 include data on gendered talk in medical encounters. In chapter 3, we see men controlling topic in unilateral ways, which would fit the cultural norms just described. But in chapter 4, the situation is more complex because female patients asked more questions than male patients—and questions are, as we have just discussed, claims to power.

In the next section, I analyze Dr. Miller's power-claiming activities.

Dr. Miller: Claims to Superordinate Rights

Interruptions

Not all overlaps of speech are interruptions (James and Clarke 1993). Dr. Miller's talk at four points (lines 169, 179, 184, and 200) does interrupt: It disruptively overlaps or cuts off Ms. Hazen's speech after she has embarked on a statement. Ms. Hazen does not interrupt Dr. Miller, under this definition.

I see these overlaps and cutoffs as violating a significant right of speakers, namely, the right to finish your point when you have the floor (Murray 1985), and therefore I classify them as interruptions. Henzl (1990) would agree; she describes these actions by physicians as "truncating" patients' talk. (Beckman and Frankel [1984] have a different, much wider definition of "interruption," as I point out in chapter 3.)

These interruptions were not necessary to accomplish the medical aims of the encounter. Even if a patient is rambling—not the case here—nonverbal ways of stopping the talk can be used without violating a speaker's rights. The physician can use gestures or facial expressions to display a desire to take a turn at talk. Non-verbal signals allow patients to finish what they were saying and then hand over the floor to the physician.

Questions

Questions claim the turn-taking right of determining who will be the next speaker. They also claim the right to control over the topic. Questions have frequently been seen as a rough index to participants' power in medical encounters (Ainsworth-Vaughn 1994b, 1992b; Frankel 1979; Maynard 1980; West 1984b).

Dr. Miller asked five of the eight true questions in the encounter; they are listed below. His questions were unmitigated. All five were marked as questions by changes in word order (auxiliary verbs switch places with the subject: "did he" instead of "he did"). Four of those five were also marked with rising intonation at the end of the sentence (indicated with the ? symbol):

Line	WH	Aux	Subject	
8–9		Did	you	do anything exceptionally . heavy?
18		did	you	l-lift a PATIENT? .
85		Did	Dr. MARSH	uh . put a *needle* in that?
109	What	*DOES*	Dr. *Marsh*	think that is.
169–172		Does	THIS	*BOTHER YOU* enough . . that if they could go in and REMOVE that sometime would you want that done?

Questions that work by changing word order and intonation are known as "direct" questions. They are interactionally strong; because of their obvious word order and intonation markings, they demand a response. These discourse forms claim speaker rights by choosing the next speaker and choosing that speaker's topic. In contrast to Dr. Miller's interruptions, Dr. Miller's questions claim rights that are an expected consequence of his social role in the event. Knowledge of medical encounters includes the expectation that physicians will directly question patients in order to accomplish medical aims.

Invoking structural affiliations

Social identity is constituted by claims to speaker rights and also by invoking structural affiliations. (The two are related—structural affiliations can be the basis for claiming speaker rights.) Dr. Miller emphasized his Aesculapian knowledge by repeatedly invoking his affiliation with other providers (lines 85, 109, 122, 141, 231–242), who also were socially legitimated as possessors of Aesculapian knowledge.

By doing this, Dr. Miller was suggesting that physicians have the right (structural power) and the ability (Aesculapian power) to solve riddles such as the one Ms. Hazen was posing. Certainly physicians' medical training provides Aesculapian tools for these tasks, as well as structural legitimacy for physicians' decisions. Claims to Aesculapian knowledge, however, were at times viewed skeptically by Ms. Hazen. Her repetitions of concern about the hard tissue, in spite of Dr. Miller's suggestion that it was only muscle or scar, are evidence of her skepticism. Ms. Hazen was also skeptical about the physician who later replaced Dr. Miller. In her 1994 interview, she stated that she did not "trust" Dr. Miller's replacement, and so she changed physicians. When I asked for an example of the problem, she said that she disagreed with this physician's position on the use of bone scans.

None of the participants in this process correctly diagnosed Ms. Hazen's pain. Dr. Marsh eventually discovered, by reopening the incision, that the pain was caused by fluids accumulating in Ms. Hazen's chest.

By the time Dr. Miller left town, Ms. Hazen had been given reason to view claims to Aesculapian knowledge skeptically. In the preceding year, her two physicians both were mistaken about the nature of her pain. Dr. Marsh thought the pain and hard tissue were part of the healing process. Dr. Miller thought the pain might be muscle strain from heavy lifting. Actually, as surgery disclosed, the pain was caused by fluid accumulation.

These contradictory and mistaken opinions are nothing to be ashamed of; they are inevitable, in a complex medical problem. But they do suggest that the difficulties of diagnosing and of healing are so great that Aesculapian power is limited. Aesculapian power (knowledge that brings about healing) may accompany the structural power (medical license) of the physician erratically or not at all. Patients such as Ms. Hazen can learn this and become justifiably skeptical of Aesculapian knowledge. In that case, invoking affiliation with other providers may not be an effective way of laying claim to power in medical encounters.

At the end of the excerpt, when Ms. Hazen asked for the whirlpool bath, Dr. Miller made his structural affiliations extremely overt. He juxtaposed the whirlpool with chemotherapy and radiation, which are developed and dispensed by the medical establishment he represents. In lines 231 through 242, he made it plain that Ms. Hazen's suggestion would have to be legitimated by the medical establishment: "we'll lo- think that *through*, and then *I THINK* if this is CAUSING you dis*COM*fort . . we should maybe have PHYSICAL therapy or somebody e*VAL*uate you to *SEE* if a WHIRLPOOL treatment" would help. Dr. Miller here overtly constituted physicians and physical therapists as having, but patients as lacking, structural access to procedures and structural rights to make medical decisions, resting upon Aesculapian knowledge.

He produced a similar effect through pronoun use. In these same lines, he moved from "we," which is ambiguous in voice ("we medical people" or "we two"; cf. Henzl 1990), to "I", a voice that was his alone, with which he claimed the right to make a decision. Thus Dr. Miller appropriated Ms. Hazen's suggestion for treatment.

Topics and future action

At one point, Dr. Miller failed to respond to a topic initiated by Ms. Hazen: He insisted on pursuing the topic "reasons for surgery" when Ms. Hazen was clearly trying to introduce the topic "reasons against surgery." Dr. Miller proposed surgery as possible future action and laid out a plan of future action in which he and his medical colleagues would determine whether or not Ms. Hazen was entitled to use a whirlpool bath. These were claims to both speaker rights and structural power.

However, Dr. Miller did share the decision-making power with Ms. Hazen by posing the surgery option to her in the form of a choice ("would you want that") and by agreeing to her veto of surgery. These were particularly important ways of sharing power because they conceded to Ms. Hazen control over her future treatment.

Ms. Hazen: Passive or Deferent?

Distinguishing passivity from deference

Patients' discourse has been described as "passive and powerless" (Roter 1977:283). Ms. Hazen used hesitation phenomena and mitigated forms of questions, and her overlapping talk was not disruptive; these discourse features might be interpreted as passivity. However, she asked a substantial number of questions, and she actively worked to control the topic and to secure the treatment she preferred. She emphatically vetoed Dr. Marsh's suggestion of treatment (surgery) and issued her own suggestion of treatment (the whirlpool).

Mitigation can be used to display deference. Deference is a universal cultural phenomenon whereby speakers acknowledge others' socially conferred authority. Deference is not necessarily evidence of passivity, although it can dilute one's claims to speaking rights and attempts to control treatment, as we shall see in regard to Ms. Hazen's mitigated questions.

Schiffrin says that in a couple she studied, "Surface forms of competition and disagreement often disguise underlying cooperation and sociability" (1984:322). But it can work the other way around: Surface forms of cooperation and sociability can disguise underlying competition and disagreement—deference is not the same as acquiescence.

It is patients' awareness of structural, charismatic, Aesculapian, and social bases for power that creates their need to show deference to physicians. Being deferent does not imply that patients are relinquishing all control over their actions. A deferent patient may walk out the door planning not to follow the physician's orders. Patients thus can remain agents in their own stories.

I define passivity as a refusal to claim power. Ms. Hazen was not passive. She did make significant claims to power. She did so in a deferent way, by mitigating her questions and other comments. The mitigation was accomplished with hesitation phenomena, noncanonical syntactic and phonological question forms, ambiguity of discourse function, and other forms such as the respect term "doctor" (line 176). This mitigation constitutes deference.

Hesitation phenomena

In much of this encounter, Ms. Hazen's speech incorporated brief pauses and repetition of initial sounds or syllables. These hesitation phenomena have been seen as evidence of patients' powerlessness in medical encounters (West 1984b). I would suggest instead that they are deferential. They are not passive; they do not prevent Ms. Hazen from keeping on topic and suggesting treatment.

On the other hand, this hesitancy is risky. It opens the way for Dr. Miller to see Ms. Hazen as unsure of herself. Though I have not compared types of deference, I suspect that some are less risky than others. Using a question to formulate a proposed action is probably not as open to this sort of misinterpretation as hesitation phenomena are. Similar problems arise with other types of deference, as I discuss below in regard to some of Ms. Hazen's heavily mitigated questions.

Interruptions

Ms. Hazen's overlapping talk consists almost entirely of "yeah" and "m-hm," without subsequent attempts to introduce a new point or topic. These utterances (known in the literature as "backchannels") are not considered by discourse analysts to be interruptions because they do not disrupt the topic or claim the floor (James and Clarke 1993). But avoiding an interruption is polite behavior, not passive behavior. Ms. Hazen's noninterruptive style was in accord with social rules of appropriateness for overlapping talk. On the contrary, it was Dr. Miller who was violating rules of appropriateness by truncating Ms. Hazen's topics (e.g., her attempts in lines 176, 178, and 183 to explain why she did not want surgery).

Questions

An important, sometimes problematic way of constituting deference appears in the fact that Ms. Hazen's three questions were mitigated. Dr. Miller's questions were marked with changes in word order and also with rising intonation. Ms. Hazen's questions instead were marked with only one of these two signals or with other, less overt, signals.

One of her three questions was marked with rising intonation and with a questioning word but not with a change in word order: "you think maybe that may be it? Gettin' back to work?" (lines 23–24). One was marked with a change in word order but not with rising intonation: "How does *that* look today." (line 33). The third, most mitigated one, was linguistically marked as a question only with a questioning word: "*I know my KIDS WAS WONDERING* if . *you* thought I should ah . be advised to have a . >let me . um stand for that< . . to ah have . get a *whirl*pool . hot tub or a *whirl*pool . to *massage* that." (lines 206–211). This last question was also mitigated with several indications of uncertainty: "ah," hesitations, and the correction of "have" to "get."

These mitigated questions are less likely to be answered than unmitigated ones (Bonanno 1982; Weijts 1993b). Of course, unanswered questions can be reinstated or upgraded in strength.

Norms for medical encounters include the expectation that patients will ask questions eliciting the doctor's opinion. Therefore, Ms. Hazen's first two questions could be unmitigated without violating social rules of appropriateness. But the third one is a special case; it requires a high degree of mitigation because it has two discourse functions—question and proposal—and the proposal may be face threatening to the physician. Rather than just asking for his opinion, it suggests what he should do.

This third question was mitigated in sentence structure, intonation, and markers of uncertainty, as mentioned previously. It was also mitigated in two more ways. Ms. Hazen provided another layer of mitigation by attributing the question to her kids rather than to herself (cf. J. Brody [1991] for discussion of this form of mitigation). Yet another type of mitigation was provided by the dual function of the utterance. The proposal function of the remark was mitigated by the presence of the question function.

The whirlpool utterance functioned both as a question and as a suggestion or proposal for treatment. Ms. Hazen may have genuinely wondered whether a whirlpool would help, and so requested that information (the question function).[1] But by raising the possibility, she also proposes the whirlpool as a possible treatment (the proposal function). The question function mitigates the proposal function, which would encroach on the physician's traditional identity as the proposer of treatment. The presence of two possible functions for this remark allows the doctor to choose which will be acknowledged, so that he is not confronted with a direct suggestion as to what treatment should take place.

Because the whirlpool question/proposal was a potentially threatening discourse move, all this mitigation (deference) may have been effective, getting the proposal on the table in such a way that the physician's social identity was not threatened. In this way, Ms. Hazen collaborated with the construction of the physician's identity as having Aesculapian and structural power.

In quantitative terms, Ms. Hazen claimed power by asking a substantial proportion of questions: 37.5% (three of the eight) questions in the encounter. This is a far cry from the 9% in West's (1984a) comparable counts of patients' questions, but it is not unrepresentative. In my quantitative study (chapter 4), patients asked almost 39% of the 838 unambiguous questions in the 40 medical encounters (including Ms. Hazen's encounters).

The best-known studies of questions in medical encounters are West (1984a) and Frankel (1979). They found patients asking 9% and 1% of total questions, respectively. As I point out in chapter 4, Frankel's definition of "question" was extremely restrictive (the question had to be the first utterance in a turn, and it had to raise a new topic). His results cannot be compared with those of other researchers.

West's definition is directly comparable with mine, and the disparity between the 9% she found and the larger numbers I found is discussed in chapter 4. However, in the rest of the (less well-known) literature I examined, patients' questions have ranged from 25% to 50% of the total. Roter, Hall, and Katz (1988) summarize the results of nine quantitative studies of medical encounters in which some form of questioning was studied; by my count of their reported figures, patients asked 25% of the questions. In Roter's own 1984 study, patients asked 43% of the questions. In one pediatric encounter, Tannen and Wallat (1983) found the physician asking 19 questions and the mother asking 18, or 50%. So Ms. Hazen's 37.5% and the overall 39% reported in chapter 4 are fully consistent with the literature overall.

Topics and future action

Ms. Hazen responded to the topics raised by Dr. Miller, but she then returned to her own topics. Ms. Hazen exerted significant control over the topics of this discourse. She first set the topic (chest pain and the hard tissue, with possible implication of a cancer recurrence) and then pursued it with determination. For example, in lines 49–157 she insisted on maintaining the topic of cancer in the hard place, in the face of Dr. Miller's suggestion that the hard place might be either scar tissue from the way the incision was repaired or muscle from her "hard physical labor."

Ms. Hazen was clear and emphatic in rejecting the possibility of future action in the form of surgery. She introduced her own proposal for future action, the whirlpool bath. Topic control and control over plans for future action are critical aspects of the encounter. Topics, after all, are the substance of the encounter. And if we were ranking the importance of these various types of control, surely control over plans for future action would be among those types at the top of the list.

Summary

Ms. Hazen and Dr. Miller collaborated to construct social/structural identities, to develop an understanding of the meaning of Ms. Hazen's pain and hard tissue, and to develop a treatment plan. All these meanings and plans were negotiated between the two speakers. Overall, Dr. Miller was dominant in the moment-to-moment construction of social identities, laying claim to superordinate speaker rights. He asked more questions and he interrupted Ms. Hazen. At times, he ignored the topics she introduced.

Dr. Miller also claimed superordinate rights regarding diagnosis and treatment—the possible use of the whirlpool—based on his structural affiliations and Aesculapian knowledge. But he accepted Ms. Hazen's suggestion that a whirlpool might be an appropriate type of treatment, and he saw Ms. Hazen as having the right to choose whether or not she would have surgery.

Ms. Hazen was active. She asked a substantial number of questions. She behaved in a deferential way, using hesitation phenomena and mitigating her demands upon Dr. Miller, especially when her action might be construed as in conflict with a physician's structural rights to determining treatment. She did not interrupt.

Ms. Hazen was not passive (i.e., she did not refuse to claim power). She laid claim to important speaker rights, including the critical right of choosing the topic. She also claimed the important right to suggest and to veto types of treatment.

In fact, Ms. Hazen set topics and pursued them persistently. She deferred to Dr. Miller's topic of surgery long enough to reject surgery, and then she returned to her concern about the hardness of the lump in her breast. So Ms. Hazen succeeded in pursuing her agenda for the encounter. I picked this encounter for close analysis because my impression of this doctor–patient pair was that they fit the usual depiction of an asymmetrical relationship between doctor and patient. And, in fact, the discourse was asymmetrical in many ways. Ms. Hazen had to work hard to maintain her topic and propose treatment. But it was not so asymmetrical in outcome: Ms. Hazen may have worked hard to implement her agenda, but she succeeded.

A word on implications for medical practice is appropriate. Should Ms. Hazen have to work so hard to realize her agenda? Should her topic be set aside? Should she be interrupted? Should her suggestion for treatment be appropriated? Was it necessary for Dr. Miller to reiterate his authority, his identity as the socially legitimated source of ideas about treatment? I think not. These behaviors risked disenfranchising the patient by taking over the topic and silencing her.

Are these behaviors by Dr. Miller paternalistic? I believe so; they suggest disrespect for Ms. Hazen and an inability to see the physician–patient relationship as a partnership.

These behaviors also run the risk of leaving Ms. Hazen unhappy with her encounter. There were at least two points of view among Dr. Miller's patients in regard to satisfaction with their encounters. Ms. Hazen stated in an interview that she was satisfied. Ms. Ivey, in her interview, was not: "There's only one of us in a room when there's two of us, the doctor's doing all the talking" {IJ-I, 11–19}.

By describing the many ways physician and patient lay claim to different kinds of power, I have suggested here that analyses of only one type of discourse move can never capture all of the power constructed as the emerging discourse, an understanding of the problem, a plan for treatment, and social identities are all negotiated by the participants. Ms. Hazen and Dr. Miller drew on a repertoire of discourse moves, including interruptions, questions, topic control, and symbolic invocations of social identity.

Making the picture more complex, any one of these discourse moves (such as the whirlpool question/proposal) can have multiple meanings. Analyses of a single discourse move are fruitful only when their results are kept in perspective, as part of a larger, much more complex theory of the construction of power. And the teaching of medical interviewing needs to rest on such broader theories, in order to help new physicians understand the many ways they and their patients claim power through talk in encounters.

II

QUANTITATIVE STUDIES OF POWER-CLAIMING TALK

3

Gender and Topic Control

One of the most frequent complaints patients make about physicians is that physicians do not listen well. This complaint implies—quite accurately—that listening is an activity. However, most of us, physician and patient alike, have done very little analysis of what it means to carry out this activity. Probably most patients and physicians identify listening with silence. It is true that silence can be important. But in listening, certain kinds of brief talk are even more important than silence.

Silence by one speaker makes time available for another speaker to talk. But silence by itself cannot in any way demonstrate that the first speaker heard, understood, or cared about what was said. Talk can do that.

Listening is often displayed at the start of the hearer's turn, in the way the hearer's words relate to the speaker's topic. When the hearer's words reflect what the speaker was saying, we have clear proof that the speaker was heard. When the hearer affirms what the speaker said, we have evidence that the two people agree. When the hearer goes on to maintain the speaker's topic, we have proof that he or she cares about it enough to keep it on the table: It is a valued topic. These ways of treating another person's topic unambiguously demonstrate listening, whereas silence can have a variety of meanings.

Ways of dealing with another speaker's topic are the subject of this chapter. Because topic control is complex, this chapter looks only at the precise ways of closing down a topic.

By involving the other person in the decision to close down a topic, a speaker can avoid cutting off the other speaker before hearing everything that needs to be said. This is power-sharing behavior. Or, the speaker can claim the power to unilaterally change topics, and suddenly make the switch. In that case, one speaker makes the decision to close the topic and does so without securing agreement from the other. In this way, the speaker claims power over the content of the conversation.

Gender may be a factor in the ways topics are changed.

Gender and Power in Medical Encounters

In chapter 2, I introduced the role of gender in discourse and the common finding that women are more likely to be cooperative in discourse, whereas men are more likely to be competitive. The studies of gender in medical discourse tend to support that finding.

There are indications that male and female physicians claim power to different extents and in different ways. West suggested that U.S. female physicians were interrupted more often than men (1984c) and were more egalitarian in the way they issued directives, or commands (1990). Pizzini (1991) found Italian female physicians more egalitarian than men in the number of directives they used (if a smaller number of directives from the physician implies a more equal balance of power) and less likely than male physicians to use humor to stop patients from talking.

Another indicator that physicians' behavior differs with their gender appears in patients' satisfaction: Both male and female patients evaluated care from female residents more favorably than care from male residents (Linn, Cope, and Leake 1984). Apparently this is not caused by differences in the residents' modes of treatment; a review of the literature by Arnold et al. (1988) found no reported differences between male and female physicians in actual therapeutic actions taken. Arnold et al. suggest that ways of communicating, discourse behavior, probably are the source of this difference in patients' satisfaction.

However, the data on gender and medical discourse is not yet extensive. Discourse studies (and conclusions) have been based on very small numbers of female physicians. K. Davis's (1988) study of gender and power involved a review of 315 tapes with 52 physicians, but all the physicians were men (63% of the patients were women). In West's (1984c) well-known study mentioned earlier, 21 medical encounters were analyzed, but only four encounters involved female physicians. All four female physicians were white. Two of the four encounters were with black women patients, one encounter was with a black man, and one was with a white man. The ethnic diversity of the patients is a complicating factor in evaluating West's results; did differences arise from gender, from ethnicity, or from some combination?

In Pizzini's (1991) study, mentioned earlier, again only four female physicians were studied. The comparison was between four female gynecologists and four male gynecologists, in a total of 40 encounters. Pizzini did not say how many encounters took place with each gender of physician, so the scope of her data is unclear.

To some extent, small numbers are a by-product of the labor-intensive nature of discourse study. Transcribing and analyzing tapes and transcripts is time-consuming. The number of speech activities performed during a very short period of time is huge. The tapes must be played over and over again, both during transcription and during analysis. Interactions among phonology, syntax, semantics, pragmatics, and numerous contextual features are very complex. For these reasons, a discourse study cannot examine many hundreds of speakers and tapes, as do coding studies which omit analysis of speech activities.

Nevertheless, studies of gender in medical discourse can be carried out with attention to comparability of the data on men and women. Though encounters and participants will never be identical, they should be chosen for contextual similarities. For this chapter, I matched encounters not only according to gender but also according to the seriousness of the medical issues and (as much as possible) according to specialty.

Why Study Topics, and What Are They?

The importance of topic control

K. Davis thinks that "control over topicality is one of the primary ways that power is exercised by professionals in institutional encounters" (1988:304). Mishler (1984) would agree. In discussing a transcribed medical encounter, Mishler praises a physician who links utterances to previous discourse:

> Listening is a necessary condition of the joint construction of meanings, but it is not sufficient. . . . This physician ties his questions and comments to the patient's accounts. In this way, he shows that he has not only listened, but that he has heard. He refers explicitly to what she has said. . . . This is the reverse of what we found in typical medical interviews. (1984: 182–183)

This discussion sounds like the topic transition activity described by Maltz and Borker as characteristic of women: "Women at the beginning of their utterances explicitly acknowledge and respond to what has been said by others. . . . women attempt to link their utterance to the one preceding it by building on the previous utterance or by talking about something parallel or related to it" (1982:210).[1]

The widely cited study by Beckman and Frankel (1984) also is relevant to topic control. Their study of interruptions was based on a definition of interruption which appears to include topic control. Beckman and Frankel suggest that patients' topics were often lost because physicians took control early in the encounter.

So we see in the literature suggestions that topic-affecting conversational activities are important, and that there is a relationship between gender and ways of changing topics. There are, however, no previous in-depth studies of topic-changing talk in medical encounters. One reason for this absence of studies may be found in the troubles analysts have had in defining topics.

Definition of "Topic"

Studies of topic outside of discourse analysis define the word loosely. Within discourse analysis, the notion "topic" is problematic. Brown and Yule say that "formal attempts to identify topics are doomed to failure. . . ." (1983:68). The problem for Brown and Yule rests in the difficulty of determining an overarching abstract topic of the discourse (the macro topic), on the one hand, and the difficulty of drawing boundaries for micro topics, on the other. In referential content, the micro topic consists of the new bits of meaning presented sentence by sentence (Schegloff and Sacks's "topic shading" [1984:82]).

"Topic" means something either too large or too small to be analyzed when it refers only to meaning (referential content). This is a fact which must be confronted in analyses of topic; its avoidance clouds the findings of Crow's (1983) and Fishman's (1983) studies of topic changes in couples' conversation.

Sequential versus referential ties to preceding discourse

Although it is difficult to deal with referential meaning, some of this difficulty can be avoided by dealing with social actions as well as referential content. It is also helpful to focus on the micro level of emerging discourse—one move at a time rather than the entire event.

Topicality is not only a matter of content but also a matter of speakers' social actions, their ways of connecting to previous talk (Maynard 1980:263). We can look at the actions speakers take to construct transitions from topic to topic, not the referential shifts alone (Schegloff and Sacks 1984). West and Garcia (1988) brought this approach to bear on topic transitions made in conversations between 10 students, 5 women and 5 men, who just met as part of a sociology experiment.

West and Garcia define topic transitions as lacking "sequential or referential" relationship to the preceding discourse. They provide a detailed discussion of sequential topic transition activities, focusing on a contrast between *collaborative* (also called *reciprocal*) and *unilateral* activities; men initiated all the unilateral transitions. West and Garcia's work on these sequential activities is a primary point of departure for the present study. At the same time, there are problems with West and Garcia's unqualified use of the phrase "sequential and referential."

West and Garcia acknowledge the difficulties of dealing with referential content and focus on speakers' social activities instead. However, their analysis still must partially rest on referential content.

Brown and Yule (1983) would suggest that it is problematic to attempt to find breaks in the referential path. Almost all gaps in the referential path can be crossed by doing inferential work. For instance, in one of West and Garcia's (1988:565) examples, students first discuss the fact that one participant is majoring in sociology, with plans to go to law school. The other participant then says, "Did ju take this fer- did you sign up for this test to impress?" (transcription by West and Garcia).

This sequence is offered as a unilateral topic transition, and I agree with that categorization. However, I do not agree with West and Garcia's *justification* for the categorization.

West and Garcia are claiming that the referential path has been broken. But this is not necessarily so. There are inferential relationships between this statement and the previous discourse. If sociology is your major, you wish to impress the sociology faculty in order to do well in your major. This topic change therefore violates West and Garcia's own definition, which requires that the new topic lack referential relationship to the preceding discourse.

Inference is the key issue. In the example of "sudden topic change" given later in this chapter (excerpt 6), there are inferential relationships between the patient's question whether life in pain is worth living and the physician's question whether the patient will soon see her therapist. Those inferential relationships are complex, including both semantic information about the nature of therapists' work and social information about the obligations of the physician (which, he implies, do not include therapy). But it would be inaccurate to say that the referential path had been broken. There are referential relationships between the two utterances, in both excerpt 6 and West and Garcia's example about signing up for the experiment in order to impress.

For medical discourse—perhaps in partial contrast to the less-focused discourse analyzed by West and Garcia—virtually all participants' contributions can be inferentially related to one another and to the medicosocial task at hand.

West and Garcia define topic transitions in terms of both referentiality and sequentiality. So I am in the position of agreeing with West and Garcia that a topic change has occurred in their example but finding that their definition of topic change does not apply to the example in terms of referentiality. How about sequentiality?

It may be helpful, in defining topic transitions, if we follow Widdowson's (1979:96–99) hierarchical model of discourse. A hierarchical model goes beyond the sequential model implicit in West and Garcia (1988; based in turn on Schegloff and Sacks [1984]).

In a hierarchical model there are larger units, usually known as speech events, which are made up of smaller discourse units, which we will call speech activities. Discourse exists in two ways: (1) as speakers' abstract knowledge of the nature and order of the usual speech activities that make up a speech event, and (2) as the actual emerging activities (the only dimension in a sequential model).

Widdowson distinguishes between coherence, or relationships on the abstract level between discourse units, and cohesion, or surface level relationships between linguistic features of actual emerging activities. Because coherence and cohesion overlap, distinguishing between them will not solve all our problems. However, the distinction allows us to move closer to a workable definition of topic change, because with it we can include and exclude certain kinds of sequentiality based on coherence. We can also specify at least some of the cohesive devices at issue.

COHERENCE: ENACTING NORMS FOR SEQUENCES OF ACTS   Coherence occurs on the abstract level at which participants construe relationships among discourse moves and structures. It is on this level that the medical encounter is understood by speakers to be a genre (ten Have 1989). Genres are known as norms participants have developed for the typical structure of the event. These norms have to do with the purpose of the interaction, permissible topics, act sequences (e.g., history taking or the physical exam within the encounter), and social rights and obligations of the participants (Hymes 1972).

So, in this hierarchical model of discourse, a new topic can be sequentially related to previous topics because it is in accord with abstract norms for the act sequence of the genre. In this view, West and Garcia's definition again is not specific enough, because breaks in this sort of sequential organization of the event are rare indeed.

For example, a patient may expect the physician to change a topic unilaterally. Past experience with medical encounters may have built up the expectation that sudden topic-changing by physicians is a norm in medical encounters. In that case, when the physician does suddenly change topics, the patient will not perceive a break in the sequential organization of the speech event as a whole.

COHESION: TYING TOGETHER ACTUAL UTTERANCES   On the other hand, ties between turn-by-turn speech activities can also be seen as *sequential*. This is an entirely different matter from the abstract norms by which coherence is judged. *Sequential* here instead refers to turn-by-turn organization, and this is the meaning West and Garcia had in mind.[2]

Ties between turn-by-turn speech activities constitute *cohesion*. Sometimes a topic is not tied to the preceding turn, either by meaning or by related words. In that case, the second turn is not cohesive with the first.

Cohesive ties are important to my definitions of topic transitions. Some easily identified and extremely common forms of cohesion are anaphoric pronouns, repetition (cf. Tannen 1989c), and use of a synonym or closely related term ("I have a *pain* in my back" followed by "Show me where it *hurts*"; mention of a specific medicine after mention of the class, "medications"). In the discourse examined here, the huge majority of turns at talk were tied together by these common cohesive devices. But when they were missing, the possibility of topic change was raised by their absence.

Inference is again the problematic issue. How much inferential work should have to be done for the analyst to say that the topic was changed?

For instance, suppose the patient mentions that her cholesterol has been high, and the physician says, "There's a medication called Mevacor that might help." The cohesion is not expressed through repetition or anaphora. In many of these cases, we can imagine an underlying word or syntactic structure[3] which does establish cohesion directly. In the example just given, the underlying structure would be, "There's a medication called Mevacor that might help *lower the cholesterol*." Or, we can say that *Mevacor* is a "closely related term" (i.e., a medication for high cholesterol levels). These are inferences on the part of the analyst, and there were a few cases such as these that led to disagreement among raters. So some of the problems with referentiality encountered by previous studies remain here. Because we can specify cohesion in many ways, however, the issues may be clarified and the problems reduced in number by introducing cohesion as a defining feature and by specifying types of cohesion.

The important point is this: *When talk is not cohesive with the preceding turn, a shift will occur in the immediate focus of participants' attention. Participants will have to do more inferential work in order to find coherence.*

As well as making demands on inference, lack of cohesion can send a negative social message. The quote from Mishler in the first section of this chapter suggested that cohesion between physicians' and patients' utterances may legitimize patients' concerns and that cohesion always displays listenership. When cohesion is lacking, however, the person who changes the topic has claimed power by claiming the right to direct the encounter without displaying attention to the previous speaker's topic.

To sum up: Coherence may be present without cohesion, but cohesion is important as a display of listenership. Listenership displays imply respect for other speakers' rights to co-construct the topic.

Referential and social meaning are profoundly connected in these encounters. The point is often made that conversational activities display social relationships. But social activities also have consequences for referential content (cf. Clayman 1992).

If both participants contribute to closing down a topic, these activities are reciprocal and move toward parity between the two (the social consequences); at the same time, they ensure that each participant has finished contributing information (the referential consequences). When one person successfully attempts to shift the topic in a relatively unilateral way, that is, without reciprocal topic-closure activities, that person has claimed control over the topic rather than control being shared. At this point, the other person's topic may be lost.

If this means that the patient loses the opportunity to add information, the result may be an incorrect diagnosis. The way topics are closed down has both social and referential/medical importance, and the social act of changing the topic cannot in fact be separated from its referential/medical consequences, though we may do so for analytical purposes.

My definition of topic transitions uses specific criteria that are both referential and sequential. First, a new topic will lack referential cohesion—realized through repetition or related words—with immediately previous discourse.

Second, I follow West and Garcia (1988) in examining sequences of social activity and whether or not those sequences involve reciprocal behavior. These activities may be unilateral, reciprocal, or somewhere in between. I introduce some new categories of these sequences.

Instead of using only two categories—unilateral and reciprocal—as West and Garcia did, I place these two categories at opposite ends of a continuum and add some new categories along the continuum. Intervening between the extremes I place the sequence described by Mishler (1984), which I call "links," and one which I call "minimal links" (figure 3-1). All these sequences are *topic-transition activities*. Movement along this continuum may represent increasing claims to power over discourse (i.e., control over emerging talk).

Examples of these four types of activities appear in a later section.

```
---Reciprocal---------        ------------------Unilateral-----------------------------------
Reciprocal Activities     Links     Minimal Links     Sudden Topic Change
```

Figure 3-1   Continuum of Topic-Transition Activities

Joint versus unilateral action

This discussion of topic transitions as placed along a continuum, becoming less and less cohesive with previous discourse, raises the crucial theoretical issue of shared versus unilateral action in conversation.

Ethnomethodologists point out the cooperative nature of discourse, and ethnographers of speaking agree that discourse is constructed by participants. If discourse is always cooperatively constructed, is it even possible for a sudden topic change to be unilateral? The same question phrased somewhat differently is an issue in chapter 6: If discourse is always cooperatively constructed, how can one sort of talk be characterized as co-construction when another is not? The answer is: It is a matter of degree. Technically, nothing in talk is wholly unilateral and everything that happens is co-constructed. Nevertheless, it is important to ask what degree of control each speaker has, and to what degree each participant's speaker rights are acknowledged. In other words, where does the encounter fall on the continuum between power-sharing (reciprocal) activities and power-hoarding (unilateral) activities?

A participant can attempt suddenly to shift the topic, but other participants must cooperate if the attempt is to succeed. This does not imply that the others always cooperate willingly. Patients may feel that they must cooperate with physicians because physicians can provide life, health, or at least information important to achieving life or health. Even though all events are jointly produced, some are produced with one party feeling coerced and cooperating only to the degree of withholding protest.

If one participant attempts to change the topic without securing overt agreement from the other, we have no way of knowing whether the other participant is silent from choice or because of the coercive nature of the situation. "Unilateral" is shorthand for this situation.

Also, in my analysis the three right-hand stops on the continuum (links, minimal links, and sudden topic change) are assumed to represent differing degrees of acknowledgment of the previous speaker. Links represent a greater degree of acknowledgment than minimal links, and minimal links represent a (slightly) greater degree of acknowledgment than sudden topic change.

Being the silent partner in a unilateral topic change, or hearing little acknowledgment of one's contribution, can damage a patient's self-respect, which is important in its own right. This damage will inevitably also hurt the physician–patient relationship.

Data

Participants and settings

I analyzed topic transitions in 12 encounters, involving eight physicians (four men and four women) and eight patients, all women. Eight of these encounters were recorded during the initial small-scale study described in chapter 1, and the other four (the oncology encounters) were recorded in the second, large-scale study described there.

Table 3.1 lists the 12 encounters by patient and physician and gives physicians' specialties. These encounters were matched not only for gender but also, as nearly as possible, for comparability in terms of seriousness of the medical purpose. Specialty was matched in 10 of the 12 encounters. Four encounters involve Ms. Lane, two with a male physician (Dr. Mey) and two with a female physician (Dr. Fife). These visits by the same patient to two physicians of different gender (data unique in the literature) are especially comparable.

There are two encounters with Ms. Jubb, one with a male physician (Dr. Moltner) and one with a female physician (Dr. Floyd). There are two encounters with Dr. Miller, seeing Ms. Mesler and Ms. Hazen, and two encounters with Dr. Finn, seeing Ms. Kijhell and Ms. Earley.

The 12 medical encounters comprise some 31,000 words.[4]

Evolving stages of analysis

I passed through several stages of analysis of these medical encounters, with new analytical tools changing the developing picture at each stage. In my first analysis of the data, I tried to use only two categories, West and Garcia's (1988) *collaborative activities* and *unilateral topic transitions*. (These categories have survived in the final analysis as *reciprocal activities* and *sudden topic change*, respectively.) After one two-hour training session, two research assistants[5] and I independently went through all the data attempting to place topic transitions into these categories. At the end of this effort, we were all dissatisfied with only two categories.

Table 3.1 Matched Encounters

Patient	Doctor and Speciality	Date	Purpose	Length (No. of Words)
Male physicians				
Lane	Mey,I	4/18/90	diabetes.meds	3,403
Lane	Mey,I	5/22/90	diabetes.meds	3,724
Jubb	Moltner,Em	3/5/89	sprained ankle	2,192
Kelly	Midgard,FP	no date	respiratory	2,084
Mesler	Miller,O	3/27/91	oncology	3,163
Hazen	Miller,O	3/27/91	oncology	1,275
				15,841
Female physicians				
Lane	Fife,I	10/30/89	diabetes.meds	4,130
Lane	Fife,I	11/17/89	dizziness	4,343
Jubb	Floyd,S	2/6/89	breast exam	1,916
Evans	Fouts,FP	9/28/89	vaginitis	2,095
Kijhell	Finn,O	4/18/91	oncology	1,143
Earley	Finn,O	4/4/91	oncology	1,877
				15,504

Em = Emergency care; FP = Family practice; I = Internal medicine; O = Oncology; S = Surgery

I then added *links* and *minimal links* to the system. I defined a link as a statement at the first of the turn which explicitly acknowledges the previous speaker's contribution, followed by a topic change by the same speaker within the same turn. A minimal link meets the same requirements (at first of turn, followed by topic change by same speaker within same turn) but consists only of an affirmative token (e.g., "Okay" or "All right").

The significant issue is that links and minimal links are done without giving the other speaker an opportunity to show agreement with the attempt to change the topic. Following West and Garcia's (1988) line of argument, these should count as being unilateral.

By adding links and minimal links, I elaborated on West and Garcia's system. Now there were four categories, one for reciprocal activities and three for unilateral activities. This required a change from West and Garcia's term "unilateral topic transition" to "sudden topic change" (now one of three "unilateral" activities). These categories claim, in progressively greater degrees, control over the topic. Therefore, they can be placed on the continuum in figure 3-1.

After three more two-hour training sessions, three research assistants and I used these categories to account for topic transitions in the data. After we had finished, I compared our differing results. Disparities were often caused by lack of background knowledge on the part of an analyst, knowledge which affected judgments of both cohesion and formulation. For instance, one analyst might count a switch to discussion of some particular medicine as a sudden topic change, while other analysts recognized the medicine as a common one for the condition being discussed and so perceived cohesion between turns. Further, one of the three analysts apparently had not understood the system, as her decisions were strikingly different from those of the other three. As qualitative researchers so often suggest, strictly quantitative measures (four analysts' tallies) would have been misleading and therefore could not be translated directly into a measure of interrater reliability.

I was also becoming convinced that the four-category system was not adequate but, rather, that topic changes were warranted in connection with certain question sequences and with negative statements, making a six-category schema. As a final stage of analysis, then, one of the analysts (a doctoral student focusing on discourse analysis) and I went through the transcripts and tapes again with the new six-category schema (table 3.2). We moved formerly-agreed-on topic transitions into the two new categories (warranted by questions or negatives) when necessary.

The counts reported here are those on which at least three of the four analysts agreed. The points on which we did not agree rested on the old problem of inferential distance between the topics (is it cohesive?) and on the related problem of what counts as a "formulation," one of the types of reciprocal activities.

We counted topic transitions within conversational parts of these medical encounters. We did not count topic transitions that are warranted by a separate speech activity within the encounter. Therefore, we excluded topic transitions that occurred during history taking; during the physical exam; those within a discussion of a list, unless one of the items on the list underwent topic development; and those that occurred on the end boundaries of side interactions (e.g., when a nurse opened the exam room door for a brief discussion with the physician). These decisions all flow from an ethnography-of-speaking theoretical stance, which leads me to regard certain prepatterned sequences as having a different force and interactional status from more conversational discourse.

I was interested in the exercise of power by one participant over possible actions of another, and, therefore, we did not count a topic transition in which a speaker changed his or her own topic within a turn.

We did, as mentioned previously, count topic changes occurring after a negative statement (*Neg*) and those occurring after a minimal answer to a question outside of a list (*Q*). It is not clear where *Neg* and *Q* might fall on a continuum of increasing power, so they were not assessed farther than a count, but they are presented in table 3.2 in order to display the range of topic transition activities and their frequency.

Discourse Examples

At one end of the continuum, we have symmetrical behavior: *reciprocal activities*, identified by West and Garcia (1988; West and Garcia call these "topic closure activities"). These are sequences in which the two speakers both contribute a move; there is an exchange between them.

Second, moving away from symmetrical behavior, *links* are attempts by a participant to refer explicitly to the content of the previous turn before changing a topic. This is the strategy identified by Mishler (1984). This topic-transition activity produces a significant degree of cohesion with previous discourse, by acknowledging the substance of what was said by the previous participant.

Next come *minimal links*, markers such as "Okay," "M-hm," or "All right" followed immediately with a change of topic by the same speaker. These terms are known as *discourse markers*. Discourse markers frequently have multiple functions (Schiffrin 1987:64). "All right," "M-hm," "Okay," and other affirmative terms are commonly used as backchannels, confirming the reception of a message as it is being delivered. When they are placed at the front of the first sentence in a turn, these terms may retain the function of acknowledging reception of the preceding message while adding the function of marking topic transition.[6] In this interpretation, the speaker acknowledges (though in a minimal way) the previous discourse.

Finally, we arrive at the other end of the continuum: When cohesion with a previous utterance is absent, and there are no reciprocal activities, links, or minimal links, I call the transition a *sudden topic change*.

Examples and discussion of these strategies follow. Topic-transition activities are in boldface type; topic changes are marked with an arrow.

Reciprocal activities

Reciprocal activities are those in which both speakers have an opportunity to participate in closing down the topic. West and Garcia (1988) suggest that speakers may do this by exchanging affirmative terms such as "Okay" and "All right," or by going through a sequence in which one person formulates the topic and the other agrees, or by participating in making arrangements for future action.

In the following example, Ms. Lane and Dr. Fife are reading and discussing test reports. They repeatedly exchange affirmative terms. The "Um" in line 141 signals that Ms. Lane believes that the reciprocal affirmative terms, "All right," "Yeah," "Okay," have closed down the topic. With "Um" Ms. Lane passes up the opportunity to introduce a new topic. Then in lines 142–143, Dr. Fife introduces a new topic (protein in Ms. Lane's urine).

(1a)   Dr. Fife, an internist, and Ms. Lane, a diabetic, are going over the results of some previous tests

136   Dr. Fife: I THINK you've got [all of *this*].
137   Ms. Lane: [I've GOT all] of that.
138   Dr. Fife: **>All right.<**
139   Ms. Lane: **Yeah.**
140   Dr. Fife: **>Okay.<**
141   Ms. Lane: **Um.**
142   Dr. Fife: **<All right.<**
143   → And this *URINE* . is spilling protein

                                                          {LAD2,4-136}

In 1b, Mr. Dunham and Dr. Miller exchange affirmative terms twice.

(1b)   Dr. Miller, an oncologist, and Mr. Dunham, a lung cancer patient, are discussing pain in Mr. Dunham's chest

51   Dr. Miller: *That* would be very UNusual to have it at
52   that level,
53   but it *COULD* be.
54   But *WHATEVER* . it IS that made your heart
55   JUST a *LITTLE* bit weak,
56   not *BAD*,
57   just a *LITTLE* weak,
57   . . u:m . the *PLEURISY* . may have tipped
58   it over the . edge.
59   Mr. Dunham: O:h.
60   Dr. Miller: Okay?
61   Mr. Dunham: Made it SHOW *UP* more.
62   Dr. Miller: **Sure.**
63   Mr. Dunham: **Yeah.**
64   Dr. Miller: *AGG*ravated it.
65   Mr. Dunham: **Yeah.**
66   Dr. Miller: **Okay?**
67   Mr. Dunham:→   NOW I won't need any more anti*biotics* or
68   any of that . *pleurisy* or (???).

                                                          {DW1,3-51}

In a second type of reciprocal activity, first one speaker formulates—summarizes or assesses—the preceding topic, and then the other speaker affirms the summary or assessment. Both Mr. Dunham and Dr. Miller did this in the previous example, in lines 61 and 64, respectively. Mr. Dunham's "Made it SHOW *UP* more" (line 61) and Dr. Miller's "*AGG*ravated it" (line 64) both summarize (formulate) the point of the previous statements.

Each of these summaries is followed by an affirmation from the other speaker, and the affirmation in turn receives affirmation, as was pointed out earlier. Again, this is reciprocal behavior. One speaker affirms, then the other reciprocates by affirming also.

It is interesting that Dr. Miller, in line 66, says "Okay?" with rising intonation, the questioning intonation. This questioning "Okay?" both asks for confirmation and turns the floor over to the other speaker. Like Ms. Lane's "Um" in the previous example, it suggests that Dr. Miller believes the old topic to be fully closed down but that he is passing up the opportunity to introduce a new one. Mr. Dunham then introduces a new topic.

These summaries and assessments, or formulations, are a very common way in which speakers signal their willingness to bring a topic to a close. They are so common because they are the best way of displaying receipt of the other speaker's message. If you can rephrase the message, you undoubtedly heard it.

So far we have seen just how cooperative topic transitions can be. These speakers do not just affirm the others' contributions; they engage in cycles of repeated affirmation. Even Dr. Miller—who in this book is my example of an old-style, somewhat authoritarian physician—engages in these long reciprocal sequences with his patients.

We have also seen that discourse actions are composed of multiple layers of functional meaning (cf. chapter 5). More than one function is invoked at a time. Dr. Miller's "Okay?" both affirmed the previous remark (helping to close down the old topic) and, with its questioning intonation, asked for Mr. Dunham's involvement in the closedown.

A third type of reciprocal transition activity consists of making arrangements: There is a proposal for some future action, followed by agreement from the next speaker. The agreement establishes a topic boundary and a new topic can be raised. In the following example, Ms. Lane, in lines 356–358, is suggesting a certain arrangement for the way tests will be handled "the next time" she takes them. In lines 359–361 Dr. Fife affirms the arrangement, and then in line 362 she changes the topic.

(2)   Dr. Fife, an internist, and Ms. Lane, a diabetic, are going over lab tests

346	Dr. Fife:	is *always* a problem with diabetics,
347		and you're running really [high] there.
348	Ms. Lane:	[>O:h<]
349	Dr. Fife:	Now they didn't *DO* a tri*G* [*LYC*erides].
350	Ms. Lane:	[*GLYC*erides].
351	Dr. Fife:	And *that's* . mm
352		[*Our*] lab automatically always *DOES* that,

353 Ms. Lane: [Hm]
354 Dr. Fife: but generally *THAT'S* pretty high in
355   diabetics also.
356 Ms. Lane: **So I guess the *next* time we'll hafta . um**
357   **I'll have to make sure that they**
358   **[. DO] one of those.**
359 Dr. Fife: [*Right*]
360   **Right.**
361   ***That* would be helpful.**
362   → **YOU can have that.**

{LAD1,9-346}

In the tables, "use" of reciprocal activities is attributed to the speaker who changed the topic after the reciprocal activities took place.

Links

I suggest the term "link" to describe a remark that acknowledges the previous speaker's contributions but is then followed immediately by a change of topic, without giving the other speaker a chance to agree or disagree with the change. A link is placed at the first of the speaker's turn. It can be preceded by an affirmative word such as "Yeah" but not by a substantive comment.

Links can summarize or affirm what has just been said, but they do not substantially develop the topic. (When substantial topic development took place, followed by a topic change, we considered a within-turn topic change to have occurred instead.)

These topic transitions are highly cohesive with previous discourse and provide a high degree of social acknowledgment of the previous speaker, but they are not reciprocal activities and they carry the possibility of losing the other speaker's topic before it has been fully explored.

In the following example, Dr. Floyd affirms what Ms. Jubb has just said. Usually hospital gowns are put on with the ties in the back, as Ms. Jubb remarks in line 47. But in Dr. Floyd's office, they are put on with ties in the front. In lines 48 and 49, Dr. Floyd links her turn with Ms. Jubb's turn by continuing the topic of which way the ties go. In this link, Dr. Floyd affirms Ms. Jubb's view that gowns should open in the back by describing her own way of putting on gowns (opening in the front) as "backwards."

(3)   Dr. Floyd, a surgical oncologist, is beginning a routine breast examination of Ms. Jubb, a 25-year-old woman

45 Dr. Floyd: >Okay,<
46   I'm *JUST* going to *remove* your gown *here.*
47 Ms. Jubb: >I *always* think it's in the *back.*<
48 Dr. Floyd: *Yeah.*
49   **We put 'em on *backwards* here.**

50	Okay.
51	→ Bring your arms up *OVER* your *head*,
52	*GOOD*, and DOWN onto your hips and PUSH
53	'em in *real* tight.

{JBO,3-45}

Minimal links

Minimal links are affirmative terms at the first of a turn, followed immediately by a topic change, without giving the other speaker the opportunity to agree or disagree with the change. "Okay," "All right," "M-hm," and other affirmative do provide cohesion with—and acknowledgment of—the previous speaker's contribution, but the cohesion and acknowledgment are minimal.

(4) This is a regularly scheduled appointment between Dr. Miller, a medical oncologist, and Ms. Mesler, a lymphoma patient. Ms. Mesler is afraid that tenderness in her breasts may be a symptom of breast cancer. She is illustrating the extent of soreness she feels.

37	Ms. Mesler:	Dr. Smith had suggested . you know .
38		POSSIBLY waiting a month and then,
39		*um* there's *TIMES* in which . I-I have
40		*VERY* restful g- uh nights,
41		and then there's *other* times when *I* CAN'T
42		get any rest because . . I'm too *SORE*.
43		I- y'know
44	Dr. Miller:	M-[hm].
45	Ms. Mesler:	[I] *HAVE* to LAY on my back-back,
46		in which . *I'm* not *com*fortable in
47		[lay]ing on my back.
48	Dr. Miller:	[Yeah].
49	Ms. Mesler:	I LIKE to lay on my sides .
50		[so]
51	Dr. Miller:	[**Okay**].
52		→ *WHEN ARE WE GOING TO DO ANOTHER* . CT
53		scan.

{MS1,4-37}

Sudden topic changes

In *sudden topic changes* a participant does not acknowledge the preceding discourse (and by implication, its speaker). In the 12 encounters I studied, both physicians and patients produced sudden topic changes. But the male physicians produced eight sudden topic changes, compared to none by the patients in their encounters. The female physicians produced two sudden topic changes, balanced with the two sudden topic changes produced by the patients in their encounters.

In the following example, Dr. Mey shifts the topic when Ms. Lane asks whether life in pain is worth living. Of course, we can infer a path of meaning from what Ms. Lane said to Dr. Mey's topic of the therapist. But his new topic is not cohesive with the immediately preceding turn. Dr. Mey does not refer to prolonging life, or reasons for prolonging life—Ms. Lane's topics. He chooses to treat the question as rhetorical, so he does not link with the question by providing an answer. His remark can be read as implying that the question would be appropriately addressed to a therapist rather than to him.

By doing this, Dr. Mey suggests that Ms. Lane's remark has no relevance to this medical encounter. But, in fact, her remark arises from her despair at coping with new side effects from the new medications prescribed quite recently by Dr. Mey (this interaction is also analyzed in chapter 5). So her remark is relevant to the medications he might continue (or not) at the end of the encounter.

(5)   Ms. Lane, a diabetic, is seeing Dr. Mey, an internist, because the side effects of her medications—especially the medication for high cholesterol levels—are making her very uncomfortable.

8   Dr. Mey: If we're going to [*really*]
9   Ms. Lane: [Yeah] I *know* that.
10   Dr. Mey: *CHIP* away at your cho*lester*ol,
11   if you decide that you want to *DO* that .
12   uh TOGETHER with me,
13   then . . I say there's *NOT* a whole lot of
14   other options in *terms* of medications
15   *FOR* your cholesterol.
16   Ms. Lane: Yeah so you pro*LONG* your life for WHAT,
17   you know?
18   (3 sec)
19   Dr. Mey: → *DO YOU* have a-*do you* have an *appoint*ment
20   to see a therapist soon?
                                                              {LAF1,8-8}

Eventually, Ms. Lane herself suggested a plan for reducing these uncomfortable side effects: She suggested discontinuing one of the new medications while simultaneously increasing amounts of an old medication which she tolerated well. Dr. Mey agreed to the plan.

Dr. Mey expressed the superficial aspects of a therapeutic partnership: "if you decide that you want to *DO* that . uh TOGETHER with me." But in this encounter he spent long stretches of time in a lecturing style, explaining points which Ms. Lane, a diabetic for more than 30 years, may have already known (he did not check to see what she knew on these subjects). In my interview with Ms. Lane, she mentioned that she knew a great deal about her disease. I asked for her impression of Dr. Mey; she characterized him as a "smart aleck." When I asked exactly what she meant, she replied, "He *thinks* he knows a LOT, but he *DOESN'T*."

In this encounter, the reciprocal topic changes made by Dr. Mey and Ms. Lane were about equal in number: Dr. Mey made four, and Ms. Lane made five. But Dr. Mey made seven unilateral topic changes, while Ms. Lane made none.

Ms. Lane came back to see Dr. Mey two more times and then changed physicians.

Counts of these topic-transition sequences appear in table 3.2.

What Does It All Mean?

Theory: New analytical categories

In this chapter, I elaborated on previous definitions of topic, adding an ethnographic assumption (cf. Moerman 1988) that speakers know and orient to norms for speech activities and speech events. In this view, the medical encounter is known as a genre which is organized to serve specific medical purposes, such as exchanging information about symptoms and their meaning.

The norms for sub-sequences within an event also are known by participants. For that reason, topic changes within history taking (and other list sequences related to medical information) are seen as warranted by participants.

Table 3.2   Continuum of Topic-Changing Strategies

				Unilateral Activities								
		Reciprocal Activities[a]		Links		(Neg)		(Q)		Minimal Links		Sudden Topic Changes
P	D	D	P	D	P	D	P	D	P	D	P	D	P
Male physicians													
Lane	Mey	4	5	1	0	0	0	1	0	5	0	1	0
Lane	Mey	7	7	1	0	1	1	0	0	2	0	2	0
Jubb	Moltner	9	5	0	0	0	0	1	2	0	1	2	0
Kelly	Midgard	7	4	2	0	0	0	0	0	0	0	1	0
Mesler	Miller	1	1	0	0	0	0	0	0	4	1	1	0
Hazen	Miller	5	4	0	0	0	2	1	0	0	1	1	0
	Totals:	33	26	4	0	1	3	3	2	11	3	8	0
Female physicians													
Lane	Fife	9	7	1	0	1	0	0	0	0	0	0	1
Lane	Fife	16	11	0	0	1	0	0	0	3	0	2	0
Jubb	Floyd	5	2	1	0	1	0	0	0	1	0	0	0
Evans	Fouts	6	2	0	0	1	1	0	0	1	0	0	0
Kijhell	Finn	8	2	1	0	0	0	0	0	0	0	0	0
Earley	Finn	6	4	0	0	0	0	0	0	0	0	0	1
	Totals:	50	28	3	0	4	1	0	0	5	0	2	2

a. "Use" of reciprocal activities as a topic-transition device is attributed to the speaker who changed the topic after the reciprocal activities took place.

D = doctor; P = patient

For instance, topic change often happens after a medical question to which the answer is minimal; that is, the answer closes down that possible line of discussion ("What was your last cholesterol reading?" "One eighty"). Topic changes after negative statements work the same way. My exclusion of such topic changes in history taking and other sub-sequences, then, rests on the notion that discourse acts are organized hierarchically—into genres and sub-sequences—as well as sequentially.

Maynard (1980) and West and Garcia (1988) point to reciprocal and unilateral social activities which signal the possibility of closing down the topic in progress. I have subdivided the unilateral activities. Instead of counting only STCs, I also counted links and minimal links.

Besides coherence and social activities, a third dimension of topicality is that of cohesion. I have attempted to specify some ways in which cohesive elements can construct topicality—through repetition, anaphora, and semantically linked lexical items.

Repetition and anaphora are easily identified. However, the degree to which lexical items can be inferentially associated varies. How can inferential distance be assessed? Having more than one analyst is one way of addressing the problem. But, if cohesion is to be a criterion for topicality, the problem of assessing inferential difficulty can only be reduced, not completely solved.

These three dimensions—coherence, cohesion, and social activities—are interrelated, inseparable in reality, but distinguishing them allows clarification of the possibilities and difficulties in defining topics and topic changes.

Doctor bashing and paternalism

Purely qualitative analyses of discourse have illuminated the creation of meaning in discourse processes. But analysts of medical discourse face special problems, ethical and pragmatic problems, when they offer strictly qualitative analyses of discourse fragments.

Within medicine, and in its sphere of influence (medical anthropology, medical sociology, and so on), purely qualitative analyses can be used to portray physicians in ways that may not be fair. The other side of the coin is portrayal of patients as being more passive than actually is the case.

Without any sense of the frequency with which physicians and patients claim power in medical encounters, we run the risk of reifying cultural expectations regarding doctors' paternalism, patients' passivity, and male physicians' dominant behavior. By contrast, West (1984a, 1984c) and Silverman (1987) provide models for the use of simple quantitative measures. This sort of assessment also protects against having legitimate descriptions of paternalism dismissed as "only anecdotal."

We need to describe precisely the ways in which power is constructed in this discourse. I believe that the way in which topic transitions are made is part of the construction of power.

If my assumption is correct, table 3.2 provides evidence supporting the general suggestion that physicians realize far greater interactional power than patients in medical discourse, and also that male physicians play a more dominant role in the discourse than do female physicians.

For patients, the ratio of reciprocal to unilateral topic transitions is 54:4, or about 13.5 to one. For physicians, it is 83:33, or about 2.5 to one. These figures document asymmetry in physicians' and patients' successful attempts to claim power by unilaterally changing the topic.

Is this asymmetry paternalism? If paternalism consists of inappropriately making decisions for someone else, then unilateral topic transitions are risky speech activities because they do not provide the other speaker with an opportunity to participate in deciding what will be talked about. The decision to change the topic is made by only one participant, and that increases the risk that the decision is inappropriate.

Patients' relatively infrequent use of unilateral transitions is not the whole story, however. If we look at the numbers of topic transitions per se, rather than just at the unilateral ones, we find that patients are doing a significant amount of topic changing (about 40%).

To understand the relation between topic control and paternalism, we need more qualitative analyses. Chapter 2 provides a qualitative overview of ways of claiming power, including topic control. In chapter 2, Ms. Hazen managed to set and pursue her topic throughout the encounter, in spite of Dr. Miller's interruptions, topic shifts, and appropriation of her suggestion for treatment.

I would say that his behavior was paternalistic, and that this paternalism impeded Ms. Hazen's attempts to pursue her topics. Nevertheless, Ms. Hazen appears to have been an active patient who succeeded in securing Dr. Miller's opinions about her lump and in securing his serious attention to her proposal that a whirlpool might be appropriate treatment for her pain. The physician's paternalistic behavior did not entirely determine the shape or outcomes of this encounter.

We have been discussing the overall results of this analysis, the contrast between physician and patient without regard to gender. But the ways in which gender and role are constituted are relevant to the question of paternalism. It appears that female physicians claim interactional power in proportions closer to that of their patients than do male physicians.

Constituting gender and role

We have seen that the overall ratios of reciprocal to unilateral activities are quite different for physicians (2.5 to 1) compared to patients (13.5 to 1). The ratios also differ widely for male physicians as opposed to female physicians. For female physicians, the ratio was 50:10, or 5 to 1. For men, the ratio was 33:23, about 1.4 to 1. Male physicians unilaterally changed the topic almost as often as they changed topics with reciprocal activities. Female physicians were much less likely to change the topic unilaterally.

Female physicians are negotiating their roles as they move into the medical establishment; for instance, Dr. Finn never wore a white jacket, the badge of medical authority. I asked why. She said that she did not see the purpose of wearing the white coat. Because one of the purposes of the coat is to differentiate those with medical authority from those without it, Dr. Finn's rejection of this symbolic division partially redefines the way a physician constitutes her authority.

Female nurses also are participating in the renegotiation of the physician role when it is filled by a woman. (All nurses in this study were women.) One nurse in Dr. Finn's office leaned close to her and squeezed her arm while passing by. In a different office, I heard a nurse relate a lengthy anecdote about a personal issue to a woman physician (not in the study). I never observed similar events between nurses and male physicians.

If female physicians avoid unilateral types of transitions, this may indicate that they do not regard the medical encounter as a "power struggle," as it has been characterized in studies of male physician–female patient interaction (Fisher and Groce 1990; K. Davis 1988). Tannen (1995) explores similar ideas in relation to women's workplace language in general.

A female physician simultaneously constitutes role and gender; the two cannot be separated. Because women will make up one-third of all U.S. physicians by the year 2000 (Epps 1991), the ways women constitute being a physician will surely affect social and sociolinguistic norms for the role and for the encounter. The numbers in this chapter may be early documentation for a major change in medical discourse, a discourse change now in progress.

This chapter suggests that listenership is cooperative. A good listener allows for and encourages participation by the other speaker by (whenever possible) using a reciprocal, participatory process to make the decision that a topic should be closed down. The study of topic control has implications for sharing and claiming power and establishing listenership in medical discourse. This study shows again that the details of talk are important in creating a therapeutic partnership in medical encounters.

4

A Genre of Questions?

The number of questions doctors and patients ask is a central issue in research on medical discourse because questioning both gains information and claims power over emerging talk. Well-known studies of medical discourse find patients producing few questions. The usual conclusion is that medical encounters are an "interview" genre—one in which one person asks questions while the other passively answers. My research suggests that this conclusion needs to be modified.

When the idea that patients are passive—they do not question—is overgeneralized and becomes a stereotype, it may become a self-fulfilling prophecy. Physicians may expect patients to neither want nor be capable of involvement. The physician may then act to fill the vacuum, and the prophecy is fulfilled.

As chapters 2 and 5 suggest, we cannot assume that the quantity of questions asked serves as a direct, one-to-one index to the entire power balance in medical encounters. There are many kinds of questioning behavior, and many ways of realizing power other than through questions.

Nevertheless, questioning has crucial functions in medical encounters, and its use gives important information about the efforts of the speakers—especially patients—to claim control over the discourse. Quantity of questions has been studied in a limited number of medical settings. In this chapter, I extend the research context for questioning in several ways, notably to private-practice settings, in regard to gender of the physician, and in regard to diagnosis.

This chapter describes a quantitative study of total numbers of true questions asked by physicians and patients in 40 encounters. The chapter is contextualized (its suggestions qualified) by chapters 2 and 5. Contextualizing works both ways, however. This chapter, in turn, contextualizes the more qualitative approaches in chapters 2 and 5 by documenting the extent of the use of questions in my data.

True questions control topic and speaker in emerging discourse. By asking questions, a speaker constitutes his or her self as a speaker who has the right to exert control over the encounter at that point in its development. By questioning, a patient or doctor does make significant claims to speaker rights.

In this chapter, I report data in which patients ask about 40% of the total number of true questions in the encounters. This percentage is at odds with well-known previous findings, although it is in accord with less well-known figures. I end the chapter with discussion of possible reasons for the differences among these findings.

Questions and Power

Questions are directives. By using directives, a speaker proposes to exert control over other conversational participants (M. Goodwin 1990) (i.e., to direct their actions in the discourse).

Questions claim power in several ways. First, a question chooses the next speaker. Who will talk next? A questioner tries to make that decision. It nominates the next speaker by asking a question of that person.

Second, a question calls for a particular type of response from the other speaker. What topic will that speaker discuss? What the next speaker says will relate to the question asked. A question, even an "open-ended" question, always in some way restricts the topic of the response. And so the question is an attempt to control what the addressee will talk about, the referential content of the conversation. In these ways, a questioner claims notable power over the emerging discourse.

A third claim to power questioners sometimes make has to do with what will happen after the question is answered. Some questions entail the expectation that the floor will be returned to the questioner, and again control will have been exerted. And finally, questions aim to elicit information, and information empowers its possessor.

For all these reasons, sociolinguists and discourse analysts see questions as claiming power over the emerging discourse and over other participants. The link between questions and power has been made in many disciplines, not just in ethnographic discourse analysis. Questions have been linked with power in such important settings as the political (Bennett 1982), educational (Mehan 1979; Walters 1984), and legal (Philips 1987; Walker 1987) arenas.

The quantitative data on questions are striking. In studies of asymmetrical dyads in institutional settings (attorney–witness, teacher–student, physician–patient), typically the speaker who has the power to reward asked the most questions (Dillon 1982, 1990), and the imbalance in numbers is dramatic. In one study, social studies and science teachers in a U.S. elementary school were observed to ask two questions per minute, but their students averaged only one question per month (Dillon 1982).

Questions are not solely claims to power over the emerging discourse. In some ways, they propose to share or give up that power. Notably, a question can hand over the floor to other participants and demonstrate the questioner's interest in the answer (Goody 1978).[1]

Because opinion across disciplines converges on the point that questions claim power in institutional discourse, it makes sense to carry out quantitative studies of questions when their definitions are discourse based, and when the studies are contextualized with qualitative analysis. The aim of this chapter is to examine numbers of questions asked by patients and physicians in a private-practice setting, with special attention to gender, diagnosis, and other contextual influences. Simple quantitative methods are used. These methods are grounded in definitions based on discourse sequence and conversational inference, as well as on linguistic form.

Questions in Medical Encounters: Differing Definitions

Studies based on the assumption that questions are powerful have been done by both physicians and researchers in associated fields such as public health, but for many of these researchers, the nature of questions is assumed to be relatively transparent and unproblematic. Some of these studies have no definition for "question" at all (Bain 1976; M. Davis 1971; Korsch and Negrete 1972). The lack of a definition does not make these studies valueless, but it prevents comparison with their findings.

For other researchers, questions and their subtypes have been defined narrowly in ways that further the analyst's research aims but do not allow comparability with studies in which the term is more broadly defined (Frankel 1979; Roter 1977, 1984).

An example of a narrow definition of "question" appears in Frankel (1979[2]). Frankel began with the "adjacency pair" definition of a question, that is, that the utterance called for an answer. He then narrowed his focus to "patient-initiated" questions. He counted questions in audiotapes of 10 ambulatory-care visits. The patients were adults, and the practitioners were in general internal medicine and were "long-term" practitioners. No other contextual details are given about the participants, such as gender, ethnicity, or diagnoses. Frankel found that fewer than 1% of the total number of questions asked by physicians and patients were "patient-initiated."

In Frankel's study, to be "initiated" by the patient the question had to be the first utterance in the turn and also had to introduce new information. In addition, Frankel excluded "'normal' troubles such as requests for clarification, information, etc." (1979:239).

Unfortunately, there has been a widespread tendency to generalize Frankel's 1% finding to all questions, when in fact it only applies to narrowly defined "patient-initiated" ones. The finding that only 1% of questions are in this category is not surprising because, to be counted, the question had to meet three criteria: be the first utterance in the turn, introduce new information, and not be about "normal" troubles.

Frankel's study was not just a study of questions but a study of questions in a certain place in the turn, with certain topics. The study does not propose to count questions in general. Similarly, Roter's (1977, 1984) study uses narrow definitions of "direct" and "indirect" questions and therefore cannot be compared to other studies.

West (1984a) does count questions in general. She used a widely inclusive definition of questions (the adjacency pair definition, discussed later), excluding only repairs (requests for repetition because one person did not hear the other) and markers of surprise ("Oh, really?").

As it appeared that my operational definitions of questions were similar in most ways to West's, I contacted West, who generously contributed the time to discuss her criteria in detail. She and I separately analyzed and then discussed one of my transcripts, comparing our identification of questions. In spite of our differing theoretical orientations, we agreed on all but one minor category in deciding what counted as a question. The disagreement was well defined and thus easy to consider when comparing results. Thus my counts of questions can be compared directly to the counts made by West.

West studied questions in 21 encounters in a clinic whose population was primarily drawn from lower socioeconomic strata. The clinic was staffed largely by residents (i.e., physicians who had completed medical school very recently and were still in training). There were 18 physicians, all of whom were white. Fourteen of the physicians were men and four were women. There were nine male patients (five white, four black) and 11 female patients (six white, five black). West found 773 questions, of which 91% (705) were asked by physicians. Only 9% of the questions were asked by patients.

West's data may suggest that medical encounters in a subsidized clinic do in fact belong to the "interview" genre, with doctors asking questions and the patients' role being largely limited to answering. But there is little contextual information on these 21 encounters. West does not say what the diagnoses were or whether the patients and doctors had met before. Along with those two unknown factors, the clinic setting, gender, and ethnicity are complicating factors in evaluating West's results; it is unclear what effect they had, and so it is unclear how West's results can be generalized. I will return to the possible significance of these contextual factors later in the chapter.

The Importance of Context

Silverman's (1987) British study provides excellent examples of the way questioning behavior may change as the situation changes. Silverman gathered audiotapes of 102 sequential encounters between pediatric cardiologists and their patients and patients' parents. Silverman points out the difficulties of deciding what a question is and gives two very brief examples, but he says little about his definition of questions. There are hints (Silverman 1987:87) that his working definition depended on both linguistic form and the way the utterance functioned in the context.

Silverman says that encounters (and within them, questioning) "vary according to their place in a patient's career-trajectory" (1987:34). For instance, there are changes in parents' questioning, depending on whether the encounter is pre-inpatient, post-catheter, or post-operation. The nature and severity of the illness also have an effect (1987:86 ff.); for example, the mean number of parents' questions was 1.14 per encounter for children with the least severe problems, 4.28 for those with moderate severity, and 2.9 for those parents whose children had the most serious problems. Notice that common sense fails us in predicting these numbers. It is unsurprising that the least number of questions occurred when the children's problems were least severe, so common sense would predict correctly in that case. But we might have expected that the number of questions would rise proportionately to the severity of the illness, which was not the case.

Biesecker and Biesecker (1990) also found that specific contexts make a difference. Biesecker and Biesecker studied correlates with the "information-seeking comments" of 106 patients (42 men and 64 women) in an outpatient clinic.[3] Their work raises the issue of socioeconomic status; in contrast to Waitzkin (1985), Biesecker and Biesecker found that socioeconomic status did not correlate with the number of patients' questions:

> Situational factors surrounding the physician-patient interaction better explain patient information-seeking behaviors than do patient demographic variables, patient attitudes, or even the physician seen, especially for patients with interactions lasting at least 19 minutes. . . . The length of the interaction, the patient's diagnosis, and the specific reason for the patient's visit proved to have an important impact on the number of information-seeking comments made by the patient to the physician. (1990:27)

Occasionally, when I have talked with physicians in the field (not the ones quoted in this book), I have noticed a tendency to attribute patient behavior either to socioeconomic status or to vaguely defined personality types. The research I am surveying here, and my own research, discounts these explanations in favor of a more complicated picture.

The interaction as it takes place can, of course, be affected by both physicians' and patients' perceptions of socioeconomic status, and no doubt there are broad types of personality that play some role. But many other contextual variables are in play, and most important of all is the way the living discourse of the encounter unfolds—the way power and identity are negotiated on the spot. Later in this chapter, we see Ms. Hake, Mr. Frisell, and Mr. Brade exemplifying some of the complexity of this issue.

The studies just reviewed converge on the notion that the balance of power in medical encounters is locally negotiated, and that questions are a crucial part of that negotiation. These studies leave a great deal of room for further research on questioning, however. Definitions varied. Gender was not studied; none of these studies included gender balance in physicians or patients, in spite of the fact that gender is widely thought to make a difference in power-claiming talk (Graddol and Swann 1989; Tannen 1993b; chapter 2). The diagnosis was considered only in Silverman's finely differentiated study. In this chapter, I address each of these research problems.

Data and Participants

The 40 encounters studied here (table 4.1) were chosen (from the larger body of data described in chapter 1) for gender balance. There were 20 encounters with male patients, 20 with female patients; 20 encounters with male physicians, 20 with female physicians. Eleven patients were male, 12 were female; four physicians were male (Mey, Midgard, Miller, and Myhill), four female (Fife, Finn, Floyd, and Fouts). The setting was oncology in 28 of the 40 encounters. Table 4.1 lists the encounters that were analyzed and gives the gender of physician and patient. (Refer to tables 1.1, 1.2, and 1.3 for details about these patients and physicians.)

Six tapes used in this chapter are from my initial small-scale study, and the other encounters analyzed here (28 oncology, 6 hematology) were recorded as part of the second, larger study (see chapter 1).

There were three stages of analysis. First, my research assistant and I repeatedly tested definitions of questions against a subset (5) of the 40 encounters. We examined the linguistic structure, referential content, and discourse function of the utterances we had identified as possible questions. We then used the resultant sets of criteria in independent analyses of the entire body of 40 audiotapes and transcripts. Finally, a second research assistant and I compared and discussed the two independent analyses, line by line.

Our definitions were sensitive to context, and at every stage of analysis we listened to all 40 audiotapes while reading and marking written transcripts, replaying important segments repeatedly.

Defining Question

Questions are strongly associated with changes in word order and with intonation. "Will you go with me?" contrasts with "You will go with me." The contrast is created by the reversal of the subject pronoun with the auxiliary verb (a syntactic, word-order change) and by rising intonation at the end of the sentence (a phonological change). These linguistic markers raise the strong possibility that the utterance is intended to elicit information—that is, it calls for an answer.

But linguistic markers such as these are not enough to tell whether a remark actually functions as a question. We can also ask questions by making a statement, a remark not marked as a possible question by syntax or phonology. Thus, we leave the hearer to infer that this statement *in context* is intended as a question.

Or we can ask rhetorical questions (chapter 5). Rhetorical questions are linguistically marked as questions but can function as some other kind of action, such as a command.

In other words, context makes all the difference in deciding whether some utterance is a question. Linguistic markers alone are only part of the picture. But this makes it difficult to articulate any universal definition of questions—and of discourse acts in general.

Although discourse acts depend on culturally agreed on signals, they also depend on interpretations made by the participants. Interpretations are made by

Table 4.1 Encounters

Tape Code	Date	Gender P	Gender D	Length (words)
Female patients				
EA1	4/04/91	F	F	1,877
EA2	7/10/9	F	F	1,066
EAA1	9/28/89	F	F	2,095
EAA2	11/21/89	F	F	1,217
FB1[a]	4/17/91	F	M	1,760
FB2	5/02/91	F	M	2,906
FG1	10/16/91	F	M	1,216
FI1	11/27/91	F	F	3,034
FI2	1/23/92	F	F	4,236
HK1[a]	4/04/91	F	F	6,376
HK2	5/02/91	F	F	2,648
IJ1[a]	4/17/91	F	M	4,322
JBO	2/06/89	F	F	1,916
KE6	n.d.	F	M	2,084
KJ1	4/18/91	F	F	1,143
KJ2	5/22/91	F	F	1,556
LAD1	10/30/89	F	F	4,130
LAF1	4/18/90	F	M	3,403
MS1	3/27/91	F	M	3,163
MS2	5/22/91	F	M	2,391
Male patients				
AG1[a]	4/17/91	M	M	839
AG2	5/08/91	M	M	1,864
BE1	5/22/91	M	F	819
BE2	7/17/91	M	F	1,090
BR1	3/27/91	M	M	2,930
CR1	4/18/91	M	F	1,237
CR2	5/16/91	M	F	1,335
DW1	4/17/91	M	M	1,319
DW2	5/01/91	M	M	1,395
FR1	4/04/91	M	F	1,760
FR2	5/02/91	M	F	2,198
HEK1	5/08/91	M	M	723
HEK2	11/06/91	M	M	1,129
JR1	n.d.	M	M	1,546
JR2	n.d.	M	M	2,239
LC1[a]	11/27/91	M	F	5,063
LC3	3/11/92	M	F	929
MP1[a]	3/27/91	M	M	4,430
MP2	4/17/91	M	M	2,031
PR1	3/27/91	M	M	<u>2,522</u>
				89,937

a. Initial visits
P = patient; D = doctor.

assessing talk within its local context. So speakers are assessing widely varying combinations of syntactic, referential, discourse, and other features. These combinations cannot be reduced to brief definitions. Referential meaning is particularly difficult to delimit with a definition (chapter 3).

It is this situated character of meaning that makes any quantitative study of discourse essentially tentative. In discourse study, quantitative research serves the same purpose that qualitative research serves—to raise questions and provide partial answers.

However, a definition can capture large numbers of cases. It can identify a number of frequently occurring types of questions, for instance.

West (1984a) uses a discourse-based definition. Her well-known study defines questions as part of a sequence of utterances. The sequence is an *adjacency pair*. This concept, from conversation analysis, suggests that the first member of an adjacency pair establishes the expectation that the second part of the pair will follow. A question is an utterance which establishes the expectation that an answer—not just a response—will follow. If an answer is not forthcoming, there is warrant to reinstate the question.

The adjacency-pair notion is to some extent controversial. Stenström (1984:24) points out that the adjacency-pair formulation suffers from circularity. She also points out the difficulty of distinguishing an answer from a response. Answers are even more difficult to define than questions, and this creates problems for defining questions by their relationship with answers.

Also, I would point out that answers often are not adjacent to questions, which makes a question different from other adjacency pairs such as greetings, in which the second part immediately follows the first. And finally, Tsui (1989) argues that the adjacency-pair formulation cannot account for third utterances bound to the first two.

The term "adjacency pair" remains influential, however, and it points to a critical dimension of questioning: the relationship between questions and answers. An important contribution of this definition is to force attention to the sequential construction of a question. It makes us recognize that a sequence of utterances by two speakers is involved, not just the initial utterance by the first speaker.

A strength sometimes implies a corresponding weakness, however. In focusing on sequential collaboration by speakers—joint action—the adjacency-pair definition must neglect actions of speakers as individuals.

In discourse, speakers are faced with the somewhat paradoxical fact that they are both individuals and members of a collaborative team. Speakers can, as individuals, claim power, whether or not other members of the group then accept the claims. If we focus only on a sequence, we may lose the ability to describe individuals' attempts to claim power.

Another case of strength implying weakness is that the adjacency-pair definition is focused on the uniqueness of each concrete discourse sequence, and therefore it does not specify abstract culturally agreed on signals that support a hearer's interpretation that an answer is wanted (cf. the discussion of defining topic control, chapter 3).

For my purposes, the central issue is: Who is claiming power? Therefore, I focus on the questioner—the claimer—and ask how a question can be raised, how power can be claimed.

I wanted to count unambiguous requests for information—that is, utterances that could be interpreted as expressing the speaker's wish for an informative answer of a certain type. Much of the preparation for counting questions in my data consisted of attempting to specify the various types of information that might support interpreting a remark as a question.

Linguistic markings are part of the information that speakers use in making this judgment. Linguistic markings include subject–verb inversion, WH movement (movement of words such as "what" and "when" to the front of the sentence), and phonological markings, especially rising intonation at the end of the sentence. These markings raise the possibility that the utterance is a question, a possibility that must be verified by examining the context (especially talk that surrounds the utterance).

Terms and phrases expressing uncertainty, such as "I was wondering whether" and "I didn't know if," also play a role in raising the possibility that a question is intended. When the phrase expressing uncertainty is used by one speaker to another speaker who does know about the topic, it is usually heard as indicating a question (Stenström 1984).

In developing a system of identifying questions and classifying their content and linguistic structure, my research assistants and I were aided by West's (1984a) list of examples and Stenström's (1984) list of lexical, grammatical, and discourse (contextual) criteria, with examples. It should be emphasized that we were developing criteria for utterances functioning *unambiguously* as questions. We omitted doubtful cases.

Table 4.2 summarizes the major linguistic and contextual criteria we used to identify possible unambiguous questions. This summary cannot convey the vari-

Table 4.2   Linguistic and Discourse Indicators of Possible Question Function

Linguistic markings

WH	When will the test results be back? (WH includes *what, why, how,* etc.)
SWH	The test results will be back when? ("search" WH question)
Yes/No	Are the test results back? (inverted auxiliary)
TG	The test results are back, aren't they? (tag question)
QF	The test results are back, right? (elliptical question; appended query form)
PH	The test results are back? (various intonation patterns, including rising intonation)

Discourse/contextual criteria

D	The test results are back. (pause) (new topic and addressee can be expected to have the information)
DD	I wonder whether the test results are back. (addressee can be expected to have the information)
QQ	I have a question. It seems important to know the test results. (addressee can be expected to have the information)

ety of phonological markers to which we attended, or the relationship between discourse and syntactic or phonological markers. Discourse context was always the determining factor. For instance, in certain discourse contexts stress on one word signals a possible question. Referential content in relation to the surrounding discourse also cannot be briefly specified. Nevertheless, table 4.2 captures the primary types of possible questions we considered.

In tables 4.3 and 4.4, the unambiguous questions we identified are categorized according to the criteria listed in table 4.2. For tables 4.3 and 4.4, when there were redundant defining features, the question was credited in the following order of priority: syntax, phonology, then discourse. For example, if the question was marked phonologically and also met discourse criteria, it was credited to the phonology category.

This is not because I value syntax and phonology over discourse but because *all the utterances were required to meet discourse criteria for a question.* All had to function as requests for information, regardless of linguistic markings. If I had used the reverse order of crediting, every question would have been counted as defined by discourse and none by any other criteria.

In fact, most questions are marked redundantly—that is, by more than one of the three types of features (syntax, phonology, and discourse). The tables cannot show the confluence of more than two of the criteria.

The total number of questions asked by each physician and patient, per encounter, can be figured by adding horizontally the numbers of each question type.

About 10% of the utterances that functioned unambiguously as questions were declaratives—that is, they carried no syntactic or phonological markers of possible question function. Questions with declarative syntax were introduced in discussion of the "whirlpool" transcript in chapter 2. Utterances in this category (category D) carry more potential for ambiguity of discourse function than do more strongly marked questions. Because they are not prominently marked as questions, they place few overt demands on the hearer and thus are deferential.

In the following sequence, Dr. Myhill used this deferential form, the declarative functioning as a question: "NObody drew any blood off of you . a pint . " This is a statement by speaker A (Dr. Myhill) about events known only to speaker B (Mr. Ager). Mr. Ager confirms that Dr. Myhill's guess about these events is correct (i.e., Mr. Ager answers the question).

Usually, analysts point out patients' deference to physicians. Certainly patients are more deferential than physicians. But physicians, too, are deferential, trying to preserve patient's face. In this sequence, I suggest that Dr. Myhill uses deferential forms first to mitigate the fact that he is explaining the meaning of a medical term (phlebotomy) to someone who may already know it, and second to mitigate the fact that he is restating the question. Restatement by itself might be seen as demanding or as implying that the listener is a less-than-competent speaker.

(1)   Declarative functioning as question

55   Dr. Myhill: So, at *this* point . u:h
56   the smoking MAY be adding to it,

Table 4.3 Patients' Questions Categorized by Linguistic/Discourse Structure

Tape Code	N/O	D	DD	Ph[a]	QF[a]	QQ	SWH[a]	TG[a]	WH[a]	YN[a]
AG1	N									
AG2	N			1						2
EAA1	N	1		1	1					3
EAA2	N			2					1	2
FB1	N			1					1	
FB2	N			1				1	1	4
HEK1	N									2
HEK2	N		1		1				1	2
JBO	N	1							2	3
KE6	N	3		2				1	1	6
LAD1	N		2	2					1	6
LAF1	N			1					3	5
BE1	O			1			1		1	2
BE2	O			1						1
BR1	O	1	1			1			2	2
CR1	O			2	1				2	
CR2	O									2
DW1	O			3				1		3
DW2	O									
EA1	O					2				6
EA2	O								1	3
FG1	O			1						3
FI1	O			2	1				2	2
FI2	O			1					2	2
FR1	O							2	8	5
FR2	O			2	1			1	8	13
HK1	O	3	2	10	1				12	32
HK2	O			1					3	4
IJ1	O	2	1	1				1	1	8
JR1	O								1	
JR2	O							1	2	
KJ1	O	1		2				1	1	
KJ2	O	1								3
LC1	O	2		5					10	11
LC3	O			1						4
MP1	O			4	1				2	2
MP2	O	1		2						
MS1	O	1	1	3					3	4
MS2	O			3						
PR1	O			1					3	
		17	8	57	7	3	1	9	75	147

a. Linguistically marked questions
N = non-oncology patient; O = oncology patient

Table 4.4 Physicians' Questions Categorized by Linguistic/Discourse Structure

Tape Code	N/O	D	DD	Ph[a]	QF[a]	QQ	SWH[a]	TG[a]	WH[a]	YN[a]
AG1	N			1	1					1
AG2	N	1							1	3
EAA1	N	1		3						2
EAA2	N			1	1				2	9
FB1	N			5					1	7
FB2	N	2		6					5	9
HEK1	N	3			1				1	3
HEK2	N	2							1	2
JBO	N			2					4	8
KE6	N	1		1	1			1	5	8
LAD1	N	2		12				1	7	12
LAF1	N	9		4					9	12
BE1	O			1					2	
BE2	O	1		1	1				2	
BR1	O			10	2		2		7	3
CR1	O			3				1	1	1
CR2	O			8					1	1
DW1	O			1					1	2
DW2	O			3					2	1
EA1	O			7					2	6
EA2	O	2		1	1			1	5	5
FG1	O	4		5					5	3
FI1	O			5					2	7
FI2	O			2					1	1
FR1	O			2					2	
FR2	O			5	1			1	3	1
HK1	O	1	1	1					3	1
HK2	O	2		1	3				4	4
IJ1	O	2		1					7	5
JR1	O			1				1	1	1
JR2	O			1					1	6
KJ1	O	1		2	1				1	3
KJ2	O	1						1	3	
LC1	O	1	1	6					3	9
LC3	O	1		2	3					2
MP1	O	2		8	1		1		12	2
MP2	O	1		1						
MS1	O	3		6	1		2	1	5	2
MS2	O	6	1	6					8	12
PR1	O	1		3	2		2		13	11
		50	3	128	20	0	7	8	133	165

a. Linguistically marked questions
N = non-oncology patient; O = oncology patient

57		but . uh: it's not *high* enough that I
58		think it-we can be *certain* . .
59		and your values are just kind of BORder-
60		line,
61		so I'm going to get a-get the, uh .
62		the *blood* testing done toDAY:
63		and we'll just *see* if your HEmoglobin
64		and heMAtocrit are as high as they
65		once were.
66		Did *you* have a phlebotomy, last time,
67		or,
68		they . they, **NObody drew any blood off**
69		**of you . a pint** .
70	Mr. Ager:	[No,]
71	Dr. Myhill:	[**before**] you came today.
72	Mr. Ager:	No, no
73	Dr. Myhill:	Okay, because our LAST value wasn't too
74		bad,
75		because the-the ((clears throat)) *other*
76		aspect that I'm LEFT with is . . u:m .
77	Mr. Ager:	She took it *twice* last time,
78		took it *once* beFORE I saw you,
79		and then, after I LEFT you she took
80		[it again.]
81	Dr. Myhill:	[took it] again.

{AG2,1–55}

This excerpt illustrates the complexity of defining and counting questions. Again, questions cannot be defined by syntax or phonology alone. We considered three utterances in this fragment as possible questions. One was marked syntactically, and two were not.

"Did *you* have a phlebotomy, last time" is syntactically marked as a possible question by inversion of the auxiliary verb with the subject ("Did you" rather than "You did"). The context confirms that it is a true question, not a rhetorical one.

Immediately after posing this question, Dr. Myhill restates it. We considered whether declarative was a question and concluded that it was. It is defined not by syntactic markings (or phonological ones) but by discourse criteria.

The first discourse criterion for this declarative question was that it was an A statement about a B event, where A needs to know about the event. Dr. Myhill made a statement about events that Mr. Ager experienced, and Dr. Myhill needed to know about those events (the blood draw). Another discourse criterion was its presence in a sequence. A declarative occurring after other questions may be more likely to be viewed as a question because repeated questioning establishes the expectation that a new utterance will also be a question. This is true of "NObody drew any blood off of you . a pint . ", which is preceded by an unanswered, syntactically marked question.

Should Dr. Myhill's "She took it again" in excerpt 1 be counted as a declarative question, requesting confirmation that he had heard Mr. Ager correctly? After all, it is an A statement about a B event. But this one violates the part of the definition of a declarative question which requires that A needs to know the information. Here, Dr. Myhill does not need to know because he already knows. Mr. Ager had just made it very clear that the nurse had drawn blood a second time ("she did it again"). Dr. Myhill could not have been questioning whether or not the nurse did this. So we defined Dr. Myhill's utterance as a summary of previous discourse.

Even then, we wondered whether the statement might express doubt on Dr. Myhill's part. It might relate to the question whether the blood draw was an ordinary one or a phlebotomy. Mr. Ager had explicitly denied having had a pint of blood taken ("No, no") but then stated that his blood was taken twice on the same visit—which certainly sounds as if a phlebotomy took place. No more was said on this subject; perhaps Dr. Myhill decided to consult the written records, after Mr. Ager's contradictory statements.

So excerpt 1 illustrates the fact that more than one criterion is considered when we identify discourse units. It is not a simple matter of, say, a zebra having stripes while a horse does not. In discourse, we have to consider where the animal is and what it is doing as well as what it looks like.

A second type of declarative question also illustrates the pile-up of contextual features that can lend authority to an interpretation. This is a declarative question in which the questioner produces an incomplete sentence followed by a pause. The hearer has to decide whether the speaker has simply decided not to go on with a dubious assertion, or the speaker has lost the train of thought, or the speaker is asking a question—in which case the hearer is expected to fill the pause with the end of the sentence.

In discourse, such a choice is sometimes easy to make because there are many redundant cues present. The following example provides a redundant combination of several discourse criteria just described: presence of just previous questions, an A statement about a B event, lack of completion of the statement, and a pause by A to allow B to complete the sentence. A phonological cue (level intonation) was present as well.

(2)

40	Dr. Miller:	Have you *LOST* any *weight?*
41	Ms. Ivey:	Well I *DID*,
42		but I *THINK* I gained it back.
43		I *lost* about ten pounds . >um .
44		I think.<
45	Dr. Miller:	**Your appetite's been** ((level
46		intonation))
47	(2 sec)	
48	Ms. Ivey:	Fine.
49		@I *haven't* lost it or anything.@

{IJ1,6–40}

Discourse redundancy such as this is parallel to morphological redundancy; both allow hearers greater opportunity to interpret speakers correctly. In making discourse judgments, such pile-ups of possible indicators of questioning are particularly important because changing the number of possible indicators allows the speaker to make delicate adjustments in the degree of ambiguity in discourse function, to match the possible risk of asking questions inappropriately.

These excerpts illustrate discourse complexity. Excerpt 1 illustrates methodological questions which are continually raised by discourse complexity, such as the question whether a declarative statement by speaker A about an event known to speaker B is a question, a summary/formulation, or perhaps nonserious.

Another issue illustrated by excerpt 1 is whether to count similar questions in a series as one or two. For instance, should we count the two adjacent utterances about drawing blood, in excerpt 1, as only one question, because they have much the same referential content? Because these differ in several ways, the decision was not difficult. But speakers often produce two adjacent utterances that are identical, word for word. When there were two such separate and complete sentences, we counted them as two questions. But we did not count parts of sentences (false starts) as separate questions.

All this illustrates the complexity of defining a discourse event.

Quantitative Findings

Variation in genre

Compared with other studies, patients asked a high percentage of the questions in these encounters. Of the 838 questions physicians and patients asked one another, physicians asked 61.3% (514) and patients asked 38.7% (324). This statistic is in striking contrast with West's (1984a) findings that patients asked only 9% of the questions. My method of counting differed from West's in only one minor way,[4] and if we eliminate that difference, we find that patients' percentage of questions actually goes up slightly, to 39.1% of the total.

These quantitative data suggest that medical encounters do not universally belong to the interview genre. The genre of medical encounters can vary between two very different types of discourse. On the one hand, there are encounters such as the ones West studied. These encounters can be primarily interviews, or even interrogations. On the other hand, encounters can be "almost like conversation" (ten Have 1991).[5] Between the two extremes are those encounters Ferrara (1994) describes as "consultations."

Therefore, the generic term for these events should be "medical encounters" rather than either "interviews" or "consultations." The overall impression of a specific encounter may fall at one end of the continuum or the other, or anywhere along the way. The place of a specific encounter in this variation will be negotiated by physician and patient, through discourse features such as first-naming, interruptions, floor holding, topic changes, storytelling, and questioning.

Comparisons between West's and my patients' socioeconomic status cannot be made; West had no data on her patients' socioeconomic status, and my information was fragmentary, emerging from the content of the encounter or interview. However, I do have socioeconomic and ethnographic information suggesting anecdotally that social power may be a basis for asking high numbers of questions.

The two patients who asked the most questions, in my data, were both in money-handling professions. Their access to information and resources important in getting money gives them structural power, which of course implies social power.

Ms. Hake was a loan officer at a bank. In her two encounters, she asked 68 questions, with an astonishing 60 questions in her first encounter (which lasted about an hour). In her second encounter, the conversation turned to ways of reducing her fatigue while she was on chemotherapy, and the following interchange took place (excerpts which are not part of the analysis of questions are not numbered):

17 Dr. Finn: What *KIND* of work do you *DO* at the bank?
18 Ms. Hake: *UM* . I MANAGE all the *lending* functions?
19   >at the bank?<
20 Med Student: She takes care of the student *loans.*
21 Dr. Finn: Oh [really]?
22 Ms. Hake: [YEAH.]
23 ((general laughter))
24 Ms. Hake: That's *RIGHT.*
25   [(??)]
26 Dr. Finn: [Which] bank *is* it?
27 Ms. Hake: First National?
28 Dr. Finn: Oh.
29 Ms. Hake: Yeah.
30   In Concordia? ((affluent suburb))
31 Mr. Hake: Need some MONey?
32 ((general laughter))
33 Dr. Finn: Uh . doesn't *EVERY*body?
34 ((general laughter))
35 Ms. Hake: It might be a *conflict* of *interest*
36   right *NOW.*
37   I don't know if I could MAKE you a
38   loan.
39 ((general laughter))

{HK2,6–17}

Here Ms. Hake and her husband invoke her structural/social power by jokingly role playing the superordinate position of loan officer to client. Although it was Ms. Hake's husband who began this role play, Ms. Hake concludes it with a mock refusal to grant a loan—in reality, a very important exercise of the power to reward, and a complete switch of roles. It is usually the physician who has the power to reward, with treatment that heals.

Mr. Frisell, discussed in chapter 5, is a certified public accountant who explicitly connected his profession with his ways of speaking to physicians. I asked him whether he had ever encountered communication problems, with any physician. This was his reply:

43	Mr. Frisell:	Oh, of COURSE.
44	NAV:	*Okay.*
45	Mr. Frisell:	When I was young*er.*
46	NAV:	Well .
47	Mr. Frisell:	Age . made a big difference.
48		And I don't know that that's the case
49		for *everybody,* but MY case. .
50		Certainly . when I was . *younger,*
51		I was in*timi*dated by people in white
52		COATS.
53	NAV:	M-hm
54	Mr. Frisell:	Ah: but over the YEARS,
55		you start to learn .
56		*I* think it had something to do with
57		GETTING in this proFESSion. .
58		You start to deal with . u:h . the
59		DOCTOR-types on more of an *equal*
60		basis.
61		Or you find them more *often* coming in
62		acting like little hurt CHILDren,
63		and . and "*What do you MEAN . I have to*
64		*pay my taxes?*" ((high whiny voice))
65		And you *suddenly* realize that .
66		*yeah* . THEY'RE no big deal.
67	NAV:	Uh huh.
68	Mr. Frisell:	*They're* like everybody *else,* . and .
69		an:d . you make a *point* of u:h .
70		CALLING them . *SPEAKING* to them with
71		their FIRST name.
72		NEVER call them "Doc*tor.*"
73		DON'T let the *EGO* get in there.

{FR-I,2–34}

Mr. Frisell asked a total of 40 unambiguous questions in the two encounters I studied, quite high numbers (see tables 4.4 and 4.5). Many of Mr. Frisell's questions were unusually personal, e.g., "Why don't you wear blue jeans?" {FR2,1–27}. Mr. Frisell's rhetorical questions, not counted in this study, are particularly interesting as claims to power. Some readers see Mr. Frisell as using rhetorical questions to sexually harass Dr. Finn, a possibility discussed in chapter 5.

Both of these upper-middle-class patients, Ms. Hake and Mr. Frisell, may feel their structural/social status to be a basis for claiming more speaker rights (more questions; personal, even sexual questions; joking putdowns) than other patients claimed. It is interesting that both of these patients (like all of Dr. Finn's patients) were extremely positive about Dr. Finn in my interviews with them. Whatever claims to power these patients may have made, their strategies did not arise from antipathy toward Dr. Finn.

However, any association between socioeconomic status and exercising power through questioning is not automatic (a fact that explains the contradictions between the findings of Waitzkin and those of Biesecker and Biesecker). Mr. Brade, one of Dr. Miller's patients, was quite low on the socioeconomic scale.[6] He asked 7 questions, 22.5% of the 31 total asked by physician and patient in the encounter. This percentage, though significantly higher than the 9% found by West, is lower than the overall average of about 39% in my study.

However, three of Mr. Brade's seven questions were "treatment" questions (Ainsworth-Vaughn 1992a), including the example that follows. A treatment question exploits ambiguity of discourse function (question/suggestion) in order to suggest treatment (Ms. Hazen's "whirlpool" question in chapter 2 was a treatment question).

(3)

30	Dr. Miller:	I can *HEAR* it.
31		I mean I can JUST hear the . in the
32		*LUNGS,*
33		so you can hear the .
34	Mr. Brade:	((coughs))
35	Dr. Miller:	*PHLEGM* . rattling around in there.
36	Mr. Brade:	**Is there *ANY*thing that I can . *uh* . *take***
37		***uh* .**
38		**like *these* people with uh bron*chit*is *have***
39		**y'know .**
40		**those *spray* bottles or SOMEthing .**
41		**to help BREAK that.**

{BR1, 2–30}

Only 24 of patients' 324 questions (about 7%) were treatment questions, probably because they are powerful discourse moves. Low socioeconomic status did not prevent Mr. Brade from exercising significant power in his encounters; whatever we may make of his 22.5%, the type of questions he asked was quite powerful.

Besides socioeconomic status, speakers have other bases on which they may ascribe to themselves the right to exercise power by first-naming, interrupting, holding the floor, and questioning. In this study, it appeared that these bases might include ethnicity, gender, diagnosis, and position of the visit in an interactional history (i.e., initial or repeat visit).

Ethnicity

It has long been recognized that ethnicity makes a difference in medical encounters. As early as 1963, Zola found that diagnoses of psychosocial problems were different according to the patients' ethnicity, even when patients described similar symptoms. Similarly, Roter, Hall, and Katz (1988), in a summary of results of 38 quantitative studies of medical interaction in which ethnicity was reported, found that "non-whites received less information and less positive talk than whites" (1988:112). In that climate, perhaps nonwhite patients are less likely to ask questions. West found several patterns in her data suggestive of the influence of ethnicity (e.g., more black patients than white were first-named by the physician).

These two studies measured changes in doctors' behavior in relation to patients' ethnicity. Ethnicity may also be a factor in the way patients talk in encounters. Doctors' and patients' talk is interrelated. The way patients participate in encounters would seem likely to be affected by the amount of information and positive talk they receive.

This suggests that the difference between West's and my quantitative results might have something to do with the ethnic makeup of the two different patient populations we studied. Approximately half of West's patients were white, half were African American; all the patients I studied were white. If ethnic identity is one of the bases for negotiation, the fact that all patients in the present study were white may be related to the high number of their questions.

As to the direct effect of ethnicity on patients' questioning, general ethnographies of African-American communication say little about questioning (Labov 1972a; Kochman 1981; Smitherman 1986). However, many other important discourse differences were described in these ethnographies, which suggests that cultural differences in questioning by white and African-American patients cannot be ruled out.[7]

Two other bases for negotiation which may have influenced questioning are gender and diagnosis.

Gender

Female patients asked more questions (9.65/visit) than did male patients (6.55/visit), but this finding is qualified by the differences among gender dyads described below. From these counts, it would appear that the genders of both the physician and the patient have significant effects on question asking.

When the physician was a woman, male patients asked 10.9 questions per encounter, and female patients asked 10.8 questions per encounter (see table 4.5 for numbers of participants and encounters in these dyads). When the physician was a man and the patient a woman, the patient asked 8 questions per visit. Finally, the man–man dyad produced only 3.7 patient questions per visit. These are striking findings.

The percentages of physicians' questions in these same encounters are equally interesting. Overall, when the physician was a woman, 49.9% (216) of the 433 questions were asked by the physician, with different proportions for male and female patients (table 4.5). In encounters with male physicians, 74.3% (297) of the 405 questions were asked by the physician.

Linn, Cope, and Leake studied patients' satisfaction: "The most dramatic and consistent finding in the study was that both male and female patients evaluated care from female residents more favorably than care from male residents, especially on items pertaining to the art-of-care" (1984:966). As I mention in chapter 3, Arnold et al. (1988) concluded that differences in patients' satisfaction were not caused by differences in the actions taken by these male and female residents. Arnold et al. (1988) suggest that differences in the ways male and female residents communicate probably are the source of differences in patients' satisfaction.

To sum up, gender is one possible source of the difference between my finding of patients' 39% of questions and West's 9%. In the present study, the number of encounters with physicians of both genders was equal. In West's study, only four of 17 encounters were with female physicians; in mine, 20 of 40 encounters were with female physicians. With female physicians in my study, patients asked about 50% of the questions; with men, about 26%. If patients feel freer to ask questions of female physicians, as the percentages suggest, then proportionately more questions would be asked in my study than in West's, simply because more of the encounters I studied were with female physicians.

This suggestion must be qualified by the possibility of individual differences in the physicians studied. However, when these data are considered together with the various findings of gender differences in discourse in other settings and in medical settings, and with my analyses in chapters 3 and 5, it seems unlikely that the gender differences in numbers of questions are idiosyncratic.

Chapters 3 and 5 explore further the ways in which gender is constituted in these encounters. Chapter 3 provides quantitative data on gender and topic control, and chapter 5 provides a qualitative analysis of the gendered interaction between Mr. Frisell (introduced in this chapter) and Dr. Finn.

Initial visit, diagnosis

Initial encounters are different from repeat encounters. In the 80 encounters studied by Boreham and Gibson (1978), questions about treatment were twice as frequent in the initial encounters.

In table 4.1, the six initial visits are marked; all others are repeat visits. At first glance, the six initial visits appear to differ markedly according to whether the patients were oncology or non-oncology patients. However, a qualitative look at these encounters raises some other possible reasons for the difference.

Two of the six initial visits, AG1 and FB1, were encounters with non-oncology patients—Mr. Ager in AG1 and Ms. Feblen in FB1. Mr. Ager asked no questions in AG1, and Ms. Feblen asked two questions in FB1. This low number stood in contrast with high numbers of questions asked in the four initial visits with oncology patients.

Table 4.5   Percentage of Questions by Gender Dyads

	Patients			
Physicians	Female		Male	
Female	(12 Encounters)		(8 Encounters)	
	4 D	7 P	1 D	4 P
	53.6%	46.4%	43.5%	56.5%
Male	(8 Encounters)		(12 Encounters)	
	4 D	6 P	2 D	7 P
	72.8%	27.2%	74.3%	25.7%

D = doctor; P = patient

There are other situational contrasts between these two initial visits and the other four, however. Mr. Ager and Ms. Feblen each came in without a final diagnosis, and so the consequences of diagnosis could not be questioned. After history taking was partially accomplished by a resident, the attending physician finished history taking and then asked the patients to return after the results of specialized blood tests had been received. In their second encounters with Dr. Myhill—with a firm diagnosis at hand—these patients asked more questions; Mr. Ager asked three and Ms. Feblen asked seven.

Dr. Myhill's social/structural power, based at least in part on his Aesculapian power (see chapter 2), also may have had something to do with patients' small number of questions; Dr. Myhill had an international reputation as an authority in hematology, and his patients were often referred to him on the basis of that prestige.

The other four initial visits involved patients who had been referred with an established diagnosis of cancer, so the purpose of the visit was to discuss what to do about the disease. These patients asked 14, 9, 28, and 60 questions, an average of 27 questions per encounter.

Overall, oncology patients asked an average of 11.57 questions per visit. Within oncology, 17 encounters were repeat visits by established patients with no pressing medical issues. These patients asked an average of 6.5 questions/encounter, not so far removed from the non-oncology average of 5.75 questions/encounter.

These figures suggest, once again, that medical discourse is fine-tuned to its context. Diagnosis, current condition, and the place of a visit in the physician–patient interactional history all make a difference.

Length of encounter

Silverman (1987) and Biesecker and Biesecker (1990) found variables such as length and purpose of visit, diagnosis, and initial versus repeat visits to be related to the amount of information patients sought. In my data these factors were confounded; initial visits with a diagnosis of cancer were also the longest visits (table 4.6).

If patients have a longer time with the physician, they have more opportunity to ask questions. But opportunity alone is not enough. Roter, Hall, and Katz (1988)

Table 4.6 Number of Patients' Questions by Length of Transcript

Tape Code	Length	Questions
HEK1	723	2
BE1	819	5
AG1[a]	839	0
LC3	929	5
EA2	1066	4
BE2	1090	2
HEK2	1129	5
KJ1	1143	5
FG1	1216	4
EAA2	1217	5
CR1	1237	5
DW1	1319	7
CR2	1335	2
DW2	1395	0
JR1	1546	1
KJ2	1556	4
FB1[a]	1760	2
FR1	1760	15
AG2	1864	3
EA1	1877	8
JBO	1916	6
MP2	2031	3
KE6	2084	13
EAA1	2095	6
FR2	2198	25
JR2	2239	3
MS2	2391	3
PR1	2522	4
HK2	2648	8
FB2	2906	7
BR1	2930	7
FI1	3034	7
MS1	3163	12
LAF1	3403	9
LAD1	4130	11
FI2	4236	5
IJ1[b]	4322	14
MP1[b]	4430	9
LC1[b]	5063	28
HK1[b]	6376	60
	89937	324

a. Initial visit (non-oncology patient).
b. Initial visit (oncology patient).

surveyed 61 studies of medical encounters; overall, clinic patients had visits twice as long as private patients, but they asked fewer questions than private patients. This fact calls into question the importance of length of visit as an explanation for questioning.

Apparently, for patients to question, they need not only an opportunity to question but also some bases on which they can negotiate an interactional status which gives them the right to question. Patients in subsidized clinics usually lack two of those bases: shared interactional history and the fundamental reciprocity of full fees for medical services.

If It Isn't an Interview, What Is It?

In the literature, the interview nature of some medical encounters, with patients asking fewer than 10% of the questions, has been overgeneralized to all medical encounters. By contrast, in the present study we find patients asking almost 40% of the questions.

The definition of "question" must be considered in reviewing studies of questioning in medical encounters. Definitions of language phenomena should attend to the entire range of linguistic and contextual features. Questioning is a speech activity, a discourse phenomenon, and therefore, its definition must be primarily discourse based, with other linguistic features, such as syntax, playing a subsidiary role.

No single feature of an utterance in context can be used to define a question. We—both speakers and researchers—assess a number of features as we try to assign a discourse function (e.g., that it is a question) to the utterance. An interpretation can be more confident, or less confident, depending on the number and type of contextual and linguistic features that support the interpretation.

Because ambiguity is a pervasive feature of discourse, ambiguity in questioning must be acknowledged in the process of defining and identifying questions. I sought to count only utterances that were unambiguous in their function as questions. To some extent, this decision may have underrepresented the number of patients' questions, because patients are more likely to use ambiguity in questioning than are physicians (Weijts et al. 1992; see also chapter 5).

This study supports the small and often-ignored body of data that finds patient activity in the discourse of medical encounters (cf. Tuckett et al. 1985). If asking questions realizes control over other participants and the topic, then my data show that some patients do claim a high degree of these two types of power.

The question becomes, what are the resources participants used in negotiating their rights to the kind of power claimed by questioning? Among the possible answers, I have discussed and presented data on gender, length, diagnosis, and the place of the interview in a sequence of visits.

I assume that the private-practice setting (though not quantifiable) also plays a role. Biesecker and Biesecker (1990) believe that patients' demographic influences, such as socioeconomic class, are less influential than situational variables, such as the medical setting. But situational variables cannot be neatly separated from demographic influences. Because the setting for this discourse was private practice, in which patients are either insured or paying their own way, patients' socioeconomic level can be assumed to be higher than in previous studies of clinic settings. With higher socioeconomic status comes lessened social distance between patient and physician and, thus, perhaps, more questions.

These are the first data on questioning in medical encounters in which gender dyads are balanced in number. The data also are unusual in including two interactions with most patients.

Diagnosis, gender, and initial versus repeat visit all appeared to make a difference in the numbers of questions patients asked. On the average, oncology patients asked more questions than non-oncology patients; women patients asked more questions than men; all patients asked more questions when the physician was a woman; and initial visits, at least in oncology, contained more questions from patients than did repeat visits. For many patients, in certain contexts, the medical encounter was not simply an interview in which physicians asked, and patients answered, questions.

If the medical encounter is not simply an interview, with all power held by the physician, what is it? The answer is that it often *is* an interview—to varying degrees, in varying contexts. Subsidized clinics and hospitals are much more likely to fit this description than other settings. The structural power of physicians is so great that if the physician invokes that power, the encounter can become an interview in any setting. Tannen and Wallat (1987) speak of the multiple frames that are in effect in a medical encounter, including a social frame as well as the frames related to medical purposes (chapter 6 describes stories that play a role in framing). So we might say that the medical frame is never absent, and physicians do have asymmetrical power in that frame.

On the other hand, the encounter may *not* become an interview. Instead, other frames may be invoked. The encounter may become a consultation between mutually respectful speakers (Ferrara 1994:199; Tuckett et al. 1985), a friendly conversation, or some combination of frames. Ten Have (1991) says that the medical encounter may alternate between types of discourse with patients and doctors negotiating this alternation on a turn-by-turn basis. We have much to learn about the ways frames are invoked or disinvoked and how they can exist simultaneously.

We can be sure that questions will play an important role in framing medical encounters and in the construction of institutional and conversational discourse. This chapter has shown that medical encounters can include substantial numbers of questions from patients.

In chapter 5, I describe the role of rhetorical questions, which usually are not considered to be questions at all. Rhetorical questions allow both patients and physicians to invoke multiple frames (friendship, challenge, authority) without having to take overt responsibility for doing so. In this way the participants show deference toward one another while still actively pursuing their agendas.

Questioning is an assertive act, and no doubt many patients' questions go unexpressed in medical encounters that are extremely asymmetrical. But in my data, patients—of varying socioeconomic statuses—did question extensively. The common stereotype of the passive patient was not substantiated. We cannot know the precise role—in confounding this stereotype—of any one discourse behavior, or of diagnosis, ethnicity, gender, or medical setting. Doctors can, however, become sensitive to differing types of questions (such as the declarative question) and can assess the effect their discourse behavior has on the numbers of questions patients ask. There will always be some patients who prefer to play a passive role. However, as the role of doctors in U.S. society continues to change away from the all-knowing paternalistic figure (Starr 1982), I suggest that there will be an increasing percentage of active, questioning patients.

A Final Caution about Power and Quantity of Questions

The particular kind of claim to power measured by counting questions is the claim to determine who speaks next and what topic that speaker will discuss. This is clearly an important kind of power to claim in the dynamic, emerging talk of the encounter. However, it is only one sort of power, as I pointed out in chapter 2. In this chapter, I defined and counted questions. But we need qualitative analyses to see the precise effect of questions in their local context. A question may claim power over who speaks next and what topic will be spoken about, but, if we simply count it without looking at its role in the event, we have said nothing about the ethical use of the question.

There are critical dimensions of claiming power which cannot be addressed by a quantitative study such as this one. I have said that power is essentially ethically neutral. This means that it can be used for desirable or undesirable purposes. Two observers of the same question might have different opinions about its ethical status, depending on their ethical systems. Discussions of ethical status are critical in the real world. For instance, let us return to excerpt 1, in which Dr. Myhill questions Mr. Ager about drawing blood.

Remember that there were two adjacent questions about drawing blood. Each was counted, in my analysis in this chapter, as an exercise of power. We have two encounters between Mr. Ager and Dr. Myhill in the data. In the first (AG1), Dr. Myhill asks three questions, while Mr. Ager asks none. In the second (AG2, from which excerpt 1 was taken), Dr. Myhill asks five questions, and Mr. Ager asks three. So Mr. Ager asked 37.5% of the total number of questions in the two encounters. One observer might conclude that Dr. Myhill's 62.5% of the questions constitutes domineering behavior; another might think that 37.5% was a high percentage, and come to the opposite conclusion.

When we see patients asking almost 40% of the questions, we can be sure that they are frequently trying to claim power over the encounter's discourse in contrast to the 9% asked by patients studied by West. But there are many other aspects of power that are simply absent from quantitative data.

For instance, Dr. Myhill's questions in excerpt 1 can be interpreted in positive or negative ways.

To begin with the positive view: Dr. Myhill's questions were an appropriate exercise of power. The second of the two adjacent questions appears to be Dr. Myhill's attempt to clarify the first, and thus to communicate clearly with Mr. Ager by explaining medical terminology.

Now the negative view: Physicians often are seen as constructing medical dominance (cf. C. Heath's review [1992:236]). The sequence of two questions in excerpt 1 could be seen as an example of dominance: The doctor first intimidates by using the medical terminology and then condescends to explain the terminology.

Based on factors listed below, I take the positive view. Dr. Myhill used the term "phlebotomy" as an everyday term in this medical setting, one he uses as a matter of course with the staff, with medical students and residents in training, and with patients who have learned the term. Dr. Myhill then realized that this patient did not fit any of the audiences just listed, so he attempted to clarify the term. I would go further: I think that the second question was phrased as a declarative in order to mitigate both the act of clarifying and the act of restating. His behavior was face saving for the patient. So, not just the number of questions but their purposes and how they are phrased are significant in assessing ethical status.

My interpretation of Dr. Myhill's talk is based in part on its phonology (which, of course, is only partly captured by transcription, for the readers of excerpt 1), on the rest of the discourse between Dr. Myhill and Mr. Ager, on discourse between Dr. Myhill and the rest of his patients, and on my observation of Dr. Myhill before and after his seven recorded encounters. Dr. Myhill listened carefully to all his patients and supported their claims to power. Specific evidence of his supportive approach appears in chapter 7, in his extended talk with Ms. Feblen. There Dr. Myhill takes Ms. Feblen's talk seriously as he works with her to co-construct a diagnosis.

Another example of the problems in discussing numbers of questions as an index of power is given in my discussion of Ms. Hake, Mr. Frisell, and Mr. Brade. Socioeconomic factors correctly predicted that the first two would ask large numbers of questions, but Mr. Brade (excerpt 3) had no claims to socioeconomic power. Indeed, he asked few questions, at least compared with Ms. Hake and Mr. Frisell. Yet, three of his seven questions served to propose treatment, usurping the physician's role of prescriber—a very strong claim to power.

No researcher, including those who have focused on abuse of power by physicians, would wish that physicians should stop asking the questions that need to be asked in caring for patients. What everyone, researchers and physicians alike, is hoping is that patients will also feel free to ask questions—in other words, that the talk in medical encounters will create a therapeutic partnership, not a one-sided interview. The present chapter suggests that we have considerably more reason to hope for such partnerships than one might conclude from previous studies focused on questions.

Asking a question does claim power over the emerging discourse and its speakers. The question nominates a next speaker and limits what that speaker may talk about. A quantitative study such as the one in this chapter can show that many questions are being asked. The frequency of questioning is important, just as the frequency of sudden topic changes (chapter 3) is important.

But it is only in qualitative analysis that we can examine what happens in a specific questioning event. The next chapter is a qualitative analysis of ambiguous rhetorical questions. These rhetorical questions are used to pose real questions and to manage such difficult issues as touching others' bodies, mentioning sexual topics, and challenging the physician's competence.

III

QUALITATIVE STUDIES: CO-CONSTRUCTING POWER AND IDENTITY

5

Is That a Rhetorical Question?

Long-term physician–patient relationships have their own kind of intimacy, created both by talk about intimate matters and by repeated interaction over the passage of time. Of the 101 encounters I studied, 99 were between physicians and patients who had, or were just embarking on, long-term relationships.[1] Even when the encounter was an initial one, the participants could project their relationship indefinitely far into the future.

Ambiguity (uncertain meanings) and polysemy (multiple meanings) play important roles in long-term relationships between intimates, mitigating potentially face-threatening acts. In the medical encounters this book describes, the physician and the patient performed an intricate dance of discourse moves with multiple possible meanings. Both doctor and patient proposed to exercise control over information, the emerging discourse, and future actions, and each deferred to the other by mitigating attempts to claim power.

Rhetorical questions were often part of the complex dance of power, mitigation, and deference. Rhetorical questions have never been counted in quantitative studies of questioning because they are usually considered to function as statements or commands, not questions. Instead of functioning as simply a command or statement, many of the rhetorical questions in my data appeared to offer hearers more than one possible interpretation. Through this ambiguity of discourse function, rhetorical questions could function as true questions. Whether or not they func-

tioned as true questions, they were part of the power negotiation, serving to mitigate the ways speakers claimed power.

In this chapter, I dissect the ambiguities in the rhetorical questions used by
patients and doctors in my data. I examine degrees and types of ambiguity and
show that rhetorical questions were used to manage difficult topics. I discuss the
appropriateness of one patient's sexual rhetorical questions and their surrounding behavior.

The rhetorical questions described in this chapter were drawn from my quantitative study of questions in 40 medical encounters (chapter 4). However, for the
present qualitative description, I have sometimes gone outside the data I used in
chapter 4. In the overall data base (described in chapter 1), three encounters were
taped for each physician–patient pair whenever possible, but in the quantitative
study described in chapter 4, no more than two encounters from a given pair were
analyzed. For the present chapter, I have drawn on data from the third encounters, as well as data from field notes and interviews of patients.

Definitions

Rhetorical questions

Traditionally, *rhetorical questions* have been defined as:

- expecting no answer
- having nonquestion pragmatic function.

The second criterion says that rhetorical questions function as commands or statements rather than as requests for information (Ilie 1994; Stenström 1984). Stenström
says that rhetorical questions function as "forceful statements" because "responses
to rhetorical questions are supposed to be obvious to both [speaker] A and [speaker]
B" (1984:53–54). Stenström's examples include, "Is that a reason for despair?" and
"Is it necessary to shout like that?"

I will begin with the issue of whether an answer is actually given. I do this
because presence of an actual answer is an issue in defining questions.

Whether an answer is actually given cannot define a rhetorical question. Many
rhetorical questions are answered, as Johnston points out:

> As my sister and I discuss my "departure" from a five-year relationship and the need
> for my "ex" to move on, [my sister] sarcastically asks,
>
> 66   A: So the next person he goes out to coffee with has to be the person he
>   marries?
>
> Obviously, we both know the answer to this question is "no," and even though by its
> nature, this question does not require an answer, I answer the question with, "I guess
> so." Interestingly, in my conversation with my sister, [she] asked 6 [of the 7] rhetori-
> cal questions, and I chose to answer every one. (Johnston 1995:8)

So rhetorical questions can be answered, just as if they were true questions. The difference is that a true question involves a strong expectation that an answer will ensue. With a rhetorical question, that expectation is not present, and so the hearer can choose whether or not to answer. In this chapter, then, I use the first part of the traditional definition: I define rhetorical questions as utterances that are syntactically or phonologically marked as questions but whose situated interpretation is such that the expectation of an answer is not created.

I depart from the traditional two-part definition in regard to its second part—the idea that rhetorical questions are not true questions (i.e., that they always have a non-question pragmatic function). Instead, I accept the idea that rhetorical questions can have multiple possible pragmatic functions (cf. Ilie's [1994] "multifunctionality" of rhetorical questions in courtroom discourse). These many functions may include a true question—a true request for information—which is exactly the pragmatic function usually ruled out in their definition. In my data, local discourse context can make it clear that an answer is not necessarily expected while still suggesting that one might be welcome.

I use solely the "no answer expected" criterion because this identifies the crucial issue in which I am interested: whether, and in what way, the speaker proposes to exert power over the hearer. Stenström points out the difficulty of finding "a line between rhetorical questions and conducive questions" (1984:55; conducive questions are true questions that predispose toward a particular response). The implicit metaphor in this statement is one of a continuum, with items arranged one by one between two points. A continuum is not the best metaphor for the relationships among rhetorical and true questions because it is unable to represent ambiguity or polysemy, or to capture the possibility of negotiation, but Stenström's point—that the two are difficult to distinguish from one another—is still good.

Besides those rhetorical questions which can be taken as statements or commands, which Stenström points out, I will use *rhetorical question* to refer to two other types of question-marked utterances. These also meet the criterion "no answer expected."

First, there are self-answered questions. A speaker may pose a question and then immediately provide an answer. Such a self-answered question is not rhetorical in the usual sense because the pragmatic function of the question-marked utterance is not that of a statement or command. But taken together with the self-provided answer, it does make an assertion rather than requesting information from the hearer. Because no answer is expected from the other speaker, a self-answered question does not exert control over the emerging discourse in the same way as a true question (the control exerted by true questions is discussed in chapter 4).

Second, there are questions posed in another's voice (J. Brody 1991). Both Mr. Frisell and Dr. Finn in excerpt 7 question in voices of characters in the movie *Young Frankenstein*. Responsibility for posing the question can be displaced from the proximate speakers (the ones now present) to the prime speakers (the original ones). This displacement of responsibility provides deniability to Mr. Frisell in one of the questions, which is a direct sexual invitation.

Defining ambiguity

Ambiguous language has been defined as language having more than one meaning or being unclear as to meaning (Grimshaw 1987).[2] The meanings can be social
as well as referential; we can have utterances that are ambiguous in discourse function (social meaning), as well as those ambiguous in referential meaning (J. Brody
1991; Grimshaw 1987). A third "level of ambiguity" is the ambiguity of voice described previously (J. Brody 1991); that is, who is talking? I deal here with ambiguity of social meaning (is this a true question, or a statement?) and ambiguity of
voice (who is talking, the original or the present speaker?).

Schegloff (1984) suggests that analysts of ambiguity suffer from an "overhearers'
problem": A (nonparticipant) analyst may think that an utterance is ambiguous when
it is not ambiguous for participants because of their knowledge of preceding discourse
and events. Schegloff thinks that a great deal of the ambiguity suggested by analysts
falls in this category.

In this chapter, I will argue that just the reverse may also be true. Participants'
knowledge of preceding discourse (and of other contextual features, such as known
interactional history) also may *add* ambiguity to utterances, making possible multiple interpretations. This might be called the "in-joke problem"; nonparticipant
analysts may miss ambiguity that is apparent to the speakers, who have shared
experience of preceding events and discourse.

Schegloff (1984) also argues that the only ambiguities we can confidently identify are those treated as ambiguous by the speakers (i.e., both possible meanings
are acknowledged in the local discourse). But ethnographic discourse analysis suggests that ambiguity is a linguistic resource often used *precisely for the purpose of
allowing a meaning to go unacknowledged.* Important ambiguities are excluded if
we accept Schegloff's criterion. This issue of what evidence to accept (only what is
acknowledged in the local discourse, or evidence outside the local discourse as well)
is discussed in chapter 1.

I agree with Grimshaw's position that "potentially interactionally significant
ambiguities should wherever possible be identified and disambiguated precisely
in order to permit assessment of that significance" (1987:187). In my view, not just
local discourse context, as Schegloff requires, but also the ethnographer's knowledge and observations and participants' statements in interviews, can provide evidence for the existence of ambiguities in discourse.

Physicians' Rhetorical Questions

Rhetorical questions were common in my data; in 40 medical encounters, my research assistants and I counted 74 rhetorical questions. Rhetorical questions had a
critical function for both physicians and patients: to mitigate participants' proposals
to exert power.

There was, however, a difference between physicians' and patients' uses of
rhetorical questions. Physicians most commonly used rhetorical questions to mitigate their commands, their requests to intrude on patients' bodies, or the fact that
they were producing long, explanatory turns. Patients had different uses. They used

rhetorical questions to suggest treatment (intruding on the physician's right to prescribe), criticize physicians, or otherwise engage in face-threatening behavior.

There were other uses of rhetorical questions, such as displaying playfulness, listenership, or membership. These rhetorical questions might be seen as enhancing the speaker's charismatic power. They do not fall within the present focus of analytical interest. Where they happen to appear in the excerpts below, they are termed "phatic" without further analysis.

Mitigating commands

Some rhetorical questions fit the classical definition quite well. They do have far fewer possible meanings than others; in context they do not create the expectation of an answer because they have only one prominent pragmatic function and it clearly is not that of a question. In my data, these were more likely to be used by physicians than by patients, and they were likely to function as a command.

By our count, physicians issued 50 of the 74 rhetorical questions. The largest category of physicians' rhetorical questions (21) was a command, mitigated with "Why don't [pronoun]."[3] Even these rhetorical questions sometimes took on more than one possible interpretation, as in excerpt 2. But when they had only one compelling interpretation, as a command, the question marking served to mitigate the command, as a superficial gesture toward allowing choice. This can be seen either as condescension or as courtesy, depending on the context of the particular use.

Even when rhetorical questions are largely unambiguous, they mitigate the use of power by displaying deference. Medical examinations in general abrogate people's right to control over the viewing and touching of their bodies (Young 1989). I suggest that it is for precisely this reason that Dr. Feit, in excerpt 1a, uses a rhetorical question which superficially reinstates that right.

The question form implies co-construction of the decision by the patient, a courtesy which—like Dr. Feit's playful metaphor "have a seat on the throne here" for "get up on the examining table"—provides a face-saving redefinition of the situation. We know that there is no significant ambiguity in this rhetorical question because the patient is in fact fully capable of getting up on the examining table.

In this excerpt, and throughout the chapter, rhetorical questions are in boldface type.

(1a)

31　Dr. Feit:　*So::* . *why don't you* **have a seat on the**
32　　　　　　　　**THRONE here.**

{MC1,1–31}

In 1b and 1c, "Why don't" is used to mitigate physicians' commands regarding the actions in the encounter (1b) and the medications patients will take (1c).

(1b)

77　Dr. Fife:　**Why don't we just do** *this* **first** .

{LAD1,2–77}

(1c)

29   Dr. Midgard: U:m . at this point in time,
30   **why don't we just . have you** *continue*
31   **these medications,**

                                                    {KE6-D,4–29}

In the following excerpt, the same type of mitigation of a command occurs. The physician nominally defers to the patient's control over her own schedule.

(2)

13   Dr. Finn: [*UH*] . **Why don't I plan on SEEING you:**
14   **the day you come in for your SECOND**
15   **chemo,**
16   Ms. Hake: >O[kay].<
17   Dr. Finn: [WHICH] will be in about *four* weeks.

                                                    {HK1,20–26}

In contrast to the rhetorical questions in excerpts 1a–1c, the one in excerpt 2 does have a small element of ambiguity: The physician does not know whether Ms. Hake has other commitments on the day in question. If Ms. Hake does have other commitments, she might propose a different date, because the date of an appointment is more inherently negotiable than the actions mentioned in excerpts 1a–1c.

Though the date of an appointment may easily be negotiated, there is little room for negotiation of Dr. Finn's demand itself. Her demand for an appointment with Ms. Hake rests on her socially legitimated right to decide that an appointment is needed. So these "Why don't [pronoun]" rhetorical questions are primarily interpretable as commands, in the context of the physicians' structural power. But they do show degrees of ambiguity, however slight.

Justifying lengthy turns

In excerpt 3, Dr. Miller exploits ambiguity of voice, asking "Why" and "Why are those big?" as if he were speaking from the patient's point of view. He then answers his own question.

(3)

49   Ms. Brade: So . YOU'RE saying . when he puts the
50   bandage on,
51   fluid's gonna be pushed UP and it's
52   just going to *STAY* up there?
53   Dr. Miller: HOPEfully it then will WORK it's way
54   *through.*
55   But we *KNOW* the tumor's BLOCKING blood

56		vessels.
57	Mr. Brade:	>Mm.<
58	Dr. Miller:	And LYMPHATIC channels.
59	Mr. Brade:	>Mm.<
60	Dr. Miller:	And that's *WHY* it's making the *arm*
61		sore.
62		It's the *SAME* thing . women who: used
63		to have the mastectomies where they
64		took off EVERYthing?
65	Mr. Brade:	M-hm
66	Dr. Miller:	Y'know, not the *newer* operations .
67		but the *OLD* ones .
68		They took *ALL* the lymph glands out from
69		underneath the *ARMS*,
70		the arm would get *HUGE*.
71		Okay?
72		**Why** .
73		because the fluid that is *formed* from
74		*BLOOD* . flowing through the *ARM* .
75		has no place to GO,
76		because *ordinarily* it goes through
77		these little channels .
78		that are *LIKE* blood vessels but they
79		have *clear* fluid in 'em,
80		*not* blood,
81		but a fluid called LYMPH,
82		and it goes up through the *lymph*
83		channels.
84		You *KNOW* the blood vessels are *blocked*
85		because you can see the veins,
86		how big they *are*.
87	Mr. Brade:	(???)
88	Dr. Miller:	Those . **why are those big?**
89		Because the ones down *below* . can't
90		take the *flow*,
91		so the top ones . have *more* in them.
92		So there *ARE* alternative . places for
93		the other lymph to go.
94		I think that'll make you feel better in
95		the sense that your ARM won't be so
96		*BIG* .
97	Mr. Brade:	>yeah<
98	Dr. Miller:	but I DON'T think it's going to make
99		the *pain* any less.
100	Mr. Brade:	M-hm.

101   Well the *pain* I can . uh . . I can *cope*
102   with that.

{BR1,5–49}

I suggest that in excerpt 3, Dr. Miller asks rhetorical questions in order to legitimize his lengthy occupation of the floor and his assumption of the role of lecturer. Legitimizing is done when the rhetorical questions take Mr. Brade's voice; thus they propose to provide vicarious participation to Mr. Brade.

Dr. Miller's rhetorical questions also transfer power by teaching, because teaching empowers the person who is taught even though it simultaneously defines the other as subordinate. It could also be argued that Dr. Miller was using Mr. Brade's voice in an attempt to display understanding of Mr. Brade's likely questions, and that this was interactive on Dr. Miller's part.

I have observed these long, teaching turns in the discourse of each physician whom I have studied at length. Most physicians occasionally use this kind of turn (often with self-answered questions) in answer to a question by a patient. I observed Dr. Miller in nine encounters. He routinely used very long turns, whether or not the patient had asked for the information—and in one case, when the patient had stated that she did not need the information (about filing for insurance benefits). Mr. Brade had not asked about lymph. He was an intelligent person and had had lymphoma for three years so it is possible that he already knew what lymph was and how it was related to swelling in his arm.

I suggest that physicians are simultaneously commanding (with "Why don't you" rhetorical questions) and mitigating the commands; simultaneously teaching (with lengthy explanatory turns) and mitigating the role of teacher (with self-answered questions). Each physician needs to be aware of the fit between these actions and a particular patient's needs. Patients do want information, and hearing it from the caregiver is important, because oral language is always our first resource for understanding. But teaching works best when it is interactive.

Caregivers also can use written language and videotapes to teach patients. I am often amazed at how little medicine exploits the particular strengths of written information. It is compact; its nature is immediately clear (in contrast to a videotape); it is inexpensive to produce; it can be absorbed and reviewed at leisure; and, importantly, it is more difficult to misconstrue than is oral language. Even if the information is given orally, the written form is still valuable because written and oral information support one another.

Research shows that even illiterate people can benefit from having written explanations because they usually have access to family members or friends who will read the document and discuss it orally with the illiterate person (S. Heath 1983).

A personal note: In 1986, when I was first informed that I probably had a malignancy, I was alone. After discussing with the surgeon at length what to do next, I drove home. Then I tried to recount to my husband what had happened in the encounter.

I could remember nothing about the discussion. All I could remember was that I probably had a malignancy.

A few years later, state law mandated that women be given written statements describing treatment options for breast cancer. I testified at the hearings before approval of this law, saying that it would have been helpful to me to have something in writing to take away from that first encounter, with its mind-numbing news.

Managing Face-Threatening Acts

Mr. Frisell: Mitigating demands

Ambiguity in discourse is often identified as a resource speakers use to manage a culturally difficult situation. Black speakers use ambiguity in "signifying"—saying something critical indirectly (Mitchell-Kernan 1972; Kochman 1981; Smitherman 1986). Ambiguity is used to tease in several cultures: Tojolab'al (J. Brody 1991), Chicano (Eisenberg 1986), U.S. working-class white (Miller 1986), and Kaluli (Schieffelin 1986). In most of these cases, ambiguity is used to mitigate statements that are potentially face threatening.

Likewise, in the medical encounters I studied, both patients and physicians used ambiguous rhetorical questions to manage difficult, face-threatening issues. Ambiguity of rhetorical questions was exploited most often by patients, probably in deference to physicans' structural power.[4] The face-threatening issues involved in the following excerpts include sexuality, being cured, and dissatisfaction with medical care.

Sexuality and being cured were issues in the three encounters between Dr. Finn and Mr. Frisell (April 4, May 2, and June 6). Mr. Frisell had been treated for testicular cancer the previous year.

Much of the literature on physician–patient talk provides examples of debatable behavior by a physician. Mr. Frisell's talk is an example of debatable behavior by a patient. His actions raise important questions about the boundaries physicians may need to set around themselves, against patient encroachment. His physician did not see his behavior as inappropriate, but others in the clinic did.

Mr. Frisell was a 38-year-old certified public accountant (CPA). He was introduced in chapter 4. He asked an unusually high number of questions, many of a personal nature. I suggested in chapter 4 that Mr. Frisell may have felt entitled to question Dr. Finn extensively because of the CPA's structural/social power over finances.

Mr. Frisell, as quoted in chapter 4, explicitly connected his first-naming of doctors with his control over their finances. Mr. Frisell claimed power by not only first-naming but also nicknaming Dr. Finn. However, lack of true familiarity shows in the fact that he chose the wrong one of two nicknames commonly used for her first name.

A simple quantitative analysis of the first two encounters we recorded between Mr. Frisell and Dr. Finn would suggest that Mr. Frisell claimed a high degree of control over the discourse by asking many questions. He asked 40 true questions to Dr. Finn's 15.[5] (Note that his 40 questions did not include the rhetorical questions in the examples that follow.)

The qualitative analysis supports the quantitative suggestion. Mr. Frisell claimed an unusual amount of power; he did this by asking both true questions that were unusually personal and ambiguous rhetorical questions that introduced face-threatening topics and made available the possibility that they were true questions.

For instance, Mr. Frisell's rhetorical questions introduced the face-threatening topic of sexuality. Excerpt 4: ">So< whatta you been *doin'*, who you been *doin'* it to?" Excerpt 6: "What've you been *doin'* and *who've* you been doin' it to?" Excerpt 7: "'Would you like to *roll* in the *hay?*'"

Mr. Frisell also made a habit of telling directly sexual jokes to both Dr. Finn and the clinic nurses. Tannen (1995:266–267) points out the possibility that sexual remarks by Mr. Frisell may be an attempt to lower Dr. Finn's status, a move to gain power.

Tannen (1995) has shown that women often feel threatened when men introduce sexual topics in workplace surroundings. Sexual topics can imply that any women present are to be redefined in terms of sexuality—lowering their status—rather than in terms of whatever their roles and social attributes were before the sexual topic was introduced.

Mr. Frisell also used rhetorical questions to raise the difficult issue of whether his cancer was cured—an implicit challenge to his physician's competence. Excerpt 5: "So I'm *CURED* here *whatever it is, huh?*" Excerpt 7: "So-wha-I'm *CURED huh?*" There are problematic consequences for both doctor and patient if these are taken as true questions and answered in the negative.

I suggest that these rhetorical questions from Mr. Frisell were ambiguous in significant ways. The "who've you been doing it to" questions occurred at the first of the encounters. Because they were at the first, they could be interpreted as routinized greetings. On the other hand, if they are taken as true questions, they frame the interaction as happening between people who are so intimate that they discuss their sexual activity. In any case, the questions raise sexual topics, with the power-claiming implications mentioned earlier.

How are caregivers to respond, when patients make extreme claims to power? Dr. Finn's responses and the clinic nurses' responses illustrate quite different ways of taking up the social meaning made available in Mr. Frisell's sexual references.

In replying to these rhetorical questions, Dr. Finn chose to treat them as greeting routines. She simply ignored the sexual content. I interviewed her about this. Her views, and the nurses' contrasting views, are provided after the excerpts that follow.

The questions about being cured occurred at the end of the encounters. Dr. Finn chose to treat them as joking closing routines. Again, she was able to avoid the difficult content.

Mr. Frisell was able to introduce highly sensitive issues in a mitigated way by making ambiguous, facetious opening and closing routines out of the questions. Dr. Finn exploited the ambiguity. However, the issues had been placed on the table in spite of going unacknowledged. The reality of these encounters had been made multifaceted, and Mr. Frisell claimed power by introducing sexual topics and by requesting reassurance that he was cured—the most extreme demand a cancer patient can make.

Excerpts 4 and 5 include some of the rhetorical questions just discussed, as well as several others that are phatic, not part of negotiation of difficult topics.

Excerpts 4 and 5 were very close to the beginning and end, respectively, of the first encounter I taped between Mr. Frisell and Dr. Finn.[6]

(4)

24	Mr. Frisell:	I see you're *WIRED* for *sound.*
25	Dr. Finn:	Yes I'm wired for sound.
26		*Isn't* this LOVELY.
27	Mr. Frisell:	Oh yeah.
28		It's kind of neat.
29	Dr. Finn:	Keep that propped there.
30	Mr. Frisell:	>So< whatta you been *doin',*
31		who you been *doin'* it to?
32	Dr. Finn:	*Oh* . not *much* .
33	Mr. Frisell:	>Yeah.<
34	Dr. Finn:	Keepin' busy,
35		outta trouble.

{FR1,1–24}

In the following excerpt and in excerpt 7, Dr. Finn is noncommittal in answering Mr. Frisell's questions about being cured: "*Hey*" and "*HEY,* you're *doin'* good." Her refusal to answer the yes/no question with a "yes" or "no" acknowledges the possibility that these apparently joking questions have an element of ambiguity: To some degree, they can be seen as true questions, requesting confirmation that Mr. Frisell is cured of cancer. Dr. Finn cannot provide false hope to Mr. Frisell by giving an unqualified affirmative answer.

(5)

36	Dr. Finn:	Yeah.
37		That's all that's important.
38		All *RIGHT,*
39		well [take care].
40	Mr. Frisell:	[So I'm *CURED*] here *whatever it*
41		*is, huh*?
42	Dr. Finn:	*HEY* . you're *doin'* good.
43	Mr. Frisell:	Wh- So . did you bring me a joke?
44	Dr. Finn:	No, I'm *sorry.*
45		No joke.
46	Mr. Frisell:	Why do I *come* here?
47	Dr. Finn:	I DON'T KNOW, I DON'T KNOW.
48	Mr. Frisell:	This is the: Henny *Youngman Clinic,*
49		*right*?
50	Dr. Finn:	I guess so.@

51   Well you take *CARE* and GOOD LUCK with
52   tax season.

{FR1,7–36}

The following two excerpts are from the second encounter that we taped between Dr. Finn and Mr. Frisell. Excerpt 6 is close to the beginning of the encounter and excerpt 7 occurs during the second encounter's physical exam.

(6)

31 Mr. Frisell: You're *look*ing proFESSional today,
32   with [(???)]
33 Dr. Finn: [Disgusting] isn't it.@
34 Mr. Frisell: Oh yeah:.
35   *Do you ever wear* jeans.
36 Dr. Finn: *WE:LL* ..
37 Mr. Frisell: Yeah?
38 Dr. Finn: Occasionally on weekends.
39 Mr. Frisell: **What've you been *doin'*.**
40   **and *who*'ve you been doin' it to? .**
41 Dr. Finn: Nothin' doin' *much.*
42   Just um .
43 Mr. Frisell: Sorry to hear *that.*
44 Dr. Finn: Oh I KNOW.
45   I'm *WORKING* too hard.
46   It's *ter*rible.

{FR2,1–31}

(7)   Dr. Finn is examining Mr. Frisell's remaining testicle

28 Dr. Finn: You *KNOW* .. and I *even* thought,
29   "Well, *this* time I will check the ri-
30   the *left* one first here."
31 Mr. Frisell: Well, *you'll* be surprised,
32   I've MOVED.
33 Dr. Finn: I know.@
34 Mr. Frisell: ((laughter))
35   Ever, did YOU ever, uh::
36   you're probably not *old* enough,
37   remember "Young *Frank*enstein"? The
38   movie?
39 Dr. Finn: Oh yeah.@
40 Mr. Frisell: His hump kept [moving around].
41 Dr. Finn: [((laughter))]
42   That's right!
43   *"What* hump?"
44 Mr. Frisell: "What hump."

45		Yeah.
46	((laughter))	
47	Dr. Finn:	*GREAT* movie . . .
48	Mr. Frisell:	Oh boy,
49		It was a *class*ic.
50	Dr. Finn:	Oh it WAS.
51	Mr. Frisell:	**"Would you like to *roll* in the *hay*?"**
52	Dr. Finn:	((laughter))
53	Mr. Frisell:	Here's another classic.
54		**"*Oh.**
55		***Great knockers.*"**
56		Remember that?
57	Dr. Finn:	Oh yes.
59	Mr. Frisell:	(???) ((in high, squeaky voice))
60	Dr. Finn:	((laughter)) Oh:: ((sigh))
61	Mr. Frisell:	*So-wha-I'm CURED huh?*
62	Dr. Finn:	*Hey.*

{FR2,7–28}

In excerpt 7, Mr. Frisell was managing a situation that may have been difficult for him: A young, attractive female physician was feeling his testicle, and apparently the testicle was not in the expected place. He changed the topic to Igor's moving hump in *Young Frankenstein*, thus simultaneously making light of his own medical condition and changing the conversational focus away from his genitalia.

The rhetorical sexual invitation, "'Would you like to *roll* in the *hay*?,'" was issued by Mr. Frisell playing the role (i.e., using the voice) of a character in the movie. I argue later that this rhetorical question was ambiguous in both function (phatic quote/actual invitation) and voice (character in movie/Mr. Frisell).

The final rhetorical "So I'm *cured* huh?" was partially routinized in the context of its use in the previous encounter, and in the context of Mr. Frisell's and Dr. Finn's shared knowledge that no one knows whether Mr. Frisell is cured; it also takes on the irony of the movie topic just finished. With all this context pointing toward irony, the noncommittal nature of Dr. Finn's answer is even more pointed.

Mr. Frisell's "This is the Henney *Young*man *Clinic*, right?" is phatic, an invitation to join in play. Dr. Finn's rhetorical questions are also phatic: "'*What* hump?'" and "*Isn't* this LOVELY" are displays of membership and listenership.

I am not suggesting that phatic rhetorical questions are entirely unambiguous. "*Isn't* this LOVELY" is routinized irony, and irony plays on ambiguity. But the ambiguity is slight, as it is in the similarly routinized "What's the use of . . ." discussed later. More important for my concerns, "*Isn't* this LOVELY" does not claim either speaker rights or the right to command, propose action, or otherwise determine participants' behavior.

Mr. Frisell's rhetorical questions deserve further discussion. Evidence in the texts, interviews, and field notes illustrates the argument that his rhetorical questions offer multiple possible interpretations.

Dr. Finn herself gave two interpretations of his behavior overall. First, in the second recorded encounter (line 53), Dr. Finn said that Mr. Frisell was good at giving her a hard time. This was said jokingly—just as Mr. Frisell's talk was joking—but, in each case, the joke makes available the serious interpretation. (Because this and the following two excerpts do not contain rhetorical questions, they are not numbered.)

45	Dr. Finn:	O*kay*,
46		let me just have you lie down and see
47		your belly.
48	Mr. Frisell:	My *urge* is to just *hack* and cough when
49		I do that.
50	Dr. Finn:	I know. ((laughter))
51	Mr. Frisell:	*Just* to give you a HARD time, you know.
52	Dr. Finn:	Well you're *good* at that,
53		giving me a hard time.

{FR2, 6–42}

But Dr. Finn, in her interview, made it very clear that she did not regard Mr. Frisell as harassing her. In response to a question about whether she had been sexually harassed by any patients, Dr. Finn brought up Mr. Frisell, saying that he was the only one who told "off-color jokes." Of course, this comment acknowledges the idea that the jokes can be viewed as harassment. But then, Dr. Finn continued, "I just don't take that in terms of being sexually off*en*sive or anything." I replied, "Not putting the *moves* on you." Dr. Finn said, "No, I don't think he is at *all.* He's just coming in to tell a JOKE, and that's just the kind of jokes he *tells.*"

Dr. Finn's point of view was not shared by the nurses who dealt with Mr. Frisell; the nurse-manager wryly told me, "We draw lots to see who has to put him in the examining room."

When I interviewed Mr. Frisell, he mentioned that he felt comfortable talking to Dr. Finn. I asked him to give me details about what made him feel comfortable in these encounters. His reply suggests that he knows there is something inappropriate about his jokes:

25	Mr. Frisell:	O:h she's *very* friendly.
26		She's re*cep*tive to my bad jokes.
27	NAV:	((laughter))
28	Mr. Frisell:	Uh . but THAT'S a way of cutting the
29		ice too.

{FR-I, 13–25}

Tannen (1995) described Mr. Frisell's sexual references as attempts to lower Dr. Finn's status. It is not clear whether this is because she is a woman or because she is a physician. Certainly there is evidence that Mr. Frisell wishes to lower physicians' status. Remember that he was quoted in chapter 4 as saying that he addresses physicians with their first names, so as to keep their egos in check. In his interview, Mr. Frisell used some variant of the word *intimidated* nine times to describe his feelings toward physicians.

In their encounters, Mr. Frisell and Dr. Finn discussed her trip to Minneapolis to become a board-certified physician. Mr. Frisell attempted to lower Dr. Finn's status twice. Before the trip, he teased that she was "just a rank amateur" because she had not yet passed the exams. At a subsequent encounter after the trip, Mr. Frisell asked whether Dr. Finn passed the exams, which were held in a neighboring large city; when she replied, "Yes, I did," his immediate response was, "Yeah. Did you do some shopping while you were there?" Although he later congratulated Dr. Finn, this first response ignored the accomplishment and instead cast her in the stereotypical role of a woman interested in shopping, certainly a role with lower status than that of a board-certified oncologist.

Tannen (1990, 1993c) shows that movements toward power and toward solidarity need not be mutually exclusive. Both interpretations may be accurate, with differing salience for different observers (including the participants themselves).

One way to understand this discourse is through the theoretical concept of framing. A frame is the participants' understanding of the type of speech activity that is under way (cf. Tannen 1987, 1993a). Regarding Mr. Frisell's sexual references, we have the following different frames:

Mr. Frisell tried to frame his jokes as a socially valued speech activity, "breaking the ice," in which something is said that facilitates friendly social contact. But he invoked more than one frame. He also used the term "bad jokes," which itself is ambiguous (aesthetic quality or social offensiveness) but clearly makes available a negative view of the jokes.

Dr. Finn saw Mr. Frisell's joking as part of a different frame, a frame related to Dr. Finn's schema for therapy. Mr. Frisell was a cancer patient and Dr. Finn told me that she believed that laughter, positive attitudes, and joking are correlated with patients "doing better" (specifically said in relation to Mr. Frisell's jokes). So Dr. Finn framed Mr. Frisell's jokes as a type of therapeutic (medically valued) speech activity.

We saw earlier that, in the interview, Dr. Finn linked Mr. Frisell's name with the topic of sexual harassment, implying a possible negative frame for his jokes. Later in the interview, Dr. Finn again implied that a negative frame for Mr. Frisell's jokes was possible. She said that the therapeutic value of joking was "one of the reasons I don't discourage [him]," raising the notion that sexual joking might be framed negatively in other cases and thus need to be discouraged.

Yet another frame for Mr. Frisell's joking was invoked by the nurse-manager who was head of staff in this practice. She reported that she and the other nurses felt offended when Mr. Frisell tried to tell sexual jokes, because the nurses saw sexual joking as inappropriate in a professional setting. Tannen's point about sexual topics is relevant. When Mr. Frisell introduced a sexual topic, the professional frame of the event was disrupted for these nurses, and the disruption was such that the nurses felt forced into sexual intimacy.

The nurse-manager told me that she decided not to tolerate Mr. Frisell's sexual joking. The next time he started to tell such a joke, she interrupted with, "*I* don't want to HEAR it." He stopped. She thwarted Mr. Frisell's claim to control over the definition of the speech event (its frame) and definition of her self as someone with whom he could be intimate.

The participants' statements about their interpretations and actions are part of the data. They are important representations of participants' ways of construing the event. Of course, participants may be deceptive of others or self-deceptive, to greater or lesser degrees. Mr. Frisell may have had motives other than breaking the ice. And, although it is difficult to see one's own motives clearly, he may have had some awareness of those motives, deliberately trying to conceal them from me during his interview.

There are implications for clinicians who are faced with behavior they deem inappropriate. The caregivers I studied illustrate three ways of responding: Dr. Finn laughed at the jokes, seeing them as part of a positive attitude. The nurse-manager flatly stated her dislike of the jokes and thus stopped the behavior. Other nurses suffered in silence. It seems likely that the hierarchical status of the physician and nurse-manager affected their choices of interpretation and action. The nurses, with lower status than Dr. Finn or the nurse-manager, may have felt that their choices were limited.

These complexities illustrate the fact that encounters include negotiation on multiple levels, for power over the emerging discourse and power over identities. Patients make demands, both appropriate and inappropriate. The physicians and nurses in this clinic might have benefited from discussing Mr. Frisell's behavior and their options for dealing with it. The discourse ambiguities I describe are subtle, designed to be deniable. But they are real.

Even if these deniable rhetorical references to "who're you doing it to" and to "great knockers" were the only sexual references Mr. Frisell made, they would still raise a crucial issue. Throughout this book, I suggest that physicians can and should cooperate with patients' appropriate claims to power. Mr. Frisell's sexual rhetorical questions, and the varied responses to them, raise the question: What are the limits of appropriateness?

The limits of appropriateness may be found when one person in the encounter attempts to diminish another. We have seen many examples in the literature of physicians diminishing patients. Mr. Frisell's sexual references were felt by the nursing staff as inappropriate, a way of diminishing them. Dr. Finn did not experience the references that way.

Whether patient or caregiver, a participant in a medical encounter should not cooperate with another person's talk when that talk is felt as diminishing the self.

Challenging competence: Ms. Lane and Dr. Mey

In the previous chapter, I discussed "treatment questions," ambiguous rhetorical questions used by patients to propose treatment. Patients must use nonovert means of proposing treatment because that is the doctor's official province. A patient's suggestion for treatment might be taken as challenging the physician's competence.

In the following dialogue, Ms. Lane used rhetorical questions to pursue concerns about the doctor's competence and about her own quality of life. These concerns are extraordinarily difficult to manage. Excerpts 8 and 9 were contiguous in the encounter.

In excerpt 8, the face-threatening issues were: Are you competent as a physician? If so, why don't you answer my questions? In this encounter (LAF1), Ms. Lane, a diabetic patient in her 50s, pressed her new internist, Dr. Mey, for changes in the medications he had prescribed in the previous encounter (her first with Dr. Mey), which had taken place about one month previous to the present encounter.

At the first of the encounter, Ms. Lane said that she needed attention to these medications: "My biggest *prob*lem is my new MEDS." Dr. Mey changed the topic rather than addressing Ms. Lane's implicit request for adjustments in (or replacement of) the new medications he had prescribed.

When Ms. Lane reinstated her complaints, Dr. Mey gave her two choices: She could either take the medicines or suffer the consequences (such as a heart attack). When she again reinstated her complaints, he suggested that other drugs were just as bad as the one he had chosen, or worse.

Excerpt 8 was Ms. Lane's reply. In it, she reinstates her distress over the side effects she had come to the clinic to discuss.

(8)

552	Ms. Lane:	*WELL* do these . y'know . I-I don't *know.*
553		I've been on the Mevacor now for a long
554		*TIME* and it's like . the *side* effects
555		AREN'T easing *up,*
556	Dr. Mey:	>Well . [I]<
557	Ms. Lane:	[and] I'm . y'know . . do they
558		*EVER* . y'know?
559		(2 sec)
560		>**Who can *answer* that.**
561		Apparently nobody.<

{LAF1,13–552}

By answering her question herself ("Apparently nobody"), Ms. Lane satisfied the expectation that questions have answers and thus contextualized this as a rhetorical question. However, the rhetorical question reinstated the immediately previous true question and did so in a particularly powerful way. Given that it is the physician's role to provide answers, this remark was an attack on the physician, questioning his ability to fulfill his role.

In my interview with Ms. Lane, I asked her to say what she meant by this rhetorical question. She paraphrased, "Who can answer that? Apparently *not you.*"

Ms. Lane's use of a rhetorical question both mitigated this attack, through indirection, and emphasized it, through irony. This rhetorical question illustrates the complexity of claiming power in discourse: The remark could be simultaneously a question and not a question and simultaneously mitigated and aggravated.

Excerpt 9 takes up at the point where excerpt 8 ended. In lines 579–584, Ms. Lane asks three rhetorical questions centered on whether life is worthwhile when it is so uncomfortable (e.g., "What's the sense of . . . prolonging life," in line 579).

(9)

561	Dr. Mey:	*Well* . there are-there are *PREDICTABLE* .
562		uh . *SIDE*-effects to medications.
563		*Then* there's the so-called idiosyn*cratic*
564		reactions.
565		Okay?
566	Ms. Lane:	M-hmm.
567	Dr. Mey:	There's *PREDICTABLE* ones that if you put a
568		*hundred* people on you know a certain
569		percentage will HAVE these.
570		*Then* there's the idiosyncratic ones that
571		are *NOT* predictable.
572		It's *possible* that you *fall* into that
573		category.
574	Ms. Lane:	WELL . with the *depression* accompanying
575		*all* this and with *no* treatment for *THAT*
576		. um . .
577		I mean . . I-I *KNOW* that . . colors my
578		outlook,
579		but *what's* the *sense* of prolonging this
580		*life* if it's . if it's so *miserable.*
581		So *what's* the sense of my .
582		*YOU* know . this is *sort* of the way I *feel.*
583		**What's the sense of *TAKING* all these**
584		**medications and feeling . half *asleep***
585		**ALL the time so you can't *DO* anything.**
586		**And having . y'know . gastro-in*test*inal**
587		**pains *all* the time . day and *NIGHT* . UM**
588		**. so that you just feel *mis*erable.**
589	Dr. Mey:	>M-hm.<
590	Ms. Lane:	[Y'know]?
591	Dr. Mey:	[*I'm* not] sure the Mevacor's *causing* that,
592		but it certainly *COULD* be.
593		It's not a *usual* side-effect,
594		as I mentioned.
595		It's not a *predictable* side-effect of
596		Mevacor.

{LAF1,13–561}

Again, Ms. Lane exploited discourse ambiguity. The questions in 579 and 583 are marked as rhetorical by our cultural knowledge of rhetorical questions which begin with "What's the sense of . . . ," but which count as statements: "There is no sense in . . . ." But note, as part of these questions, the mention of specific side effects. By mentioning these Ms. Lane reinstated, in a very powerful way, her request that the side effects be addressed.

Whether or not life is worth living was conditional here; it depended on whether or not "all these medications," the ones recently prescribed *by this physician*, continued to create side effects. That was the problem Ms. Lane originally wanted to solve with her physician. While posing the rhetorical question, Ms. Lane took the opportunity to underline her agenda by repeating the list of side effects that were not being addressed by the physician, and in so doing challenged his competence.

Interestingly, Ms. Lane shortly used a treatment question to suggest substituting a drug she had previously taken with no problems; this time, she suggested, the dose could be increased, because the drug was not effective enough at the original dosage. Dr. Mey agreed immediately. The list of "other drugs" he offered just before Ms. Lane's "Apparently nobody" remark did not include the one she suggested. Perhaps he had dismissed the drug as ineffective without considering its dosage level.

In both Mr. Frisell's and Ms. Lane's use of rhetorical questions, we see ambiguity of discourse function. In these fundamentally asymmetrical encounters, with physicians holding the structural power, patients exploited the functional ambiguity of rhetorical questions in order to pursue their agendas. Because the physicians were offered a choice as to uptake of a discourse function, an answer was not required, and patients adhered to the expectation that deference will be shown to an interlocutor who has notable structural/social power.

Disambiguating voice: The role of contextual knowledge

J. Brody shows Tojolab'al women taking on the voice of an infant in order to "displace responsibility for what they say onto him" (1991:6). These women wished to make critical comments without damaging social solidarity with the object of the critical words.

In excerpt 3, Dr. Miller used a patient's voice in a self-answered question, possibly to legitimize a long turn or to teach. In excerpt 7, Mr. Frisell and Dr. Finn both issued rhetorical questions in voices drawn from *Young Frankenstein*.

Dr. Finn's "*What* hump?" was phatic, displaying the fact that she also had seen the movie. There was no ambiguity of voice—that is, we could not take the remark as possibly being in the voice of the movie character but possibly also being in the voice of the physician. The reason ambiguity of voice was not present was that neither the local context nor the interactional histories of the speakers would allow a scenario in which an alternate meaning—with Dr. Finn asking "What hump?"—would make sense.

But I argue that contextual knowledge makes possible ambiguity of voice in Mr. Frisell's "Would you like to *roll* in the *hay?*" I have already discussed the extensive sexual references Mr. Frisell initiated in these encounters. Besides these other sexual references, in the second encounter I taped, a few minutes after his rhetorical sexual invitation to Dr. Finn to roll in the hay, Mr. Frisell issued a real invitation: He asked Dr. Finn to go water skiing with him.

Dr. Finn exploited topic continuity as a way of ignoring the first implicit (line 9), then explicit (line 12) social invitation:

9	Mr. Frisell:	So are you up to uh . *water* skiing this
10		*summer?*
11	Dr. Finn::	*I* [have water skiied] .
12	Mr. Frisell:	[Or do you not] *fraternize* with
13		patients?
14	Dr. Finn:	Uh . *I* have *water* skiied ONCE in my
15		life,
16		and I spent *more* time FLOPPING in the
17		water than I did @

{FR2,9–9}

This invitation provides contextual support for my interpretation of Mr. Frisell's sexual talk, including his rhetorical question, "Would you like to *roll* in the *hay?*," as ambiguous—offering Dr. Finn the opportunity to follow up on sexual topics.

In the following excerpt, Ms. Kelly takes Dr. Midgard's and the resident's (collective) voice and poses the rhetorical question, "What are we going to do with her?"

(10)   Ms. Anna Kelly, 38, is seeing family practitioner Dr. Midgard for bronchitis. Dr. Midgard and a resident enter the room. The resident has already taken Ms. Kelly's history and current complaint.

17	Dr. Midgard:	Hi ma'am.
18	Ms. Kelly:	Hello.
19	Dr. Midgard:	Oh [we're] *recording* again . huh?]
20	Ms. Kelly:	[(???)]
21		Yeah .
22		Same old stuff.
23		((2 sec pause; Ms. Kelly laughs))
24		This is ominous.
25		*You* two standing there looking like
26		"*What* are we going to do with her?"
27	((all laugh, Ms. Kelly coughs))	
28	Dr. Midgard:	Hmm . for *stubborn* resistant cases *like*
29		this we've *always* got the .
30		a *graveyard* out back.@
31	((Ms. Kelly laughs))	
32	Dr. Midgard:	One *well*-placed bullet between the eyes
33		and we'll . ((laughter))
34	Ms. Kelly:	**Did you want me to turn off the**
35		***tape* recorder now?**
36	((laughter))	
37	Ms. Kelly:	**You'll [just bury it with me] right?**
38	Dr. Midgard:	[(???)]
39		**Or does this . have a self-addressed**
40		***stamped en*velope?**
41	Ms. Kelly:	Well as a *matter* of fact the-the tapes

42		are labelled '*Sue*,'
43		so . *you* know . they'll *never* put the
44		two together *any*way.@
45	Dr. Midgard:	Oh yeah.
46	((laughter))	
47	Dr. Midgard:	I love it.
48		What's *BOTH*ering you the *most*?
49		The [*sinuses* or the cough.]

{KE6–D,1–17}

Like Mr. Frisell, Ms. Kelly used rhetorical questions humorously, behavior reminiscent of conversation among friends. She built humor on shared knowledge of her three-year history of repeated episodes of bronchitis and pneumonia, treated by this physician.

Ms. Kelly's rhetorical questions here served more than one negotiating purpose. By invoking knowledge of an extensive interactional history and by joking, she established that the relationship was one of long standing and thus of reduced social distance, which implies more nearly equal negotiation rights.

Second, Ms. Kelly's rhetorical "*What* are we going to do with her?" implied patients' most fundamental demand, as consumers of medical care, on physicians: "What are *you* going to do about this illness?"

Again, as with Mr. Frisell's "Would you like to *roll* in the *hay*?," I am making the analytical interpretation on the basis of knowledge of the context, including participants' shared interactional history. It is because Ms. Kelly is a patient speaking to a physician and because her respiratory problems have been intractable that "*What* are we going to do with her?" can be seen as posing, in some degree, a true question. The other three rhetorical questions in excerpt 10 do not have such double interpretations supported by knowledge of the context.

As knowledge of the context expands, more interpretations become feasible; if we knew that Dr. Midgard had previously been tried for shooting an obstreperous patient, we might interpret his "One *well*-placed bullet between the eyes" as less transparently humorous than it now appears.

"Who Can Answer That?"

Rhetorical questions in my data were not simply question-marked utterances with a pragmatic function of statement or command. They were often ambiguous as to function, voice, or both. Ambiguity in physicians' rhetorical questions mitigated their uses of structural power, such as their violations of patients' control over their bodies. Patients, lacking structural power, exploited fully the potential of ambiguous rhetorical questions for mitigating face-threatening acts. Their ambiguous rhetorical questions included a sexual invitation, requests for information about being cured of cancer, and requests for the solution to the medical problem. One rhetorical question challenged the physician's authority: "Who can answer that? Apparently [not you]."

Power and solidarity are coexistent in medical discourse, constructed by simultaneous multiple meanings. Patients and physicians both have discourse strengths which they draw on in seeking control over the encounter and over the plan of medical treatment. Indirection may be one of these strengths.

Indirection, such as relying on the subtlety of a rhetorical question to pose a true question, has been criticized as ineffective in the medical encounter (Bonanno 1982); physicians have also been criticized for ignoring indirect questions (Weijts 1993b). Without disagreeing with these criticisms as appropriate to their contexts, I suggest that in the contexts examined here, indirection sometimes is appropriate. Physicians' ambiguous rhetorical questions appropriately mitigated the request to intrude on patients' control over their bodies.

Indirection can be used to mitigate extremely face-threatening talk. Mr. Frisell used ambiguous rhetorical questions to make sexual references, and Ms. Lane used them to challenge Dr. Mey's competence. Mr. Frisell exploited ambiguity of both function (routinized greeting or intrusive sexual reference?) and voice (his voice or the voice of a movie character?). Mr. Frisell's claims to power raise the question, "When does a patient go too far in claiming power in the medical encounter?"

"Ambiguity permits criticism and conflict in the context of cooperation and social solidarity" (J. Brody 1991:78). In offering a choice of interpretations, ambiguous rhetorical questions served both the need for deference and participants' profound wish to claim power in these medical encounters.

6

"*Geez* Where'd You Find *THAT?*"

Co-constructing Story and Self
in Oncology Encounters

There are both ethical and pragmatic reasons for physicians to "empower" patients (Waitzkin and Britt 1989). I have already mentioned (chapter 4) the lower blood pressure, lower blood sugar, lower rates of return visits—in short, improved medical outcomes—for patients who actively question physicians (Roter 1984; S. H. Kaplan, Greenfield, and Ware 1989). In chapter 3, I suggested that listening is one part of empowering. In this chapter, I suggest that the two concepts, empowerment and activity, should be subsumed under the concept of co-constructing an event.

Physicians' and patients' talk together constructs the emerging medical encounter (Ferrara 1994; see Jacoby and Ochs [1995] for a survey of actions that co-construct discourse). Paradoxically, this joint action has a dimension of individual action—for instance, as we saw in chapter 3, one speaker might claim power by unilaterally attempting to change the topic. Then the other speaker can cooperate—or not—with that attempt.

In this chapter, I describe physicians who cooperated with their patients' attempts to control talk and to define themselves. Two physicians—both oncologists—accepted and built on patients' possible bids to tell a story.

In my data, there is a great deal of conversational discourse that succeeds in integrating the lifeworld and medical world. Stories are the best example, as they are rich in evocative detail and in cultural meaning.

Besides co-constructing stories, caregivers have other appropriate ways of being attentive (Mishler et al. 1989). For instance, they can show listenership with an attentive gaze, nods, backchannels such as "M-hm," or requests for information such as "Really?" or "Tell me more." Elsewhere in my data, physicians often listened to stories but did not actively participate in their construction. These physicians were able to be attentive without joining in the story construction.

Why were some stories taken up by physicians differently from others? In each of the two cases described in this chapter, I think the answer rests on the fact that the patient was in distress over a new diagnosis of cancer.

Ms. Melan interrupted Dr. Finn, changing the subject, while Dr. Finn was trying to introduce talk about Ms. Melan's newly diagnosed recurrent breast cancer. I suggest that Dr. Finn abandoned her topic and took up Ms. Melan's topic to allow Ms. Melan to avoid, for a few moments, pursuing the topic of her cancer recurrence. Dr. Finn then found a way to ease into the topic of the cancer.

Ms. Wells, only a few days past her diagnosis of lung cancer, threw out a lead about her panic attacks. Her family then showed a critical attitude toward her panicky symptoms. Dr. Munn weighed in on Ms. Wells' side by co-constructing a diagnostic story that legitimized Ms. Wells' symptoms, and then he further legitimized her symptoms by telling a short story about another patient with the same symptoms. In this way, Dr. Munn showed respect and acceptance of Ms. Wells' new ill self—a self in turmoil, at least for the moment.

Each of the following stories served as a site for integration of the patient's lifeworld with the physician's medical world. There are numerous critiques of asymmetry and distancing in medical discourse (e.g., Katz 1984; Fisher 1986; K. Davis 1988; Taylor 1988; Todd 1989). By contrast, this chapter depicts medical encounters that fit with contemporary calls for patient–physician partnership in constructing medical discourse and in integrating the lifeworld and medical world (Dye and DiMatteo 1995). And in these encounters, physicians tailor their talk to patients' needs.

Background: Power, Co-construction, and Stories

Physicians often thwart attempts to introduce the patient's lifeworld into the encounter (Henzl 1990; K. Davis 1988; Mishler 1984). However, Coupland et al. (1994) describe brief sociable exchanges at the outset of encounters in a progressive English clinic. Also, ten Have (1989, 1991) and Maynard (1991) connect medical encounters with everyday talk. But none of these studies focuses on extended cooperative talk, and only K. Davis (1988) describes an extended sequence in which the patient takes an active role.

Patients who integrate the lifeworld and the clinical experience may provide their physicians with information important in understanding the presenting complaint (Smith and Hoppe 1991). They also gain a sense of control over their lives, which may contribute to their health.

A story from Maynard (1995) may illuminate the nature of the link between control and health. Maynard describes receiving a diagnosis of diabetes from a physician who informed but did not listen. Later that afternoon, Maynard spoke with a physician who elicited questions from him and listened with empathy before giving answers. The level of stress Maynard was feeling suddenly dropped, and

"I felt like I was going to be able to deal with the disease" (Maynard 1995:17). Maynard's experience may exemplify that of patients who feel stressed because illness has reduced their control over life.

For these patients, being a significant participant in the medical encounter restores some of that control, as they actively gather information and help make decisions. Being in control reduces fear. The body's reaction to fear is release of powerful hormones, hormones whose overproduction can impair the immune system and other body processes. Reduced stress would allow the body to return to a more nearly normal physical and mental state (Benson 1975, 1996).

Ethicists assert patients' rights to control over their bodies and lives (Arnold, Forrow, and Barker 1995). If patients wish to take that control, they need to be fully informed to make choices in their best interests. But full information can be gained only through participatory talk, talk in which patients make clear their beliefs. Patients' beliefs can determine their understanding of an illness (Snow 1993).

For physicians and patients to communicate fully, Waitzkin suggests that "doctors should let patients tell their stories, with fewer interruptions, cut-offs, and returns to the technical" (1991:273).

Co-construction

Discourse analysts will be quick to point out that co-construction, in the broad sense, is an inevitable part of all oral discourse. It is a fundamental tenet of contemporary language analysis that participants work together to establish and maintain purposeful talk (Schegloff 1991b; Shotter 1993). In each moment, speakers together construct both the ongoing event—lecture, sales transaction, medical encounter, and so on—and their social selves (Grimshaw 1990; Jefferson 1981). When the word is used in this broad sense, "co-construction" in medical encounters is unremarkable—nothing else is possible.

But kinds and degrees of co-construction vary, and co-construction can occur in service of differing goals (chapter 3). In this chapter, I use the term "co-construction" in a more limited sense, to describe co-construction of a highly significant speech activity, in the service of patients' ability to define their newly ill selves as worthy of respect.

Stories: Generalized versus localized

There is a large cross-disciplinary literature on stories (e.g., Bauman 1986; Josselson and Lieblich 1993; Riessman 1993). Sandelowski (1991) provides a masterly review of sources relevant to medicine and medical discourse. In the health sciences, narration has been linked primarily to patients' histories. "The patient's story," whether told by patient or physician, usually means an overview of the illness or of the patient's life history in relation to illness (H. Brody 1987; Charon 1989; Kleinman 1988; Hunter 1991).

There is another meaning. By contrast with the life-history meaning, storytelling can refer to a localized speech activity, a sequence of actual utterances which tells a particular story (M. Goodwin 1990; Riessman 1993).

In this chapter, I examine not "the patient's story," in the sense of a history of an illness or life story, but localized stories—actual discourse sequences.

Stories are a subcategory of narratives. Narratives describe related events.[1] The number of events can be as few as two (Labov's [1972b] "minimal narrative"). To turn a narrative into a story, the narrator must establish the significance of the relationship among the events—the point—otherwise, the narrative is just a report, not a story.

The point can be understood by hearers who share cultural/social values, profound beliefs about the way people should behave (Polanyi 1979, 1985; Riessman 1993). So stories can invoke shared cultural background and thus establish a link between storyteller and audience.[2]

Stories are supposed to be told in such a way that listeners can understand the teller's *evaluation* of the events. Was the teller angered, saddened, made joyous? Other narrative forms, such as reports, do not have this esthetic dimension (K. Davis 1988:145). Evaluation is a way of representing our selves; in evaluation, as its name implies, we most clearly express our values.

Hearers of a story may participate in its construction. While the story is being told, they may choose to suggest the relevance of pivotal cultural/social points and their own involvement in the storyworld, as Dr. Finn does in the encounter with Ms. Melan.

Because stories define the self, they claim power. They can be used in conflict, to disparage one's opponent (M. Goodwin 1993) (i.e., to define the opponent's self in a negative way). On the other hand, stories can be used to say something positive about another person, as Dr. Munn does regarding Ms. Wells. Another common way storytelling claims power is by attempting to persuade or teach the audience (Kirshenblatt-Gimblett 1989). Stories in the Munn–Wells encounter are also used to persuade.

In the discourse excerpts that follow, stories may not be recognizable at first glance because of their brevity and interactive nature. However, these stories fit all the criteria just listed. They present related events. The events have a point, which is indicated by evaluation within the story. The stories persuade and teach. Perhaps most important, these stories display and define the self.

STORIES IN MEDICAL TALK   Young (1989) describes localized stories in medical encounters. These stories had little overt relation to the patient's presenting illness. Young makes the point that patients were attempting to create a respected self through storytelling, albeit without much cooperation from their physicians.

K. Davis (1988) examined stories, gender, and power in Dutch medical encounters between general practitioners and women. She reports on four encounters in detail. All the physicians were men, and all the patients were women.

In K. Davis's data, "Myriad instances were available of the patient's 'lifeworld' being 'absorbed' into medical frameworks" (1988:357). Davis makes it clear that she does not mean this in a positive way—as an enriching integration of the two— but rather as the disappearance of the lifeworld. However, the picture Davis draws is quite complex. She provides one of the rare views of physician–patient interaction which asserts that one possible frame of medical encounters is friendship

(K. Davis 1988:107). Davis's choice of these four encounters was made to show that patients' storytelling can range from being successful throughout the encounter to being stymied at every attempt.

STORIES IN MY DATA   It is difficult to quantify the occurrence of stories. Stories are a subcategory of narratives, narration is omnipresent in oral discourse, and the boundary between narration and story is often indistinct. Also, stories can be episodic, with many small stories contributing to a larger-scale narration; which should be counted? All these factors make a quantitative study of stories problematic.

For these reasons, I have not attempted a quantitative analysis of stories in my data. K. Davis (1988) estimated that storytelling occurred in 75% of the encounters she studied. I would estimate that 80% to 90% of the encounters I studied contained stories.

My sense of the data is that there is no difference in frequency of co-construction of stories in relation to either gender or diagnosis. Instead, the specifics of the immediate situation, and possibly the personality and communicative styles of the participants, may have caused variation. But the great majority of encounters included stories, usually with direct or indirect relevance to the illness at hand.

Mitigating Bad News: Ms. Melan's "Cold/Christening" Story

Ms. Melan, a 70-year-old retired nurse, had recurrent breast cancer. The encounter analyzed here was the first time she had an opportunity to discuss the recurrence with Dr. Finn. At the time of this encounter, news of the recurrence had already been given to Ms. Melan over the phone by a nurse ("Cindy" in the transcript).

Ms. Melan's husband, a retired physician, came with her to all her encounters. Both were New Englanders, long transplanted to the Midwest. Ms. Melan was not an unusually talkative person; she did not typically compete for the conversational floor. Thus, it was marked behavior when, encouraged by Dr. Finn, she occupied the floor at some length with the "Cold/Christening" story transcribed here. Ms. Melan was quite direct and showed a wry sense of humor: At one point in her first encounter, she remarked, "You know you're going to have all kinds of experiences in this life. . . . I want some of the fun ones, I want to be a prostitute when I get through with this." (Her husband changed the subject.)

Dr. Finn, 36, was a board-certified oncologist. Dr. Finn participated in two oncology–hematology practices in a midwestern university town. One practice was located in the community, and one was in the university-owned clinical center at the edge of campus. Ms. Melan's encounter was at the clinical center.

Dr. Finn enjoyed excellent relationships with her patients, as well as with her staff. The three patients and one staff member I interviewed spoke highly of her. For instance, I asked one patient about the ideal doctor: "What would be the kinds of things you would like that doctor to do?" His answer: "Be like Dr. Finn" {BEI,4–12}.[3]

When Dr. Finn's involvement in this study was finished, I interviewed her. She told me that her medical education had not included any formal courses in medical interviewing. However, "listening to patients," "the humanistic approach," was "really emphasized" in her medical school. I asked Dr. Finn, "What kind of advice would you give [an oncologist just beginning to practice], in terms of communication?" Her answer bears on her willingness to join in the process of storytelling:

> Um I *think* in oncology . the patients have *SO* many psychosocial needs not related . *NOT* necessarily related to the medical problems they're having. And I *think* if you want to be efFECTIVE in oncology, you've *GOT* to let those psychosocial issues be part of your practice. Which is *ONE* of the reasons that . if somebody wants to take a couple extra minutes talking about the *christening* . that's fine, because . . a *LOT* of the family dynamics really *play* into the support team. *Especially* when there's . >you know< . metastatic disease or you *KNOW* that the *prognosis* is not going to be good. But there's just *SO* many . Yeah. *uh* . there's just so many *things* going on. And I . and I *think* if you're someone who . is JUST taking care of the *cancer*, you're going to MISS . a *lot* of the support stuff that these folks need. {FinnI,10–38}

The following excerpt, "Cold/Christening" (75 seconds long), is from the first of an encounter between Ms. Melan, her husband, and Dr. Finn. In this excerpt, and throughout the chapter, stories are in boldface type. Only Ms. Melan and Dr. Finn speak during this excerpt. It illustrates cooperation by a physician with a patient's attempts to follow her own agenda for beginning of the encounter.

The excerpt also illustrates the way stories can function to further the purposes of physician and patient. The story mitigates bad news in three ways.

First, it simply delays discussion of the news, by interrupting Dr. Finn's attempt to start the discussion. Second, it allows Ms. Melan to request and receive sympathy regarding her cold, when requesting and receiving overt sympathy for her cancer might be awkward. Finally, the sociocognitive content of the story defines Ms. Melan as anchored in a lifeworld of family, including grandchildren through whom she will live on in spite of the cancer.

In the first 12 lines of the transcript—not given here—Dr. Finn and Ms. Melan talk briefly about the fact that they are being audiotaped. Dr. Finn then begins the topic 'news of the recurrence' (lines 13–25). But Ms. Melan interrupts and starts a new topic, her cold (line 26):

(1)   Cold/Christening

13	Dr. Finn:	Okay . . .
14		*Well* ((sigh)), I GUESS Cindy
15		CALLED ya.
16	Ms. Melan:	Yeah . she . gave me the . lovely *NEWS*
17	Dr. Finn:	[Ye:::s]
18	Ms. Melan:	[((laughs))]
19		But . [[uh]]
20	Dr. Finn:	[[We::ll]], ((sigh))
21		I . certainly wasn't expe-*really*
22		EXPECTING that.

23		I just . I kept *KIND* of [HOPING maybe]
24	Ms. Melan:	[>yea::h<]
25	Dr. Finn:	it was something else that.
26	Ms. Melan:	I'm *not* gonna get NEAR you 'cause *I* got
27		such a *bad* [cold].
28	Dr. Finn:	[*OH NO*] ((laughs))

{ML1,1–25}[4]

At this point, Ms. Melan has introduced a new topic—her "*bad* cold"—but she has not clearly indicated that there is a story associated with the new topic. Some physicians might have responded by immediately asking about symptoms and what, medically, could be done to relieve them. This choice would have maintained Ms. Melan's topic but also would have moved it into the medical realm, under the control of the doctor.

Dr. Finn instead chooses to maintain Ms. Melan's topic with "*OH NO*" and a laugh. This response makes explicit Dr. Finn's sympathy and turns the floor back to Ms. Melan. Dr. Finn has not moved the topic out of the lifeworld, and so Ms. Melan continues the topic.

(2)

29	Ms. Melan:	*Oh* it's *A*Wful.
30	Dr. Finn:	**Geez where'd you find THAT?**

Ms. Melan evaluates the cold; it is "*A*Wful." This evaluative comment implies that there are reportable details which make up the awfulness. Again, Dr. Finn might choose to move the topic into the medical realm, asking about the symptoms and suggesting medical treatment. Instead, in line 30 Dr. Finn asks a question which keeps the topic in the lifeworld and asks for a story: "*Geez* where'd you find *THAT*?"

The boundaries of a story are difficult to find. Did the story start with Ms. Melan's announcement that she had a cold? With Dr. Finn's "*OH NO*"? With the evaluative "*Oh* it's *A*Wful"? Because any of those could have ended the topic, we might suggest that the beginning of agreed-on storytelling is line 30. I have marked this line as the beginning of the story by putting it in boldface type.

But notice: When Dr. Finn treats what Ms. Melan has just been saying as a bid to tell a story, what Ms. Melan has just been saying then becomes part of the story. So the boundaries of this story are moved back by Dr. Finn's remark in line 30. This change in the story's boundaries illustrates the fact that what happens in one part of the discourse can cause a reevaluation of a previous part. The encounter is known in the minds of its participants, and their understanding of it is constantly changing. So our marking of the beginning, at least in this case, only reflects part of what has happened.

The two then co-construct the story of Ms. Melan's cold, caught at a party for her granddaughter. This is a story about Ms. Melan's lifeworld. It is also a narrative construction, a small world of its own—a storyworld.

(3)

31	Ms. Melan:	I . THINK . eh one of the uh
32		uh little . uh *ANNA* was bapti-uh .
33		christened on . *Saturday* night.
34		And . *Sally* had a party for her,
35	Dr. Finn:	[Lots of little kids.]
36	Ms. Melan:	['n (??) LITTLE kids.]
37	Ms. Melan:	And *HALF* of 'em,
38		they had *RUNNY* noses n': .
39	Dr. Finn:	Definition of a *KID* . I *THINK*
40		((chuckling))
41	Ms. Melan:	*YEAH,*
42		*RIGHT.* @
43		And . *boy,*
44	Dr. Finn:	>O::h<.
45	Ms. Melan:	it started . . *Tuesday,*
46	((knock at door))	
47	Dr. Finn:	*Yes?*

At this point, the story had been under way for 32 seconds. A nurse then interrupted to confirm dates for scheduling Ms. Melan's tests. After this interruption, Ms. Melan took up the storyline where it had stopped.

(4)

54	Dr. Finn:	THANK you. ((sound of door closing))
55	Ms. Melan:	Ah . . o:h *yeah* I think . it must have
56		been Saturday night,
57		because uh . . >uh I came down with it
58		Tuesday,
59		but that's about the right . length of
60		time.<

Having located in time the onset of the cold, Ms. Melan makes a shift in the story topic. She shifts to her symptoms, a topic congruent with the medical world:

(5)

61		And it's *ONE* of those HORRIBLE ones where
62		you cough up YEUCH::
63		and you blow YEUCH [(((chuckles))].
64	Dr. Finn:	[Oh no.]
65		*WON*derful. ((laughs))
66		Any FEVERS at all?

Dr. Finn builds on Ms. Melan's shift to the topic of symptoms. Ms. Melan had mentioned specific symptoms (coughing up and blowing "YEUCH"). Dr. Finn asks about another specific symptom—a fever. Fever is a symptom that might call for medical intervention. It might indicate that Ms. Melan has something worse than just a cold; by asking about fever, Dr. Finn is engaging in diagnostic discourse.

Through these small shifts in topic (sometimes called topic shading), the two speakers have integrated the lifeworld (a child's christening party, full of runny-nosed kids) with the medical world (diagnosing and treating a respiratory illness). The integration of the two continues in the following excerpt, as Ms. Melan reports symptoms she has in the lifeworld, symptoms that might be of medical interest.

(6)

67	Ms. Melan:	I don't know,
68		I haven't BO:thered 'cause I'm . .
69		*hot* half the time anyway ((laughs)).
70	Dr. Finn:	>o*kay*<
71	Ms. Melan:	I didn't FEEL . extra feverish .
72		and I didn't ACHE all *OVER* I just hurt in
73		my back,
74		that's all. .
75		Y'know . around my chest.
76	Dr. Finn:	>Yeah.<

In line 72, Ms. Melan provides another bridge to a medical topic of special interest in this encounter: her recurrence of cancer. Both patient and doctor know that the recurrence is in her back, in her spine, and that it has been causing pain.

Line 75 is particularly interesting. Ms. Melan tries to relocate her back pain to her chest, away from the site of the cancer. Line 75 suggests to me that Ms. Melan's reference to pain in her back caused by the cold was not intended to bring up the topic of pain in her back caused by the cancer.

But, in line 77, Dr. Finn does not accept Ms. Melan's proposed relocation of the pain. Instead, Dr. Finn reinstates the topic of pain in the back, caused by the cancer. Thus she moves to the reason for this encounter: Ms. Melan's recurrence of cancer, in the spine. Dr. Finn's topic shift also is the ending boundary of Ms. Melan's story about her cold. The total time occupied by this story was 75 seconds.

(7)

77	Dr. Finn:	*HOW'S* that pain *doing* in the back.
78		About the same . or
79	Ms. Melan:	*Yeah* . it's about the same.
80		What I *HAVE* done,
81		I tried the uh . medication you gave me
82		[again],
83	Dr. Finn:	[Uh huh.]
84	Ms. Melan:	*AND* uh . now it-it *DOES* help.
85	Dr. Finn:	>Okay.<

86	Ms. Melan:	*HOWEVER*, if I try to *DO* anything,
87		y'know . if I:'m . very *active* at all,
88		then it DOESN'T help.

{ML1,1–13}

The three participants then go on to discuss what they will do next to address the problem of Ms. Melan's recurrent cancer.

Thus, the transition is smoothly made from primarily-lifeworld narration into the medical realm and specifically the purpose of the visit—cancer treatment. This process of beginning with the patient's perspective and moving toward the physician's perspective is both similar to and different from the "perspective display series" used by physicians to co-implicate the patient's perspective in diagnosis (Maynard 1991). Maynard suggests that the perspective display series is one way in which physicians construct asymmetry.

In the PDS, the physician first asks for the patient's perspective and then builds on it in presenting a diagnosis. So the physician sets the topic with a question and then uses the response as a bridge to the conclusions he or she wants to put forth. In Maynard's data, the perspective display series was used to persuade the patient to accept the physician's diagnosis.

Dr. Finn did use Ms. Melan's remark as a bridge to an overtly medical topic, but she did not initiate a perspective display series in order to do this. She began with a comment (that the recurrence was not what she had expected) rather than with a question. When Ms. Melan interrupted the "recurrence" topic with a remark about something else entirely—her cold—Dr. Finn then used a furthering question about the cold. Only later, after Ms. Melan's story was well explored, did Dr. Finn take up a topic—raised by Ms. Melan—of back pain, which served as a bridge to a discussion of the recurrent cancer.

Of course, Maynard is discussing only encounters in which a physician is attempting to gain acceptance for an unwelcome diagnosis. In Ms. Melan's encounter, the diagnosis is not at issue. But in both cases, the patient and physician must deal with a difficult topic. In both cases, talk moves from the patient's perspective to the physician's perspective. The differences lie in ownership of topics and the ways topics are initiated and developed.

In this encounter, Ms. Melan initiated a topic, and Dr. Finn cooperated in developing the topic into a storyworld that integrated Ms. Melan's life with her medical situation. After 75 seconds of storytelling, Dr. Finn attempted to move the topic back to the one she had initiated before Ms. Melan's interruption. Ms. Melan cooperated with Dr. Finn's topic shift. Both physician and patient claimed power over the topic, and both cooperated with the other's claims.

Is this really a story?

Because this talk about a cold and a christening party is not about something dramatic, such as a car wreck, we might question whether it deserves to be called a story. But it has all the features described earlier as defining stories.

Ms. Melan's story *topic* is a cold and the fact that it was caught at her grandchild's christening party. As all storytellers do, Ms. Melan and her co-narrator create a *storyworld.*

The *actors* in this storyworld are, of course, Ms. Melan herself; her daughter, Sally; her grandchild, Anna; and numerous other small children. The time *sequence* (characteristic of narratives in U.S. English) begins on a Saturday, when the party took place; proceeds through the following Tuesday, when the symptoms of Ms. Melan's cold appeared; and continues to the present day, the following Thursday.

The *story focus* is on Ms. Melan and a disturbance she had to overcome (Johnstone 1993): the cold she caught.

In any story, the storyteller has to evaluate the reportability of the story, the fact that it was worth telling. Often in this *evaluation*, the unusual nature of the event is demonstrated. Ms. Melan evaluates her story in several ways.

First, she suggests that her cold is so bad that she should not be near a doctor. This suggestion dramatizes the extreme nature of the illness because we would expect doctors, as a matter of everyday routine, to examine closely patients who have bad colds in order to rule out pneumonia, bronchitis, and so on. Ms. Melan is suggesting that her cold is far out of the ordinary by saying that it is so bad that a doctor should not get near it.

Next, Ms. Melan says explicitly that the cold is "such a *bad* cold"; *Oh* it's *A*Wful"; it is "one of those HORRIBLE ones where you cough up YEUCH:: and you blow YEUCH." Speakers can be evaluative by saying explicitly how they felt about what happened, and that is what Ms. Melan does here. A word such as "Yeuch" is particularly evaluative because it is used only to describe great disgust.

Sounds also evaluate. Pitch, loudness, lengthening of the final sound—these are phonological ways of evaluating, marking the importance of the word spoken loudly, at a high pitch, or with its final sound lengthened. Ms. Melan uses these phonological resources for evaluation throughout her description of the cold and its awfulness. Other linguistic resources she uses throughout her story include a sad tone of voice and a slow cadence, embodying her distress and fatigue.

In all these ways, Ms. Melan evaluates her own narrative, showing the importance of these events—their cultural and social point.

The storyworld as integration

The images and actions of the storyworld, along with their associations, are the site of Ms. Melan's integration of the lifeworld and the medical world.

Ms. Melan's story is about herself and her family. She characterizes herself as a caretaker of others' health and—the primary focus—as victim of a severe respiratory illness. She introduces a party scene, a christening, populated by her daughter, her granddaughter, and other small children. These images all take on significance when viewed in relation to Ms. Melan's present visit to the doctor. The images—caretaker, cold sufferer, grandmother—relate to Ms. Melan's new role as a patient with terminal cancer.

Cancer entails a loss of control over one's health and a growing dependency upon medical providers. In introducing the story topic, however, *Ms. Melan re-*

verses the roles: She adopts the role of caretaker for the physician's health: "I'm *not* gonna get NEAR you 'cause I got such a *bad* cold."

Widespread recurrent breast cancer cannot be cured; at best it will be slowed. *But a respiratory virus will run its course and go away.* This illness is controllable and thus easier to focus on than the cancer.

It is culturally difficult to request or receive sympathy for terminal cancer (any cancer, in fact). Instead, the culture praises the cancer patient who does not complain. As Sontag (1977) argued so well, cancer has become the metaphor for evil in our culture. Therefore, the topic inspires fear and is avoided. The fact that this is a terminal cancer introduces the topic of death, another taboo topic. *But it is extremely common, culturally easy, to request and receive sympathy for being the victim of a transient cold.* Having a bad cold is a manageable experience. Everyone has had this experience and can therefore empathize with its miseries.

Ms. Melan, a retired nurse and wife of a physician, knows that widespread recurrent breast cancer seldom, if ever, is eliminated. Contextualizing this fact are the images of Ms. Melan's family: *She will live on through her daughter and granddaughter.* Reinforcing the theme of survival is the fact that *a christening is a celebration of new life.*

The images in this story—Ms. Melan as guardian of others' health, Ms. Melan as suffering and thus deserving sympathy, Ms. Melan's daughter and granddaughter, a christening party—both contextualize and are contextualized by the reason for her visit to Dr. Finn: her own struggle with cancer. The present and the storyworld exist simultaneously, and thus the present medical encounter, whose goal is to discuss her long-term cancer prognosis and treatment, is integrated with Ms. Melan's storyworld.

Just as important for bringing together medical and lifeworld experience is the integration of those two realms within the story. This storyworld is like the medical realm; it includes coping with illness. It is also like the lifeworld; coping takes place day-to-day, in the context of family support and family continuity. Thus, the themes of Ms. Melan's lifeworld and the medical realm converge through co-constructed storytelling.

Specific acts of co-construction

Many stories belong primarily to one teller. Labov (1972b) analyzes stories of near-death encounters and of black teenagers' memorable fights; these are told by the person who had the experience, with little contribution by the interviewer. But co-construction—to varying degrees—also is common (Polanyi 1979).

Ms. Melan and Dr. Finn used three especially important types of co-constructing discourse moves:

- The "furthering question"
- Repetition, used to show participation and agreement (Tannen 1989c)
- Formulations (West and Garcia 1988) of shared cultural knowledge.

THE FURTHERING QUESTION   In the "Cold/Christening" story, Dr. Finn makes a crucial remark, "*Geez* where'd you find *THAT*?" I call this a *furthering question,* because it advances the narrative. Furthering questions can occur at any point in a story, asking the other speaker to elaborate. This one is particularly important because it elicits the story itself, making possible all the social functions of storytelling.

Dr. Finn asks a second furthering question in line 66: after acknowledging Ms. Melan's complaint that the illness is "*HORRIBLE,*" Dr. Finn asks, "Any fevers at all?" This question not only furthers the immediate narrative but also invokes the purposes of the encounter (i.e., to give and receive medical advice). Once these purposes are invoked, it is easier for Dr. Finn later to move on to the original topic of the meeting—Ms. Melan's recurrence of cancer.

REPETITION   In response to "*Geez* where'd you find *THAT*?," Ms. Melan describes where she found the cold—at a christening party for her grandchild.

34		And . *Sally* had a party for her,
35	Dr. Finn:	[Lots of little kids.]
36	Ms. Melan:	['n (??) LITTLE kids.]

In line 35, Dr. Finn displays her shared cultural knowledge about christening parties and develops both the scene and the story by introducing some new characters into the story: "lots of little kids." Ms. Melan repeats Dr. Finn's words, beginning to talk before Dr. Finn has finished the phrase, and finishing in simultaneous utterance of "little kids."

Repetition, as Tannen (1989c) has shown, is a powerful and pervasive discourse strategy. It demonstrates beyond question that the repeater heard the speaker, and it often implies agreement. As Tannen remarks, repetition sends a metamessage of rapport.

Moreover, when the two speakers are able to produce identical language simultaneously, as in lines 35–36, they show that their attention to what the other person has said is so careful that they can accurately predict words not yet said. This is a strong demonstration of rapport.

FORMULATIONS   Ms. Melan then brings up the kids' contagious state:

37	Ms. Melan:	And *HALF* of 'em,
38		they had *RUNNY* noses n': .
39	Dr. Finn:	Definition of a *KID* . I *THINK*
40		((chuckling))

Dr. Finn, in turn, demonstrates rapport. Ms. Melan says that these kids had runny noses, and Dr. Finn says, "Definition of a *KID* . I *THINK*." In other words, "Yes, all kids have runny noses."

Dr. Finn's remark is a formulation. Speakers commonly formulate a point for preceding discourse (West and Garcia 1988, Houtkoop-Steenstra 1995). Sometimes a formulation only sums up what has been said; sometimes it also adds some relevant information. This particular formulation displays the fact that Dr. Finn heard and also adds the relevant idea that runny noses are a general condition. By adding this generalization, Dr. Finn shows that she shares experience with Ms. Melan: They both know how children are.

In this section, I have suggested that Ms. Melan and Dr. Finn co-constructed a story that served to mitigate the subsequent discussion of medical bad news, through delay, through its elicitation of sympathy for Ms. Melan's illness, and through its hopeful lifeworld images, which contextualize the subsequent discussion of cancer. The two speakers used furthering questions, repetition, and formulations as co-constructive devices which established and maintained rapport.

This was an encounter in which the patient was active, the physician cooperated with her and yet also pursued the medical agenda, and the two cooperated in integrating the patient's lifeworld with the medical facts of her new stage of illness. In the next encounter, between Ms. Wells and Dr. Munn, the patient was less active in defining her self. Ms. Wells was under siege from her own family,[5] and Dr. Munn used stories to support Ms. Wells' claims about her experience.

Validating Another's Experience: The "Panic Attacks" Story

Ms. Wells, 47, had lung cancer. Her cancer was discovered in an X ray administered as preparation for a hip-replacement operation less than a week before her first encounter with Dr. Munn.

Although I did not interview Ms. Wells (a scheduled interview was canceled when she was hospitalized with severe complications from chemotherapy), I talked with her and her family at length just before the first encounter recorded between Dr. Munn and the Wells family. I learned that Ms. Wells's sister, Ellen, had recently died of lung cancer. Ms. Wells and other family members brought up their experience with Ellen three times during the encounter. For example, when Dr. Munn said that Ms. Wells's blood counts would have to be monitored after radiation, Ms. Wells said, "Yeah, we went through that with Ellen, remember?" This was part of the background for Ms. Wells's and her family's anxiety, as they tried to deal with the news of her lung cancer.

In each of the encounters, Ms. Wells was accompanied by her 20-year-old daughter (Daughter Wells). In the first and third encounters, she also was accompanied by her mother (Mom Wells). The third encounter is the one from which this excerpt is drawn.

The excerpt from this encounter shows the typically outspoken ways of the family and their tendency to participate actively in the discourse and decision making of the encounter. Although Ms. Wells seemed tired, sad, and sometimes apologetic, she held her own throughout. For instance, a discussion arose as to whether or not Ms. Wells should have chemotherapy, and both mother and daughter took positions, but Ms. Wells made it clear that she intended to make the decision.

Dr. Munn, 44, like Dr. Finn, was a board-certified oncologist and enjoyed

excellent patient and staff relationships. His offices were in the community practice shared by Dr. Finn and another physician.

Although I recorded seven encounters involving Dr. Munn, I was not able to
interview him. When I asked Dr. Finn why she had chosen to practice with Dr. Munn,
she said that he shared her "approach to medicine." Dr. Munn, like Dr. Finn, spent
substantial amounts of time with patients and displayed close attentiveness to their
concerns, even though his workday appeared to be overcommitted.

The following excerpt from an encounter between Ms. Wells and Dr. Munn
contains three stories. There is co-construction by participants other than just
patient and physician. Storytelling is used as part of constructing a diagnosis, to
build accord as to that diagnosis, and to validate the patient's experience.

All three family members are heavily involved in co-constructing the story of
Ms. Wells's symptoms, symptoms they construe as panic attacks. Family members
contribute reports of symptoms, such as "*She* can breathe" (line 38) and "It didn't
this morning" (line 70). The family conflict that is going on appears when Mom
Wells and Daughter Wells contradict Ms. Wells: "*NO* it's no:t" (Daughter Wells,
line 33) and "*She* can breathe" (Mom Wells, line 38).

This sequence begins in the following excerpt. Ms. Wells reports her daughter's
candidate diagnosis for problems Ms. Wells has been having since learning that
she has lung cancer.

Dr. Munn, like Dr. Finn in the "Cold/Christening" story, performs the most
basic of co-constructing strategies by pursuing the patient's topic. And, just as
Dr. Finn did in "Cold\Christening," Dr. Munn uses the co-constructing technique
of formulating and generalizing what he has just heard, naming Ms. Wells's breathing problems "hyperventilating."

(8) Panic Attacks

13	Dr. Munn:	Well . it's not *your* fault.
14		So *TELL* me,
15		how ya *doin'*?
16	Ms. Wells:	To*day* we're not *doin'* too .
17		I'm having . um . what do you call it?
18		My *daughter* calls it anxiety attacks.
19		I call it "I CAN'T BREATHE."
20	Dr. Munn:	Oh:: [h]
21	Ms. Wells:	[So] you tell *me*,
22		I don't know.
23	Mom Wells:	She's having [panic atta:cks].
24	Ms. Wells:	[I'm having a real]
25		problem.
26	Dr. Munn:	[Really?]
27	Dau. Wells:	[You're worr]ied.
28	Ms. Wells:	[They started] about *FOUR* o'clock this
29		MORning.
30	Dau. Wells:	You're *WORRIED* about EVERYthing

31		constantly.
32	Ms. Wells:	Um::m that's just >normal<.
33	Dau. Wells:	*NO* it's no:t.
34	Ms. Wells:	When I *STARTED* bout four this morning,
35		I just . I just . woke *UP*,
36		I COULDN'T breathe.
37		I-I'm BREATHING.
38	Mom Wells:	*She* can breathe. ((contemptuous))
39	Ms. Wells:	I can breathe.
40		I can't say I c[an't breathe].
41	Dr. Munn:	[Hyperventilating] [huh?]
42	Mom Wells:	[Yeah.]
43		Yeah.
44		>Hyperventilating.<
45	Ms. Wells:	Basically.

{WL3,1–12}[6]

Dr. Munn formulates Ms. Wells's experience in medical terms, "hyperventilating." This is interesting because it may function in two ways. It medicalizes, gives a medical name to, lived experience. A medical provider could use this discourse strategy to move away from the painful details of the lifeworld, and that may be one of the effects here.

But this naming is also a generalization, showing that Dr. Munn is familiar with the behavior, that the experience must have been shared by others. It is support for Ms. Wells's original suggestion (line 32) that panic attacks are "just >normal<". Ms. Wells's adoption (in lines 73–75) of Dr. Munn's "hyperventilating" term tacitly shows that she welcomes the formulation. (Later, in lines 112 and 115, after Dr. Munn has made explicit that panic is "*COMMON*," Ms. Wells again shows that she welcomes normalization of her behavior, with the explicit "Thank you" (line 112) and "*THANK* you!" (line 115).

In lines 46–67 (omitted), there is talk about previous breathing problems and negotiation of where family members will sit. Then Dr. Munn returns to Ms. Wells's symptoms and how they can be helped:

(9)

68	Dr. Munn:	Na-Now when you're HAVING it are you uh .
69		does the inhaler *help* or anything?
70	Mom Wells:	>It didn't this morning.<
71	Dr. Munn:	No?
72	Ms. Wells:	It *DIDN'T* this *MOR*ning . .
73		'cause I'm doing just .
74		well . I-I *AM* hyper*vent*ilating.
75		I guess that's [EXACTLY what I'm *Do*ing.]
76	Dau. Wells:	[She's SCARED that she's]
77		gonna stop breathing is probably what
78		it is.

Ms. Wells's daughter then returns to her candidate diagnosis of "anxiety attacks," which appeared in line 18. All in a monotone, she develops a story about Ms. Wells's fearful behavior. To evaluate how much distress Ms. Wells is feeling, how unreasonable she is being, and how difficult it has been for her family to deal with her behavior, Ms. Wells's daughter uses repetition.

The difference between this repetition and the repetition I pointed out in the "Cold\Christening" story is that here Daughter Wells is repeating herself, not the other speaker. So this repetition is used just to evaluate, not to create rapport as well, as was the repetition I discussed previously.

Daughter Wells repeats terms for fear: "she's SCARED" (line 76), "she's been *panicking*" (line 81), "she's afraid" (line 89), "she was FREAKin' out" (line 91), "she STARTED panicking" (line 97), "she *started* panicking." Ms. Wells co-constructs this story about her fears, in alternation with her daughter, offering formulations (which can be used to close a topic down, as Ms. Wells might like to see happen) and apologies.

(10)

79	Ms. Wells:	I don't know. .
80		I have *NO* idea.
81	Dau. Wells:	**She's been *panicking* about EVERYthing**
82		**lately.**
83	Ms. Wells:	Well I *was* just . I'm-I'm going through a
84		PANIC . disorder I think,
85		RIGHT lately.
86	Dau. Wells:	I just [(???)]
87	Ms. Wells:	[*I* AM.]
88		I panic [over money, *every*thing].
89	Dau. Wells:	[She's afraid she's] not gonna
90		have enough MONey,
91		she was *FREAK*in' out when she was . . *late*
92		pickin' her up,
93		she lives *right* around the [*cor*ner.]
94	Ms. Wells:	[((laughs))]
95	Dau. Wells:	It was *8:05* and she was supposed to be
96		there at *8:00*,
97		she STARTED panicking.
98	Ms. Wells:	*I* can't *help* this . this .
99		*I'M* sorry.
100		This is *just* me.
101		[(???)]
102	Dau. Wells:	[*DINNER*] wasn't done on time,
103		she *started* panicking.
104	Ms. Wells:	*I'm* just . *I'm* doing a lot of *panic* stuff
105		here.

In line 108, Dr. Munn co-constructs this diagnosis story by accepting the Wells's diagnosis and generalizing it, as discussed previously: "*Actually* that's something that's . uh *COMMON* . >you know<."

(11)

108	Dr. Munn:	*Actually* that's something that's . uh
109		*COMMON* . [>you know<].
110	Dau. Wells:	[Is it?]
111	Dr. Munn:	*WE* see a LOT of [patients] go through
112	Ms. Wells:	[Thank you.]
113	Dr. Munn:	that.
114		That's the [TRUTH].
115	Ms. Wells:	[*THANK*] you!
116	Dr. Munn:	Yeah.
117		*IT* IS.

In lines 119–131, Dr. Munn then produces brief narratives about hypothetical events (see chapter 7, in this volume, for a discussion of hypothetical and habitual narratives). Dr. Munn uses medical terminology ("you can sometimes get *FIXA*Ted on your DISEASE," "*people* can get uncontrolled *nau:*sea"). In this hypothetical world, patients "just kind of VO:Mit." In comparison with this image, Ms. Wells's panic behavior suddenly appears only mildly problematic.

(12)

118	X Wells:	[(???)]
119	Dr. Munn:	[*IT'S*] something that way you get real .
120		you can sometimes get *FIXA*Ted on your
121		DISEASE and . things going on,
122		and then you start to really st-to really
123		start to *PAN*ic with it,
124		and all *kind* of things can happen,
125		*y*'know.
126	Dau. Wells:	[>Okay.<]
127	Dr. Munn:	[You can] get . *people* can get
128		uncontrolled *nau:*sea . VOM-
129		[you know],
130	Ms. Wells(?):	[>Yeah.<]
131	Dr. Munn:	just kind of VO:MIT,
132		*or* like YOU have the hyperventi [lation],
133	Ms. Wells:	[>Right<.]
134	Dr. Munn:	and things like that,
135		so there *ARE* things that .
136		[*I've* seen] that happ[en]
137	Ms. Wells:	[*ALL* right] . [so] this is *NOT*-

Daughter Wells then interrupts her mother to co-construct this hypothetical world of panicking patients. Her co-construction here is double-edged. It raises a new topic, a problematic behavior (complaining) that Ms. Wells might have, and thus is critical of Ms. Wells. On the other hand, it carries the implication that Ms. Wells's complaints may be beyond her control, if they are part of this medicalized condition.

(13)

138		this is *not* a [(???)]
139	Dau. Wells:	[Do they compla-] do
140		they complain a lot, too.
141	Dr. Munn:	OH about [EVERYthing]!
142	Dau. Wells:	[*Nothing's*] PERfect.
143		[*Nothing's* right.]

Finally, Dr. Munn narrates a story about another patient and the patient's adult child who are experiencing "the EXA:CT same thing," similar right down to the fact that the patient's panic caused him to criticize his child. This story generalizes Ms. Wells's behavior and thus validates it. Daughter Wells's formulation in line 154 makes this explicit: "It's a *generalized* thing."

(14)

144	Dr. Munn:	[Ri- EXACTLY]!
145		*O:H* . I can *SHOW* you an indivi-,
146		and matter of fact,
147		the *only* difference is that it's a-
148		it's a MALE,
149		a:nd . the *daughter* comes in and its the
150		EXA:CT same thing.
151		I mean,
152		it's ALmost a PICture perfect thing here
153		where .
154	Dau. Wells:	It's a *generalized*[thing],
155	Dr. Munn:	[(???)]
156	Dau. Wells:	nothing was right.
157	Dr. Munn:	*RIGHT.*
158		And that's the *SAME* thing that hap-
159		matter of fact,
160		I was *tal*king to the *dau:*ghter .
161		after the patient went out to check
162		back,
163		*Y'*know to get another *appoint*ment,
164		and I was te- *y'*know,
165		SHE was telling me,
166		she says, "I don't know what to DO

167   any*MORE.*
168   I try to do *THI:S* and *THA:T* and he's
169   just always *ON* me and,
170   Y'know . *every*thing has to be *this* and
171   *that,"*
172   when you *mention* the fact that he-sh-YOU
173   were late for five minutes,
174   it *reminded* me that . *SAME* type of thing
175   happened.
176   *AL*most the same thing . yea:h.

Daughter Wells's responses in lines 126 and 154 suggest that Dr. Munn's attempts to co-construct the family's understanding of Ms. Wells's situation were successful. He first used formulations of Ms. Wells's and Daughter Wells's stories and then himself produced stories. With both co-constructing moves, but most clearly with the stories, he redefined Ms. Wells's behavior as normal for her.

M. Goodwin (1990) described stories used to aggravate social differences (e.g., a story told by one teenage boy in which another boy is defined as a coward). Instead, Dr. Munn uses stories to mitigate, rather than aggravate, social differences. The stories about patients who develop nausea make Ms. Wells's behavior seem mild in comparison. The story about the "exa:ct same thing" validates Ms. Wells's experience both in its content and in the fact that it is a story, describing experiences such as those she has just described rather than a prose statement such as "this is not unusual." By describing experiences exactly parallel to those in Ms. Wells's story, Dr. Munn displayed that he fully heard and recognized Ms. Wells's and her family's own descriptions and thus could reciprocate in kind. He affirmed the reportability of their topic (by reporting the same one), and he affirmed the accuracy of the report (by describing the same thing). In these ways, he co-constructed their story.

Like Maynard's physician, Dr. Munn gave "answers [that] were anecdotes, stories, and bits of humor that responded to a deeper level of concern than [the patient's] questions overtly revealed" (Maynard 1995:18). It should also be pointed out that he addressed Ms. Wells's anxiety directly later in the encounter, explaining that he had already given her a small prescription for anti-anxiety medicine and providing her with a larger prescription for it. She had not taken the medicine because she was not sure what it was for.

Co-constructing Story and Self

In these two medical encounters, we saw patients, physicians, and family members co-constructing medical discourse in which physicians cooperated with patients' claims to speaker rights (i.e., "empowered" patients). Because of physicians' socially legitimated authority in medical settings, they have the choice of cooperating or not cooperating—hence the verb "empower," which suggests that physicians are giving power to patients. This is close to the truth; physicians are cooperating with patients' claims to power.

Ms. Melan claimed power by interrupting and changing the topic. Dr. Finn cooperated with the interruption and topic change. She requested a story, with "*Geez, where'd you find THAT?*" She co-constructed the story with Ms. Melan until the topic was well explored. When Ms. Melan made a comment that could be used to return to the purpose of discussing Ms. Melan's recurrence, Dr. Finn took the opportunity, even though Ms. Melan might have preferred to continue delaying that discussion. So the decisions about who would talk and what would be talked about were shared. The encounter was not entirely in the hands of either participant.

Localized storytelling was a crucial co-constructed speech activity. It mitigated a transition into talk about Ms. Melan's recurrence of cancer and validated Ms. Wells' fears. Storytelling was part of the process of arriving at a diagnosis for Ms. Wells and part of the integration of lifeworld and medical world for both patients.

Stories in these encounters are important because we define ourselves and create our worlds through storytelling (Josselson and Lieblich 1993). H. Brody relates storytelling to medical discourse: "Suffering is produced, and alleviated, primarily by the meaning that one attaches to one's experience. The primary human mechanism for attaching meaning to particular experiences is to tell stories about them" (1987:5). When physician, patient, and family members co-construct stories they share a deeply human activity, that of constructing meaning.

Stories must have a point, and the point embodies cultural, social, and personal values. In Ms. Melan's story about a cold, the point was that she should receive sympathy—sympathy that would be very appropriate, but difficult to ask for, in relation to her cancer recurrence. In an indirect, coded way, Ms. Melan's talk about her cold may have been saying something important about her need for sympathy.

Like Dr. Finn, Dr. Munn pursued his patient's topic rather than imposing his own and co-constructed their story about Ms. Wells in a way that validated her experience. Maynard describes his experience with a physician who behaved similarly:

> When I revealed my fears to him, he said it was natural to feel scared. To have someone, especially a physician, state the commonness of such a reaction reduced a sense of aloneness that was fostering my fear. . . . Time after time, then, Dr. Nelsen met my deepest worries and concerns with messages that were, to my psyche, utterly like balm to an aching physical wound. (1995:17)

As medical ethicists have argued, this experience is important in its own right, regardless of any effects on subsequent medical decisions in the encounter. However, when patients' stress is reduced, medical outcomes may be improved.

Conceptualizing physicians as empowering and patients as active (or not) is accurate only when these actions are placed in context as part of co-construction of talk. Talk and action through talk do not exist as isolated utterances. Instead, medical discourse is created through sequential collaborative action.

In that collaboration participants can make greater, or lesser, claims to speaker rights, and they can accept or reject others' claims. In these two encounters, patients and family members were active; that is, they claimed the right to set a topic, to hold the floor, and to integrate lifeworld and medical world through storytelling. Physicians were empowering; that is, they accepted and cooperated with patients' claims to these speaker rights.

From an ethical standpoint, patients deserve to be heard and to participate appropriately in encounters. From a practical standpoint, physicians stand to gain more information from patients, patients stand to gain appropriate control over their medical experiences, and both stand to gain a sense of connection, when consequential medical discourse resembles the storied, co-constructed encounters between Dr. Finn, Ms. Melan, Dr. Munn, and the Wells family.

7

Diagnosis as Storytelling

In chapter 6, I introduced the idea that *story* can refer to localized storytelling—talk about an actual sequence of events. I reviewed theories about stories and narratives (the larger category into which stories fit). A *narrative* can be simply a report of events. But when the speaker evaluates the events by suggesting their cultural or emotional importance, the narrative becomes a story.

In this chapter, I will make a proposal that is entirely new in the literature on medical discourse. My suggestion is that a social, deeply human activity—joint localized storytelling by patient and doctor—can be part of developing a diagnosis. This claim specifies one way in which the speech activity of diagnosing can be carried out. It also modifies the usual view that diagnosing is solely done by the physician and is solely cognitive.

Laboratory tests and other mechanical procedures, such as blood tests and computer-assisted technology, are critical in many diagnoses. Sometimes it may seem that diagnosis is nothing but the use of tests and procedures and the report of their definitive results.

The fact is, however, that most patients' complaints (60–90%) cannot be diagnosed with tests alone (Benson 1986:49). Doctor and patient must talk. In the past, we thought that talk in the medical encounter was social only at the first and last of the discourse (cf. Cheepen 1988), and that any social talk—wherever it occurred—had nothing to do with other, medically important talk.

The diagnostic process was certainly not expected to be social. It was envisioned instead as a series of factual questions from the doctor, designed to elicit unadorned information from the patient. We thought that this talk was not social but rather was done by only one person (the physician); that it was reporting, not narrating; that it was scientific, not emotional. And indeed, this may be what happens in some encounters.

However, diagnoses also can be co-constructed through an essentially social and emotional activity—storytelling. Once acknowledged, storytelling can be examined for its ethical impact and its appropriate role in diagnosis.

Storytelling in diagnosis embodies the art, the human factor, in medicine. There is no activity more artful or more human than storytelling. It is artful because it taps our descriptive and evocative abilities, and human because it embodies our rich symbolic life—our ideas about self, about past and present, about values. Our vast symbolic life is the one attribute of humankind shared by no other species.

Because it can determine the entire course of treatment, and because it embodies our selves, storytelling claims power. No more important claim to power could be imagined than that which aims to co-construct a diagnosis (entailing treatment) and at the same time define who we are and who we will be.

The narratives and stories I describe are not the same as either "the patient's story" or the "story" of an illness (Frank 1995, Young 1989; H. Brody 1987; Charon 1989). Frank, Young, Brody, and Charon were interested in the overall life story or illness story—an overarching, abstract narrative.

Instead, I am pointing out small-scale, "localized" stories. I found two previous analyses of localized storytelling in medical encounters (K. Davis 1988; Young 1989). These studies looked at stories being used by patients. The stories appeared to have two purposes: to define the interaction so that the social distance between patient and physician was reduced and to assert a self which had been suppressed in the institutional discourse.

In other words, localized stories in the medical encounter are associated with patients and thought of as patients' actions in a fundamentally conflictual relationship with the physician. Localized stories have not previously been related to physicians or to the process of diagnosing.

Both abstract and localized stories are constructed as part of the diagnosing activities in my data. Both cognitive and social activities are taking place. These activities are carried out by both participants—when the process takes place in its maximally useful form. When things are going right, patients and physicians both contribute to the process of arriving at a diagnosis. They negotiate the meaning being constructed on both localized and overarching levels. Localized storytelling actions serve to propose, argue against, augment, or accept (i.e., to construct) an overarching diagnostic hypothesis and its associated treatment plan.

This chapter has two parts. The first is this introduction, which discusses models of diagnosis. In the second part of the chapter, I analyze an extended, complex sequence of small narratives and stories which constitute the diagnostic process in an encounter between Ms. Feblen and Dr. Myhill. Co-construction of the diagnosis is prominent in this sequence. The patient, Ms. Feblen, takes a major role in building the diagnosis through suggesting, contributing to, or arguing against three hypothetical diagnostic storyworlds: the Hemachromatosis storyworld, the Chronic Fatigue storyworld, and the Toxic Fumes storyworld.

The chapter closes with a section that illustrates what happens when doctor and patient make different claims about possible and likely diagnostic storyworlds.

The "Phase Model" of Encounters

C. Heath's (1992) analysis of British medical encounters exemplifies a common view of diagnosis. In this view, the medical encounter is made up of phases in sequential order, with diagnosis—by the doctor—occurring in one of the later phases.

Heath's particular version of a phase model is drawn from Byrne and Long (1976), who suggest six phases:

> [Phase] I, relating to the patient; II, discovering the reason for attendance; III, conducting a verbal or physical examination or both; IV, consideration of the patient's condition; V, detailing treatment or further investigation; and VI, terminating. (C. Heath 1992:237)

Heath suggests that diagnosis is embodied in the physician's remarks during Phase IV. Heath also finds patients producing candidate diagnoses, but in his data both patients and physicians discount them.

Notice the way Byrne and Long name each phase after the physician's action. In Phase I, the physician "relates" to the patient. In the other phases, the physican "discovers," "conducts," "considers," "details," and "terminates." Certainly there are encounters in which these phases do exist. But it is not appropriate for encounters to be defined only in terms of the physician's activity. Other versions of the phase model have avoided doing this (Lipkin, Putnam, and Lazare 1995).

Besides phases, there are other dimensions of the medical encounter, other ways in which it is organized. In this chapter, I conceptualize it as consisting of jointly constructed speech activities, such as greeting, topic control, questioning, storytelling, and making plans for future action. This conception is similar to that of Maynard (1991) and Cicourel (1987).

In my data, these speech activities sometimes were organized into a pattern similar to Byrne and Long's phases, sometimes not. Analysis of the entire phase model is beyond the scope of this chapter. The point I wish to make is that this model dominates the literature to the point that it is taken as factually describing typical encounters. In fact, however, it is only one theoretical model. Its applicability is probably much more limited than we have thought. For instance, it most likely works best in describing initial encounters, not the repeat encounters that make up most of my data.

Whether we focus on phases, speech activities, goals, or some other dimension of the encounter's organization, our approach must attend equally to the behavior of physician and patient, instead of suggesting that only the physician's activity characterizes the event.

Diagnosis as a Sociocognitive Activity

Physicians writing about medical encounters tend to accept the phase model, but physicians add discussion of cognitive activity (C. Kaplan 1995; Lazare, Putnam, and Lipkin 1995:10). This diagnostic cognitive activity takes place in the physician's mind while questioning (history taking) goes on during early phases of the encounter (Myerscough 1989; Smith and Hoppe 1991). The diagnosis, arrived at through the physician's consideration of hypotheses, is presented to the patient in a late phase of the encounter.

The cognitive nature of diagnostic activity is highlighted in medical writing by terms such as "diagnostic algorithms," "hypothetico-deductive," and "probabilistic," all used to describe diagnosing (Myerscough 1989, 20 ff.). Although one medical theorist, H. Brody (1987), described a diagnosis as a story, for Brody a story is an abstract overarching explanation rather than actual words—still a strictly cognitive phenomenon.

I do not quarrel with the idea that diagnosis is cognitive, that the physician elicits significant information from the patient, or that the physician uses extensive medical knowledge in arriving at a conclusion. And it seems likewise clear that in some cases only a physician could sift through the information and arrive at a proper diagnosis; the patient has no idea what is wrong.

My data suggest some additions to the picture, however. First, in my data it was common for a patient to offer a candidate diagnosis (see chapter 8 for a summary of candidate diagnoses illustrated in excerpts throughout this book). The candidate diagnoses I am discussing are not explanatory models (i.e., patients' understanding of causes of the illness). Instead, these are concrete diagnoses, and they may be offered at any time during the encounter. As C. Heath (1992) suggests, patients often were indirect in offering diagnoses (e.g., Ms. Hazen in chapter 2).

Second—as in Ms. Feblen's case, in this chapter—when the illness is not immediately classifiable, doctor and patient may go through a diagnostic process in which the doctor and patient work together to construct stories that explain what may have happened in the past and how a possible diagnosis might play out in the future.

In this process of storytelling, the patient may play a significant role. He or she may not simply answer questions posed by the doctor. Instead the patient may offer alternative diagnostic storyworlds or modifications to or negations of a storyworld proposed by the doctor.

All this activity is cognitive, and the doctor's role is critical. But it is simultaneously social, and the patient's role is also critical.

A final point is that storytelling is often used for persuasion. Doctors and patients elaborate their diagnostic stories in subtle attempts to persuade others that one diagnosis and its attendant treatment should be chosen. When doctors become aware of the way this happens, it will become easier for them to avoid trespassing on patients' rights of control over their medical experiences.

Background and Terms for the Discussion

Narrative is a term that subsumes descriptions, reports, storytelling, and other accounts (K. Davis 1988, 141 ff.; cf. Bauman 1986). A description is a narrative that aims to provide enough information about an event that the hearer can form a perceptual impression of it. A patient might describe a pain, attempting to communicate what it is like. A report is a narrative about a series of events that took place in the past; a patient might report, without comment, a series of symptoms. It is generally assumed that doctors and patients are engaged in description and in reporting as they talk about symptoms and the nature of possible explanations.

Doctor and patient do use description and reporting as they talk. But these two kinds of narratives can become a third kind: stories. A story is any narrative that is evaluated. Either person, doctor or patient, can evaluate the ongoing narrative, turning it into a story.

Evaluation is done by indicating the cultural, social, or personal significance of the events.[1] Chapter 6 includes examples of repetition and formulations, used to evaluate one's own and others' stories. To evaluate, speakers also may say explicitly that something was frightening or surprising; make the voice louder or softer when they get to the point; quote other people, or themselves, about significance (Labov 1972b; Tannen 1989a) (Polanyi 1979); or invoke culturally shared values (Polanyi 1979, 1985).

Some evaluation subtly indicates the significance of an event, some is more overt. In other words, there are degrees of emphasis the speaker can place on the many ways an event is significant. The evaluation in the Feblen–Myhill diagnostic storytelling often is subtle (especially in Dr. Myhill's talk).[2] But any linguistic way of pointing to the positive or negative impact of the storied event counts as evaluation.

Let us return to the larger category—narratives. The narratives in medical diagnostic talk fall into three types: Labovian, habitual, and hypothetical. The *Labovian narrative* is about past events, arranged in chronological order. It has the sort of organization usually associated with narratives and stories. Straightforward illness stories, told in interviews, are usually Labovian narratives.

The other two kinds of narration differ from Labovian narratives in their location in time, and they are less easily recognizable as narratives.

The *habitual narrative* (Riessman 1991) is not organized by chronological order, as Labovian stories must be. Habitual narratives depict events that are typical of a span of time. However, the events are not ordered in time, one after the other, in a certain sequence. Habitual narratives are about the way things usually are, not about a specific series of events. Habitual narratives can be set in the past, present, or future and are often used to describe symptoms.

The *hypothetical narrative* (Riessman 1991; cf. M. Goodwin 1990) is set in some hypothetical time—past, present, or future. Hypothetical narratives offer for our consideration alternative worlds. They answer the question, "What if . . . ?" In the Feblen–Myhill encounter, hypothetical narratives are used to answer such questions as the following: What would the symptoms be if the illness is chronic fatigue syndrome? What would they be if it is an allergic reaction to plastics? These hypothetical narratives are often evaluated, becoming hypothetical storyworlds.

Hypothetical narratives can present events in the order in which they took place (Labovian order), or they can present action as unordered and habitual (habitual narrative). Hypothetical narratives are often used by physicians to persuade.

In the 30 encounters I reviewed in detail looking for reports and stories, no encounters were completely devoid of evaluated narratives (i.e., stories). Participants frequently introduced evaluative signals that showed their attitudes and feelings about the events narrated. Participants in medical encounters are always in a social situation as well as a transactional one. The social forces push participants toward evaluation, turning reports into stories. For instance, stories (as opposed to reports) are persuasive. Evaluation lends credibility to an account, for either physician or patient.

Initiating the Diagnostic Process: Labovian Stories

One of the first speech activities in many medical encounters is a Labovian "Why I'm here" story, told primarily by the patient, such as "My Brothers Thought I Should Come In," told by Ms. Feblen. In chapter 6, Ms. Wells told a "Why I'm here" story ("Panic Attacks"). In both "Panic Attacks" and "My Brothers Thought I Should Come In," the patient offered a candidate diagnosis, and this diagnosis eventually was accepted by the physician.

Because "Why I'm here" stories occur at the beginning of the encounter, they carry a heavy cargo of discourse functions, both interactional and referential. They must define the participants and the possible trouble, and they must make the visit to the physician appear justifiable.

Three visits by Ms. Feblen to Dr. Myhill were recorded, on April 17, May 2, and May 25. Ms. Feblen, 45, had been experiencing a variety of symptoms, but other physicians were unable to locate the problem.

The April 17 encounter was Ms. Feblen's first visit to this practice. She was interviewed by a resident, Dr. Fedders, before seeing Dr. Myhill; Dr. Fedders reported to Dr. Myhill, and then Dr. Myhill spent 35 minutes with Ms. Feblen, pursuing possible diagnoses. Ms. Feblen's "Why I'm here" story was told during her talk with Dr. Fedders (lines 29–45 below), and the subsequent habitual and hypothetical narratives that constitute the diagnostic process were told during Ms. Feblen's talk with Dr. Myhill.

(1)   "My Brothers Thought I Should Come In"

27   Dr. Fedders: Well *ROBBIE . WHAT* brings you to the
28   clinic today.
29   Ms. Feblen: Um . . *actually* my . um . BROTHERS . .
30   THOUGHT I should come in here and
31   get a checkup.
32   I *haven't* been feeling *very* well for

33		quite a little *time* now and . .
34		I've *SEEN* a couple *different*
35		specialists,
36		*a:nd* I finally . said,
37		"Well I *GUESS* I'm JUST going to have to
38		*FEEL* bad."
39	Dr. Fedders:	Mhm.
40	Ms. Feblen:	And my *brothers* said that . uh
41		*THEY* see Dr. Myhill,
42	Dr. Fedders:	[Mhm.]
43	Ms. Feblen:	[and] they *wanted* me to *just* get a
44		checkup.
45	Dr. Fedders:	Okay.

{FB1, 1–27}

This narrative is Labovian because it starts in the distant past and moves forward, mentioning events in the same order in which the events happened in real time.

Besides chronology, past time to present time, Ms. Feblen also uses specificity to organize the sequence. The narrative progresses from general to particular. Ms. Feblen first makes a general, unspecific statement about her well-being over a sweep of time (not feeling very well). Then she mentions repeated specific events in which she carried out a particular action (seeing specialists). Then she becomes more specific, reporting her own inner speech ("constructed speech"; Tannen 1989a): "Well I *GUESS* I'm JUST going to have to *FEEL* bad."

The constructed speech in this story portrays vividly both Ms. Feblen's hopelessness and her stoic ability to deal with that hopelessness. Constructed speech is highly characteristic of Labovian narratives. It is almost always evaluative, as it is here—marking the story's significance.

Having created a small storyworld peopled with herself and her specialists, Ms. Feblen now returns to characters mentioned in the abstract, or story preface (lines 29–31)—her brothers. "And my *brothers* said that *THEY* see Dr. Myhill, that they *wanted* me to *just* get a checkup." Like the constructed speech, this indirect quote is part of the evaluative structure of the narrative. By describing other peoples' action, Ms. Feblen lets us know that other people, not just she, thought the events being narrated were significant.

This part of the story has other implications. In showing that her brothers care about her health, Ms. Feblen portrays herself as being a valued member of our most important social group, the family.

Also in this storyworld, a candidate diagnosis is implied. This takes place twice, at the first and last of the story, when Ms. Feblen's brothers are mentioned.

Both of Ms. Feblen's brothers have hemachromatosis, an inherited condition in which the body accumulates too much iron in the blood. Although Ms. Feblen's symptoms were different from theirs, the brothers saw some similarities and suspected that she might also have the condition; that is why they sent Ms. Feblen to a specialist in blood diseases, Dr. Myhill (their doctor). As it eventually turned out, they were right.

In this case, then, the initial "candidate diagnosis" (Weijts 1993a) was made not by a physician but by patients' relatives who were not even present in the encounter. Ms. Feblen presents the candidate diagnosis indirectly, attributing it to her brothers rather than to herself. Thus she avoids making a personal challenge to the physician's right to diagnose.

Three Storyworlds: Constructing a Diagnosis

After the resident, Dr. Fedders, talked with Ms. Feblen at length, Dr. Fedders reported to Dr. Myhill. Then Dr. Myhill continued the encounter.

We will follow Ms. Feblen and Dr. Myhill through part of the diagnostic process. Notice that this encounter illustrates some problems with the phase model of encounters and diagnosis: Instead of the physician first questioning and then diagnosing, the physician and patient use questions, answers, narratives, and stories to consider three diagnoses, two of which come from the patient—one introduced in the "Why I'm here" story, one introduced during the encounter.

To some extent, Myerscough recognizes that the phase model is incomplete. He says:

> In practice, the history taking and clinical examination are generally not separate consecutive parts of the consultation; they proceed alongside each other as complementary parts of the *process of diagnostic reasoning.* (1989:26; emphasis added)

Myerscough sees that there is an ongoing process of interwoven activities rather than a series of relatively discrete phases.

Our focus is on the construction of hypothetical storyworlds, each associated with a diagnosis. The diagnostic storyworlds are:

  H: the Hemachromatosis storyworld

  CFS: the Chronic Fatigue Syndrome storyworld

  TF: the Toxic Fumes storyworld

The process of diagnosing consists of moving back and forth among these three storyworlds, constructing or deconstructing each in relation to the new information that is progressively revealed as the physician and patient talk.

The Hemachromatosis storyworld

The first recorded talk between Ms. Feblen and Dr. Myhill begins with line 1 below, in which Ms. Feblen says that her brothers talked her into coming to see him. In lines 4–11, Dr. Myhill makes explicit the candidate diagnosis of hemachromatosis which was implied by the fact that Ms. Feblen's brothers sent her to him. He does this by describing a hypothetical world in which her symptoms of fatigue, weakness, and arthritic pain are caused by hemachromatosis:

(2)

1	Ms. Feblen:	They *TALKED* me [into this].
2	Dr. Myhill:	[laughs]
		Into coming down.
3	Ms. Feblen:	[Yeah.]
4	Dr. Myhill:	[*WELL*], th-the uh . . the *PATTERN* of .
5		uh . hemochromatosis is such that a
6		*lot* of symptoms can develop . that
7		are a bit unU:sual.
8		And *CER*tainly for advanced . . disease,
9		. uh fatigue, uh weakness, uh . . u:h
10		the arthritic *COM*ponent,
11		*ALL those* things could *occur.*
12		I *suspect* though that you've been pretty
13		well worked up . uh at *least* with the
14		identification of serum (???) and *so*
15		on.

{FB1, 14–20}[3]

Dr. Myhill's hypothetical narrative about hemachromatosis is also a habitual narrative. Certain symptoms are typical (habitual) in a hypothetical case of hema-chromatosis: fatigue, weakness, arthritic symptoms. The hypothetical/habitual narrative is evaluated (though subtly) with the clause "that are a bit unusual." Un-usual events are worth telling as a story. Because the narrative is evaluated, by our definition it is a story as well as a narrative.

As Dr. Myhill and Ms. Feblen continue to talk, they use the available evidence to build up narrative worlds and tear them down.

The first buildup took place in lines 4–11 of the previous excerpt, as Dr. Myhill suggested a storyworld (H) in which Ms. Feblen does have hemachromatosis—her symptoms fit that disease. Then Dr. Myhill reversed field and tore the narrative world down, in lines 12–15; in these lines he argued against H. He referred to the tests that had already been given to Ms. Feblen, tests that presumably were attempts to rule out H.

In the following excerpt, the two discuss whether lab work to rule out H was done appropriately. Dr. Myhill then reverses ground again, pursuing whether H can reasonably be construed as the relevant diagnostic storyworld. He questions Ms. Feblen about menstruation, which usually protects women from hemachromatosis (lines 25–28). When he learns that she had a hysterectomy 10 years ago, Dr. Myhill adds to the H storyworld, in lines 34–43.

(3)

16	Ms. Feblen:	Yeah, there wasn't . uh I *told* him about
17		the hemochromatosis so Dr. *BAYLEY*
18		did . some . uh *lab* work for that,
19		but I don't know *how* much or anything.

20	Dr. Myhill:	Was it-that fairly recent . uh
21	Ms. Feblen:	*U:h* . . it [was] about a *YEAR* ago.
22	Dr. Myhill:	[or]
23		>A year ago.<
24		>Okay.<
25		You're still menstruating?
26	Ms. Feblen:	No.
27	Dr. Myhill:	Okay.
28		When did you s-uh >discontinue<?
29	Ms. Feblen:	I had a *HYSTER*ectomy about *ten* years
30		ago.
31		[(???)]
32	Dr. Myhill:	[Okay.]
33		All right.
34		So . . uh you're at a point *now* where
35		*iron* accumulation *COULD* be REAL.
36		Usually you-the *protec*tion during the .
37		. . uh . early . female . menstrual
38		[cycle activity] is *such* that,
39	Ms. Feblen:	[Oh . uh huh.]
40	Dr. Myhill:	it *DOESN'T* develop like it would in your
41		*brothers,*
42		Uh . but from *your* standpoint it *still*
43		could be high.

Again, there are habitual actions: "*Usually*" women are protected (line 36). But Dr. Myhill invokes a hypothetical storyworld in which Ms. Feblen may be an exception: "iron accumulation *COULD* be real" (line 35), "it *still* could be high" (lines 42–43), if H is the correct storyworld.

In the next excerpt, Dr. Myhill links his plans for treatment to Ms. Feblen's history and feelings. In doing this, Dr. Myhill evaluates the point of her "Why I'm here" story (apparently relayed to him, at least in part, by Dr. Fedders). Dr. Myhill returns to the "Why I'm here" story and jointly constructs it with Ms. Feblen (lines 51–56).

(4)

44		We'll *re-check* that,
45		because I think that's *important* to-at
46		least for you to feel *COM*fortable
47		and we'll [know].
48	Ms. Feblen:	[Yeah.]
49	Dr. Myhill:	'Cause your *SYMPTOMS* don't . fit . into
50		any . nice *PATTERN,*
51		and I . can *under*stand if [you've] been
52	Ms. Feblen:	[Yeah.]

53	Dr. Myhill:	uh . going *up* the *wall* trying to get
54		. [u:m] some *answers* . uh
55	Ms. Feblen:	[I am.]
56	Dr. Myhill:	[for WHY the fatigue is there].

Ms. Feblen displays her awareness that Dr. Myhill has just returned to her "Why I'm here" story. She does this by returning to it herself, repeating almost word for word what she said to Dr. Fedders: "I just felt like "Well I've just got to FEEL bad." By repeating and co-constructing this important initial story, Dr. Myhill and Ms. Feblen send one another a metamessage of rapport (cf. Tannen 1989b, on the functions of repetition).

(5)

57	Ms. Feblen:	[Well I *just* got discouraged] about it.
58		I just felt like "Well I've just got to
59		FEEL *bad*."
60	Dr. Myhill:	>Okay.<

In lines 61–77 (omitted), Dr. Myhill suggests some tests to evaluate H. He then introduces the second candidate diagnosis, chronic fatigue syndrome. This candidate diagnosis is not at this point expanded into a storyworld. No habitual symptoms are given and there is no evaluation. So this excerpt shows that diagnosis need not always involve storytelling.

(6)

78	Dr. Myhill:	Um . . and *ALSO* I'm sure too that
79		they've all gone around the *STRESS*
80		situation and things of this sort,
81	Ms. Feblen:	Oh.
82	Dr. Myhill:	*TRYING* to work out some . *reasons* for uh
83		chronic fatigue,
84	Ms. Feblen:	Ri:ght.
85	Dr. Myhill:	[and]
86	Ms. Feblen:	[M-hm.]
87	Dr. Myhill:	>there *is*< there *is* a so-called chronic
88		fatigue *syndrome*,
89		but that's . kind of a um .
90		is an umbrella for a *lo:t* of different .
91		[things],
92	Ms. Feblen:	[M-hm.]
93	Dr. Myhill:	*no* one feels very comfortable in just .
94	Ms. Feblen:	M-hm.
95	Dr. Myhill:	uh . putting a *label* on it,
96		sitting back.

Although the discussion of chronic fatigue syndrome (CFS) has not so far involved storytelling, Ms. Feblen, in the following excerpt, quickly changes that.

The CFS storyworld: "I feel that bad"

In the following excerpt, Ms. Feblen pursues the topic of fatigue with an evaluated habitual narrative of her symptoms. She invokes a storyworld of her own chronic fatigue, implying that a chronic fatigue syndrome diagnosis may be the appropriate one.

One way in which Ms. Feblen evaluates her narrative is with direct statements about her feelings ("I *FELT* that bad"—lines 102, 115). Another is by contrasting the world in which she does take Prozac with a world in which she does not. In the second world, she "PROBABLY would just *stay* in bed" (line 107). All of this evaluation, showing how extreme her fatigue is, supports the idea that her symptoms may match the CFS diagnostic storyworld.

(7)

97	Ms. Feblen:	Well I *did* get to the point where I just
98		didn't,
99		I *felt like* I *just couldn't* go on and
100		that's when they put me on the *PRO*zac.
101	Dr. Myhill:	Yeah.
102	Ms. Feblen:	I *FELT* that bad.
103	Dr. Myhill:	But the *Prozac* you think *MA:Y* be helping
104		somewhat or .
105	Ms. Feblen:	I think it is *somewhat* because .
106		I *feel* like if I *didn't* take it,
107		I *PROBABLY* would just *stay* in bed.
108	Dr. Myhill:	>Okay.<
109		Well that's
110	Ms. Feblen:	THERE'S *some* days I feel
111		*pretty good,* . .
112	Dr. Myhill:	>Okay.<
113	Ms. Feblen:	and *some* days I . could . care less if
114		I got *OUT* of bed or not.
115		I feel *THAT* bad.

In response, in the next excerpt, Dr. Myhill pursues Ms. Feblen's focus on chronic fatigue by discussing a symptom of Chronic Fatigue Syndrome (CFS)—panic attacks. He defines the CFS world of panic attacks with a habitual narrative: "Where you feel . *fearful* in an area and heart beats rapidly and you get uh *frightened.*"

(8)

| 116 | Dr. Myhill: | >Okay.< |
| 117 | | Do you *ever* have uh PANIC attacks. |

118	Ms. Feblen:	Mm: no?
119	Dr. Myhill:	**Where you feel . *fearful* in an area and**
120		**. heart beats rapidly and [you] get**
121	Ms. Feblen:	[OH.]
122	Dr. Myhill:	*frightened,*
123		**and uh .**
124	Ms. Feblen:	I have claustro*PHO*bia,
125	Dr. Myhill:	Yeah, [something like] that.

In line 118, Ms. Feblen expresses doubt that her experience fits into this storyworld. Then in line 124 she does find a fit: Her claustrophobia is a type of panic attack.

In the following excerpt, as Ms. Feblen's memories about panic/claustrophobia return, she revises the suggestion that she has claustrophobia. She tells a story that attributes her rapid heartbeat to an allergic reaction rather than to claustrophobia. Evaluation consists of images about her heart jumping out of her chest, and her face swelling.

(9)

126	Ms. Feblen:	[*THAT* happened] to me when I had
127		one of my *x rays* done.
128		But it was *ALSO* . they used the *DYE?*
129	Dr. Myhill:	Uh huh.
130	Ms. Feblen:	and when they used the *dye,*
131		my,
132		it felt like my *heart* was going to
133		come out of my *chest,*
134		and I *THINK* it was the *dye* because I
135		remember my *face* started swel[ling]
136	Dr. Myhill:	[(???)]
137	Ms. Feblen:	[and] everything.
138	Dr. Myhill:	[Yeah].
139	Ms. Feblen:	So it *probably* [was] what it was.
140	Dr. Myhill:	[Kay.]
141	Ms. Feblen:	It was *probably* the [*dye*].
142	Dr. Myhill:	[Right.]
143		All right.

Alternating possible storyworlds

Just as talk consists of interwoven speech activities, diagnosing can consist of alternating among possible narrative worlds.

Dr. Myhill and Ms. Feblen have just constructed and deconstructed a possible storyworld in which Ms. Feblen has chronic fatigue syndrome. Now (in lines 144–159, omitted), Dr. Myhill and Ms. Feblen close down the topic of a CFS storyworld for the moment, because Ms. Feblen's story about dye has argued against it. In lines

160–172 (omitted), talk turned to Ms. Feblen's children and whether or not they should be tested for hemachromatosis. Dr. Myhill said that if Ms. Feblen did turn out to have hemachromatosis, then her children should be tested, but if not, "then I don't think it would be any real concern" (line 172).

Then, in the following excerpt, Dr. Myhill reopens the H storyworld, by bringing up environmental influences that might contribute to H.

(10)

173	Dr. Myhill:	Um . are you a heavy *meat* eater?
174	Ms. Feblen:	*U:m . not* particularly no.
175	Dr. Myhill:	>Okay.<
176		And you don't . *cook* in iron SKILLETS .
177		[any]more.
178	Ms. Feblen:	[>No.<]
179	Dr. Myhill:	Everybo[dy's] got the *aluminum* ones
180	Ms. Feblen:	[No.]
181	Dr. Myhill:	and . [@]
182	Ms. Feblen:	[No],

In excerpt 10 a possible event in the H storyworld was deconstructed. In the following excerpt, Ms. Feblen moves to a new possible diagnosis—a new diagnostic storyworld.

The Toxic Fumes storyworld

Ms. Feblen begins her topic shift by referring back to her talk with Dr. Fedders. In that talk, Ms. Feblen suggested a storyworld, Toxic Fumes (TF), in which the fumes in the plastics factory where she worked might be the source of her problems. These fumes are an environmental influence, like iron skillets, so Ms. Feblen is maintaining the general topic brought up by Dr. Myhill.

Ms. Feblen introduces and amplifies her candidate diagnosis of toxic fumes indirectly. She uses several coexisting types of indirection:

1. Instead of simply saying that she thinks toxic fumes may be causing her problems, she refers back to her talk with Dr. Fedders, knowing that Dr. Fedders has relayed information to Dr. Myhill.
2. Instead of using direct descriptive terms, Ms. Feblen uses nonspecific terms such as "situation," "things," and "affect."
3. Ms. Feblen interrupts her own syntax twice, in lines 184–186, indirectly indicating the possible inappropriateness of what she had in mind to say.
4. Ms. Feblen even says that she may not want to mention what she has just mentioned—that is, she expresses reluctance to suggest a diagnosis while in fact suggesting it.

She indicates that she is hesitant to mention toxic fumes because she fears for her job, should her suggestion become known at work. However, Ms. Feblen's extreme use of indirection is not fully explained by her fear, because she did talk directly about toxic fumes with Dr. Fedders. Why was she reluctant to be direct with Dr. Myhill but not with Dr. Fedders?

Dr. Fedders was a young female resident whose position clearly was not as consequential as Dr. Myhill's. Ms. Feblen used indirection when she needed to make a candidate diagnosis to the attending physician, Dr. Myhill, a tall, dignified, 60-year-old man, known by Ms. Fedders to be an expert.

In short, there are two problematic issues for Ms. Feblen: the diagnosis itself and how to suggest it. Talking about the diagnosis itself (toxic fumes) is problematic because such talk might put Ms. Feblen's job in jeopardy. But suggesting a diagnosis, any diagnosis, to Dr. Myhill is problematic because it might put her relationship with him in jeopardy. Indirection solves the second problem.

Again, it is hard to delimit the exact boundaries of a narrative. This one began in Ms. Feblen's talk with the resident, Dr. Fedders. In the Feblen–Myhill encounter, either line 184 or line 192 might be seen as making available a possible diagnostic narrative world, new to the Feblen–Myhill discourse.

I chose line 192 as opening up this possibility. This line asserts the danger of the fumes at Ms. Feblen's work and thus is evaluative. Its evaluative nature—pointing to a significant (dangerous) event—makes it available as a possible abstract of a story (story preface).

(11)

183	Ms. Feblen:	I *did* talk to the doctor about the
184		*situation* at *work* and I thought .
185		I feel *REALLY* u:m . .
186		I didn't *know* if I *really* wanted to
187		*mention* that *because* .
188		I wouldn't want it to go back and
189		*they'll* say,
190		"We:ll . you shouldn't have *said*
191		anything about that."
192		**But there *is* things there that *COULD***
193		***affect* people.**

In the following excerpt Dr. Myhill takes this up, by describing a hypothetical storyworld in which toxic fumes at work do affect Ms. Feblen, but when she goes on vacation, she feels better. He treats lines 192–193 as a story preface, and so they become a story preface; he provides the story that they preface.

(12)

194	Dr. Myhill:	Now . . when you *take* vacation time and,
195		it's a little difficult to decide,
196		at least you're *out* of that *atmosphere*,
197		do: you: *pick* up on energies and uh and

198   **uh feel more .**
199   Ms. Feblen: *U:H*
200   Dr. Myhill: *com*fortable? or .

Ms. Feblen responds by first equivocating (lines 201–204), then deconstructing the TF storyworld with a Labovian story (lines 206–215) about terrible pains in her legs. Notice the three evaluative images, images of touch, sensation, and movement, in lines 210–213. These are powerful images: The legs could not be touched, they felt like boils, walking upstairs hurt.

(13)

201   Ms. Feblen: I *didn't really* notice it.
202   If *anything* maybe I didn't feel as
203   tired,
204   but that's probably pretty normal.
205   Dr. Myhill: Yeah [well]
206   Ms. Feblen: [I was] *off* for two *weeks.*
207   But *DURING* the two *weeks* I had this . um
208   thing *here* in the calves of my *legs*
209   where I could hardly .
210   you couldn't *TOUCH* 'em.
211   They were like *BOILS.*
212   It *HURT* so bad I couldn't walk up*stairs,*
213   or anything.
214   And that was, s- so .
215   [I'm not *really* sure if I felt better]
216   Dr. Myhill: [So it would be HARD . hard to assess]
217   [it.]
218   Ms. Feblen: [be]ing off work or *NOT.*
219   Dr. Myhill: >Okay.<
220   And *THIS* has been ongoing now for .
221   s-several years
222   Ms. Feblen: *Uh* . it's *been* about a year and a *half.*
223   Dr. Myhill: Year and a half.
224   Ms. Feblen: >M-hm.<

Dr. Myhill then depicts a Toxic Fumes storyworld that is explicitly hypothetical: chemicals "might be" in the air, "you could have" people who "might be" very sensitive, in contrast to the rest who "might be" normal.

(14)

225   Dr. Myhill: Okay, **now there *ARE* some people who are**
226   ***very* sensitive to um . *fumes,***
227   **toxic . .**

228		or at least *SUBSTANCES* that uh .
229		chemicals . that might . be in the *air*,
230		and you could have . one out of a
231		*hundred* persons who might .
232		be very *sensitive* because of their .
233		BODY [chem]ical
234	Ms. Feblen:	[Right.]
235	Dr. Myhill:	*makeup*,
236	Ms. Feblen:	>M-hm.<
237	Dr. Myhill:	and the *rest* would be perfectly
238		[*nor*]*mal*,
239	Ms. Feblen:	[>Yeah.<]
240	Dr. Myhill:	so you *can't* just say if everybody *else*
241		is feeling fine,
242	Ms. Feblen:	Right.
243	Dr. Myhill:	you *don't*.
244		Um . . and so there i- *still* a
245		possibility that *exposure* . . uh .
246		to things . in the um . u:h in your
247		*work*place might be doing something.

In some omitted lines (248–252), Dr. Myhill asks whether Ms. Feblen has allergies, and Ms. Feblen says she does not.

Then, in the following excerpt, Dr. Myhill returns to the Toxic Fumes storyworld, and he and Ms. Feblen co-construct the TF world with details about the kinds of fumes she might breathe at work and their effects.

(15)

253	Dr. Myhill:	>Okay.<
254		Um . . so but I . *wouldn't* rule that out
255		as be-as being a possibility.
256		But *REALLY* to *test* it out . WELL,
257		you SHOULD be *away* from those conditions
258		for. ah . . perhaps up to a *month* and
259		and see if . uh *there's* a DECIDED
260		change.
261		And I *don't* think that's *out* of the
262		question,
263		because you've *really* been . PUT through
264		an awful lot.
265	Ms. Feblen:	*U:m* . the uh *sterilization part* of it we
266		use *E.T.O.* gas,
267		which . if you're *exposed* to it,
268		at the *right* amount long *ENOUGH*,
269		it can cause you a *problem*.

270   Dr. Myhill: >M-hm.<
271   Ms. Feblen: But . uh . the *other,* the *MAIN* thing I
272   was *REALLY* kind of,
273   getting kind of concerned about was the
274   *fumes* off the *plastic* .
275   when the plastic is *hot.*
276   It gives off like a .
277   Dr. Myhill: There's a . [plasticizer]
278   Ms. Feblen: [*boric* acid] . . fumes or
279   something, anyway . .
280   actually if that wa-*turned* into a *LIQUID*
281   it would . um . it's an *acid,* @ .
282   Dr. Myhill: >Yeah.<
283   Well the *plastic*izers are all,
284   are *volatile* to an extent and if you
285   *heat* 'em up,
286   they get *more* so, and . . this
287   Ms. Feblen: Yeah
288   Dr. Myhill: [this]
289   Ms. Feblen: [you can] we've *JUST started* using that
290   in the last . past *couple* years.
291   *That's* why
292   Dr. Myhill: So . u:m . . there are some
293   *possibilities* then [(huh?)].

Dr. Myhill and Ms. Feblen constructed three hypothetical storyworlds: Hemachromatosis, Chronic Fatigue Syndrome, and Toxic Fumes. These three are the "possibilities" Dr. Myhill mentions in line 293. Ms. Feblen suggested the H and TF possibilities, and Dr. Myhill accepted those hypotheses and added the CFS possibility. Each of these hypothetical diagnostic worlds was elaborated into a storyworld, through Ms. Feblen's and Dr. Myhill's use of evaluative comments and techniques.

In their subsequent encounter on May 2, Dr. Myhill reported that new laboratory tests showed Ms. Feblen having hemachromatosis. It would be easy to say that the diagnosis was made through laboratory tests. But such tests are often quite specific. The physician needs to have a diagnostic possibility in mind in order to choose a particular test.

The process through which the physician explores possibilities is crucial to the correct choice of tests. In this encounter, the physician gathered information through a process of joint construction and deconstruction of possible diagnostic storyworlds.

Ms. Feblen participated in the process, which was in turn part of diagnostic reasoning. She participated by suggesting, constructing, and deconstructing the narrative worlds. Her deconstruction was persuasive because it was done through multiple, memorable evaluation in her stories: legs that felt like boils, a heart that jumped out of her chest.

Though proposed storyworlds were challenged in the Feblen–Myhill encounter, these challenges were not conflictual. But the patient and physician sometimes do engage in conflict, as the following excerpts show.

Conflict: Challenges to Physicians' Narratives

Encounters with Ms. Evans and Mr. Mahon exhibited conflict between the patient and physician (cf. Maynard 1991). These conflicts were played out through storytelling about possible diagnostic worlds.

Ms. Evans: Bladder infection or yeast infection?

Ms. Evans, 23, was an articulate woman with a degree in clinical psychology. She worked part-time as a counselor in a youth crisis center. Dr. Fouts, 39, was a family practitioner in private practice.

The excerpts below come from the first encounter we recorded between Ms. Evans and Dr. Fouts. However, it was not the first visit between the two. In a previous encounter, Ms. Evans was diagnosed with a bladder infection and given an antibiotic. She returned this time complaining of vaginal discomfort.

Dr. Fouts examined Ms. Evans and took a sample of the vaginal flora and fauna. Dr. Fouts then reported that "when we looked under the scope, right now, what we see is a lot of yeast." The next excerpt begins at that point.

Dr. Fouts captures the habitual/hypothetical nature of her narration by using the word "sometimes" three times.

(16)

53	Ms. Evans:	SO, like a *yeast* infection?
54	Dr. Fouts:	Yeah.
55		It can give you *ALMOST* the same *SYMP*toms
56		sometimes,
57		you know . BURNING and feeling like you
58		got to GO all the time and .
59	Ms. Evans:	>Hm.<
60	Dr. Fouts:	sometimes you actually get a white
61		*DIS*charge that comes outside and it
62		[irri]tates and
63	Ms. Evans:	[>M-hm.<]
64	Dr. Fouts:	makes you all [red] outside.
65	Ms. Evans:	[>M-hm.<]
66		>M-hm.<
67	Dr. Fouts:	*SOMETIMES* it makes it .
68		you're *RAW* in your va*gina* and [so it]
69	Ms. Evans:	[>M-hm.<]

70   Dr. Fouts: **could HURT when you have** [*sex*] **or**
71   Ms. Evans: [**>M-hm.<**]
72   Dr. Fouts: [**Y'know,** *THAT* **kind of stuff.**]

{EAA1, 1–53}

Ms. Evans responds by challenging the Yeast Infection storyworld. She does this by denying that its habitual symptoms exist in her case. She mitigates her challenge three ways: with a false start (line 73), the phrase "I thought," indicating uncertainty (line 74), and by half-chuckling in the middle of the word "familiar" (line 77).

(17)

73   Ms. Evans: [**Right now, I haven't had** .]
74   **I thought that I was** *OVER* **with my yeast**
75   **infection because I haven't had any**
76   **of** *THOSE* **things,**
77   **y'know I'm very** *fam@il*ar **with**
78   [**those things**].

In the next excerpt, Dr. Fouts affirms Ms. Evans' knowledge of her symptoms with "*YOU'VE* had those. *OKAY*" and mitigates her own diagnosis with "it looks like." This last phrase does double duty; it is ambiguous, with possible meanings of both uncertainty (the mitigating meaning) and accuracy (from the clinician's look through the microscope).

With "we" (line 82), Dr. Fouts manipulates the participant structure of the diagnosis process, again using ambiguity. "We" may refer to Ms. Evans as Dr. Fouts' co-diagnoser or it may refer to medical authority.

(18)

79   Dr. Fouts: [Yeah. *YOU'VE*] had those.
80   *OKAY.*
81   Ms. Evans: But .
82   Dr. Fouts: But THAT'S what it looks like we've got
83   now,
84   and it's *pro*bably from the: .
85   antibiotics.

A brief discussion follows, and Dr. Fouts explains in great detail how a yeast infection can cause a burning sensation during urination. Ms. Evans then accepts the diagnosis and talk turns to ways of treating her symptoms.

Ms. Evans's challenge to Dr. Fouts's diagnosis was brief and was mitigated. But it was a challenge. Like Ms. Feblen, Ms. Evans was participating in the process of diagnostic reasoning, deconstructing the narrative world in which she has a yeast infection. Dr. Fouts acknowledged Ms. Evans's reasoning as based on her lived experience but then provided the information Ms. Evans needed to be convinced that the Yeast Infection storyworld (dramatically evaluated by Dr. Fouts in excerpt 16) was the correct diagnostic storyworld.

Mr. Mahon's heart

In the second case, Mr. Mahon is seeing his oncologist, Dr. Feit. Mr. Mahon believes that he may have heart trouble, but Dr. Feit does not accept that possibility. Here the entire conflict is indirect. No confrontation takes place because neither diagnosis is overtly chosen.

Dr. Feit, 40, interacted with her office staff in a warm and nonhierarchical way. Dr. Feit's caring and respect for her patients appeared in her friendly banter and in the fact that patients seldom waited more than a few minutes to be seen.

Mr. Mahon, 86, was in relatively good health except for his prostate cancer, which was in remission. He still drove a car and had come to this appointment alone, although on other occasions his daughter often accompanied him. Mr. Mahon had a very friendly relationship with Dr. Feit: The encounter began with jokes and compliments by both participants.

Before this encounter began, Mr. Mahon complained to the nurse of an irregular heartbeat. In the encounter, Dr. Feit listened and heard the irregularity. She offered to give Mr. Mahon a Holter monitor to wear for 24 hours, to "check it out further," but he replied, "No: . I don't like that." Dr. Feit then listed further symptoms that would signal a need for the Holter monitor: dizziness with the skipped beats, or a feeling that his heart was turning over.

In the following excerpt, Dr. Feit listens again. She tells a habitual narrative/story about the way "normal, healthy young people's" hearts might skip a beat. She contrasts Mr. Mahon's lack of symptoms with a hypothetical world in which he does have symptoms of heart trouble.

(19)

41	Dr. Feit:	LET me *take* s: . a *listen* for a little
42		bit longer now.
43		Cause it sounded regular . **and PEOPLE'S**
44		**hearts,**
45		**even NORMAL, healthy young people's skip**
46		**beats.**
47	(4 sec)	
48		Yep, *I* hear it.
49		It kinda *PAUSES* for a [second],
50	Mr. Mahon:	[M-hmm.]
51	Dr. Feit:	like it [*resets*].
52	Mr. Mahon:	[Uh huh,] uh huh.
53	Dr. Feit:	*That's* okay.
54		**As long as you're not having CHEST**
55		**pains,**

56   **SHORTNESS of breath,**
57   **SWEATiness,**
58   **LIGHT HEADEDness,**
59   **like you're dizzy.**
60   That's o*kay.*
61   'Cause it's *OTHERWISE* regular.

Dr. Feit is arguing for a storyworld in which the skipped heartbeat is not cause for action. She does so in the same way patients, Ms. Feblen and Ms. Evans, argued in previous sections: by contrasting the patient's observed symptoms with those of patients in the proposed Heart Trouble storyworld. In a Non-Heart Trouble storyworld, it is normal for healthy young people's hearts to skip beats. In a Heart Trouble storyworld, Mr. Mahon would have the list of symptoms in lines 54–59—but he is not having those symptoms, so the storyworld is denied.

But Mr. Mahon is not fully reassured, as we see in the following excerpt. Mr. Mahon's reply (lines 62–63) reinvokes the possibility of the Heart Trouble storyworld, one for which he has another symptom—water retention.

(20)

62   Mr. Mahon: **But I've-I think I've picked up a** *LITTLE*
63   **bit of WATER on my [ank]les.**

Dr. Feit acknowledges this point but changes the topic to Mr. Mahon's appetite. Whether or not his appetite is relevant to the Heart Trouble storyworld is not clear to me, and it probably was not clear to Mr. Mahon. At any rate, he reinvokes the Heart Trouble storyworld by mentioning water again, in the following excerpt (lines 74–86). The two indirectly discuss the Heart Trouble storyworld by discussing the swelling of his ankles, and Dr. Feit then suggests what to do about the swelling.

(21)

64   Dr. Feit: [Yup.]
65   How's your *APPETITE?*
66   Are you *EATING?*
67   Mr. Mahon: Yeah, *I'M* eating.
68   It's not that much *freer,*
69   but
70   Dr. Feit: OH!
71   Mr. Mahon: taken that
72   Dr. Feit: You've gained six and a
73   half POUNDS!
74   Mr. Mahon: **Some of that is just** *water.*
75   Dr. Feit: **>Yeah.<**
76   (2 sec)

77	Mr. Mahon:	It don't go . uh . *higher* than my .
78	Dr. Feit:	Mkay.
79	Mr. Mahon:	CALF.
80	Dr. Feit:	Does it go, is it *GONE* in the *morning*
81		when you get up?
82	Mr. Mahon:	Mmmm . *MOST* of it . [I]
83	Dr. Feit:	O[kay]
84	Mr. Mahon:	but I still .
85	Dr. Feit:	Okay.
86	Mr. Mahon:	carry it.
87	Dr. Feit:	I'd *PREFER* not to put you on any *water*
88		pills if we don't have to.
89	Mr. Mahon:	I don't want to, but I [still] want to
90	Dr. Feit:	[Okay.]
91	Mr. Mahon:	sh .
92		I want to TELL you.
93	Dr. Feit:	During the *DAY*?
94		when you're *SITTING*?
95		Put your feet [up.]
96	Mr. Mahon:	[Yeah,] [yeah.]
97	Dr. Feit:	[*Even*] at the
98		dinner table.
99		*PUT*'em up on another chair.
100	Mr. Mahon:	Yeah.
101		See my wife had that trouble.
102		>Water, water, water.<
103	Dr. Feit:	Yeah.

{MC1, 3–4}

Dr. Feit avoids a confrontation over this diagnosis by neither accepting nor dismissing the Heart Trouble storyworld. Mr. Mahon actively proposes this diagnostic storyworld, supporting his claim with evidence.

Who Makes the Diagnosis?

There is a prevailing narrow view of patients' discourse roles in the medical encounter. There are only two discourse roles usually suggested for patients: answering questions (providing data for the physician's diagnosis) and asking questions (becoming educated by the physician).

My analysis takes up K. Davis's suggestion that we need to "show how the patient is involved in the process of transforming complaints into a diagnosis or a treatment decision" (1988:121), beyond asking and answering questions. In my data, patients use the "Why I'm here" narrative to set the scene for diagnoses; they suggest candidate diagnoses (diagnostic storyworlds), they offer evidence for and against possible diagnostic storyworlds, and they may even challenge physicians' conclusions as to the correct diagnostic storyworld.

Maynard reviews and critiques the widespread view that medical discourse is asymmetrical in power relations (1991; see also Coupland et al. 1994). Maynard qualifies this view: "While clinical discourse may be asymmetric, it is not so in any unadulterated, comprehensive, or totalistic fashion, but in particular and specifiable ways" (Maynard 1991:485).

In the bases for claiming power in discourse, medical encounters will always be asymmetrical because physicians have both expert knowledge and socially legitimated authority. But in speech activities and self-definitions, participants in the encounter can approach or achieve symmetry.

The symmetry I described in this chapter lies in physicians' and patients' co-construction of diagnoses and treatment plans, through their co-construction of narratives and stories about past, present, and future worlds. I also illustrated patients who work toward symmetry by engaging in conflict over diagnoses.

Asymmetry in control over speech activities and emerging discourse does exist in medical encounters, and when it does exist it is not negligible. However, to develop an accurate and useful theory of the nature of institutional and medical discourse, we must examine both asymmetry and symmetry.

Descriptions of one need not imply the nonexistence of the other. In fact, as Ms. Evans's and Mr. Mahon's encounters show, conflict and agreement, symmetry and asymmetry, friendly relationships and hierarchical relationships—all can alternate or even exist simultaneously in medical encounters.

To study a social event and its symmetry or asymmetry, we must examine the crucial speech activities that constitute it. The medical encounter is a speech event that often has a central purpose of arriving at a diagnosis and associated treatment plan. I described speech activities crucial to that purpose: the construction and co-construction of Labovian, habitual, and hypothetical narratives that propose, accept, refuse, and elaborate on diagnostic storyworlds.

My description amounts to a reconceptualization of the shapes medical encounters may take and the roles their participants may play, a broadening of our understanding of possible variation in encounters.

I can imagine a continuum from decision making by caregivers to decision making by patients, with most decisions negotiated in between. Medical decisions may be made entirely by medical caregivers (e.g., in an emergency room).[4] Or, diagnoses may be made in a process that consists simply of question–answer sequences that do not invoke storyworlds or even narration. Or, the sort of joint construction of a diagnosis that I have described could take place. Or, the patient might decide to take medical decision making entirely into his or her hands, simply ignoring medical advice.

In my data, in long-term private-practice relationships, diagnosis was often constituted through habitual and hypothetical narratives, many of which became stories when they were evaluated by their tellers. In this way, the lifeworld was successfully integrated with the medical world in the encounter.

Science resides in the formation of hypotheses that simultaneously refer to and revise cognitive schemata. In medical encounters, diagnoses are hypotheses. They are often jointly developed by physician and patient through the social processes of narration and storytelling. When this happens, medicine draws upon practitioners' profound implicit knowledge about language and social life, as well as drawing on consciously held information acquired during medical training.

Perhaps this is part of what is meant by the familiar claim that "Medicine is an art as well as a science": Practitioners who make this claim know that what they are doing involves more than cognitive schemata alone. Diagnosing—and medicine in general—may be sociocognitive, not just cognitive, at the very heart.

IV

IMPLICATIONS FOR PRACTICE

8

Active Patients and Cooperative Physicians

After the introductory chapter, each chapter of this book was organized around data—transcriptions and analyses of the talk I recorded between patients and physicians. In this concluding chapter, I briefly review theories about the overall shape of medical encounters and relate my data to those theories. I then summarize the previous chapters about patients' talk—specifically, the claims to power patients made in the encounters I studied. And finally, I reflect on patients, physicians, and their attempts to share control over the medical encounter and over illness.

Central to this chapter is the description of patients' claims to power. After that description, I list some reasons why physicians often dominate, rather than cooperate with, patients' claims to power. Finally, I discuss and evaluate ways physicians can cooperate with active patients.

As I have read the literature and attended conferences on doctor–patient communication, I have been struck by the absence of attention to patients' activities. Often, it sounds (or reads) as if the only person who acts is the physician. Perhaps the most unusual contribution of this book to extant literature is its attention to patients' actions. I have shown that patients can and do take an active part in the medical encounter, in controlling both communication and illness, and I have given details of how patients do this.

At the end of this chapter, I turn to the topic of patients' resources for healing beyond the encounter. I suggest that physicians can help patients articulate the entire array of personal, medical, and community resources on which they can draw.

One important personal resource for patients is the ability to make sense of illness and to let others know how they construe what has happened. This can be done verbally or otherwise. To close this book, I provide artwork by patients and the statements the artists made about the way their work represents their understanding of illness. In this art, we can see patients doing something no one else can do: healing themselves by making sense of what has happened to them. In my book, this artwork represents patients themselves—creative, rational, and active in bringing about their own healing, both inside and outside the medical encounter.

Research on the Medical Encounter

Researchers have tended to focus on three dimensions of the discourse organization of the medical encounter: sequential phases of the encounter; its discourse genre (usually, interview vs. conversation); and its major constitutive speech activities. This book contributes detailed research to the third dimension—constitutive speech activities. My data on those activities are also relevant to the dimension of discourse genre.

Ritualized sequential phases

In the medical literature, explicit models of medical discourse usually construe encounters as consisting of sequential phases. Helman's (1984) reference to encounters as "ritualized" refers in part to their organization into phases.

Though we seldom notice ritual in everyday life, it interpenetrates conversational talk—for example, simply getting through a grocery store checkout line can involve as many as five ritualized routines of thanking and farewell. These are ritualized in three ways: the type of speech activity is culturally predetermined, its place of occurrence in sequential talk is prescribed, and its phrasing is routinized. All this operates at such a low level of awareness that we do not normally consider such encounters to have a routinized dimension.

In the medical encounter, all three of these dimensions show ritualization, but—for physicians and medical educators, at least—there is a conscious attempt to design these ritual aspects of talk. As is the case with religious rituals, the approved speech activities, their phrasing, and their sequence are taught explicitly by the ordained to the neophyte (physician in training). Another similarity to religious rituals is the fact that the design of the discourse is subject to overt debate and change (cf. Smith and Hoppe 1991, discussed below).

However, conversational discourse co-occurs with ritualized discourse in medical encounters. Medical discourse is unpredictable, and in being unpredictable, it is like conversation. Also, many of the constitutive speech activities of medical encounters are shared with conversation.

The conversational dimension of medical encounters is often ignored. Instead, many researchers—especially in the medical literature—focus on the dimension of ritualized phases and see these phases as defining encounters.

The model of ritualized phases has been adopted into the discourse literature, from the medical literature. For instance, Heath (1992) cites a phase model drawn from the medical literature—Byrne and Long (1976). Byrne and Long suggest six phases: "[Phase] I, relating to the patient; II, discovering the reason for attendance; III, conducting a verbal or physical examination or both; IV, consideration of the patient's condition; V, detailing treatment or further investigation; and VI, terminating" (Heath 1992:237). Note that Byrne and Long name each phase after the physician's activity rather than joint activity. This focus on the physician and neglect of patients' role in co-constructing the discourse is a significant limitation of both literatures.

Ten Have's (1989) sophisticated analysis avoids this limitation. Ten Have's model brings together the phase, genre, and speech activities dimensions of medical encounters. He regards "The Consultation as a Genre" (the title of his article). For ten Have, this genre is marked by orientation to phases. At the same time, it is realized through locally negotiated speech activities.

Ten Have speaks of medical encounters as organized into an "ideal sequence" of six phases: opening, complaint, examination or test, diagnosis, treatment or advice, and closing. "The sequence is called 'ideal' because one observes many deviations from it that seem to be quite acceptable to the participants" (1989:118).

Deviations, variation from the phase model, showed up in the earliest discourse studies of medical encounters. Shuy (1983) found a great deal of variation in the sequential organization of encounters. Physicians in Shuy's data apparently were filling out a written questionnaire during the encounter. Shuy expected that the topics of the encounters discourse would be clearly related to the questionnaire. Shuy reports:

> One startling conclusion faced me at the end of my examination of some 100 interviews: It would be very difficult to reconstruct the written questionnaire on the basis of the tape-recorded interviews. . . . Not all interviews cover the same topics and by no means are all questions covered consistently across all interviews. The range of variability was, in fact, gross. (1983:22)

In other words, patients' and doctors' local negotiation changed the encounter away from the doctor's previously established design for the discourse. We see such negotiation vividly illustrated in the chapters of this book, especially in the qualitative studies (chapters 2, 5, 6, and 7).

Shuy's subsequent discussion casts his results in terms of the possibility that medical encounters can be conversational to a degree. Shuy suggests that patients are more comfortable with encounters that are more conversational. This raises the issue of genre: Are encounters fundamentally interviews that can be modified toward conversation, or fundamentally conversations that have been modified to create interviews?

Genre

The question whether medical encounters are fundamentally conversational or interview-like appears in several major analyses. Frankel pointed to early studies in which researchers suggested that the encounter "is essentially conversational in nature," and he remarked that the "case [has not] been made convincingly" (1979:232, 233). Instead, he suggested, the restricted turn-taking system of the medical encounter is in contrast with that of conversational discourse, especially in regard to questions.

Ten Have's discussion of genre in medical encounters suggests that there is "simultaneous relevance of several different interactional formats" (1989:115). Ten Have sees conversation as one of the interactional formats that participants in encounters orient themselves toward, but this can be "problematic," as physicians resist the format.

Heritage appears to agree with Frankel that institutional discourse is defined by restrictions on speech activities: "Institutional interaction seems to involve specific and significant narrowings and respecifications of the range of options that are operative in conversational interaction" (1989:34). Heritage's formulation might suggest that he sees medical discourse as essentially conversational in nature.

Maynard identifies speech activities that are found in both conversation and in the medical encounters he studied. Maynard shows that "doctor-patient interaction involves sequences of talk that have their home in ordinary conversation" (1991:449). This sequence is neither problematic, as in ten Have's data, nor peripheral, as in Shuy's. The sequence Maynard finds in both medical encounters and ordinary conversations is a "perspective display series" (discussed in chapter 6).

Maynard points to the theoretical significance of finding overlap between conversation and medical encounters: "If, at the level of conversational sequencing, we find deep connections between everyday life and the medical encounter, implications [for theories of] clinical and other institutional discourses are vast (1991:449)." One such implication is that the structures of institutional discourse should be studied in conjunction with those of ordinary conversation, rather than in isolation, as is often the case now.

In this book, I examine topic transitions, questions, and stories, all of which are speech activities that are shared between conversational and medical discourse. The central issue in chapter 4 is whether the right to question is shared between doctor and patient (as in conversation) or held only by one participant (as in interviews). In chapters 6 and 7, I examine stories, another conversational structure found in both genres. My data are particularly significant for the "conversation as fundamental" approach because narration and stories are often cited as archetypal conversational speech activities.

Ferrara's (1994) list of contrasts between conversation and talk in psychotherapy sessions is relevant to discussion of genre because psychotherapy sessions are an outgrowth of medical encounters. Ferrara identifies seven differences between conversation and psychotherapy sessions: parity, reciprocality, routine recurrence, bounded time, restricted topic, remuneration, and regulatory responsibility.

Three of the seven—routine recurrence, bounded time, and remuneration—are contextual features, which unarguably constitute the event but do not directly control or define the speech activities in the event. These three contextual features are found in both psychotherapeutic and medical encounters, but not in ordinary conversation.

The other four features have to do with discourse structure. They often are prominent in medical encounters, but have varying salience. Restricted topic, for instance, is a feature of encounters; but that statement must be qualified, for both topic sequence and topic itself. Shuy's (1983) abovementioned data show the unpredictability of topic sequences in encounters. In my data on topic in oncology encounters (aspects of which are discussed in Ainsworth-Vaughn 1992b), the restriction operated to require discussion of the relevant medical topic, but not necessarily to exclude discussion—even extensive discussion—of other, nonmedical topics.

In reviewing my data on medical encounters, I find two more of Ferrara's contrasts to be borne out: lack of reciprocality (e.g., patient and doctor have unequal rights to ask questions) and regulatory responsibility (the physician has an asymmetrical right to initiate and terminate the encounter).

This leaves parity. Parity, or lack of it, in Ferrara's data refers to a client's agreement that the therapist is a helper and that the client needs help, through the discourse itself. Here therapeutic talk can differ from that of medical encounters. Since the discourse itself is treatment, the therapist has rights that may or may not be ceded to physicians in medical encounters.

In psychotherapeutic encounters, patients are presenting themselves for on-the-spot treatment through discourse, including discussion of intimate topics as the therapist deems therapeutic. So parity is relinquished, at least in selection of topics. This is not necessarily the case with medical encounters. In medical encounters, parity is negotiated among participants, apart from the genre (conversational or ritualized talk). When the physician puts forth a diagnosis and treatment plan, this act is sometimes accepted as desired help and is ratified as a plan of action. The sequence of offering and accepting then constitutes lack of parity.

But the same act may be taken as constituting an opinion, and the patient may hold in abeyance any plans for action. In my data, an oncologist suggested that a young man with testicular cancer should have an exploratory operation to see whether cancer was in the nearby lymph nodes. Because the couple had no children, and the operation could lead to impotence, the man's wife suggested a different plan, and her plan was eventually adopted. She had negotiated parity; her plan was on a par with that of the physician.

In sum, we cannot characterize all medical encounters as having a matrix of conversational features or as having a matrix of interview-like restrictions. We can suggest that encounters exist on a continuum between interrogation, as described in Mishler (1984), and friendly conversation with a small amount of time devoted to satisfying medical goals, as I found in studying unproblematic oncology checkups.

At the interrogation end, the sequence of speech activities is heavily ritualized (primarily questions and answers) and reciprocality is not present. At the conversation end, only a brief part of the sequence of speech activities is ritualized, and reciprocality may be present in varying degrees. Regulatory responsibility (the right of the physician to begin and end the event) is present throughout the continuum. Parity is negotiated locally, apart from the discourse genre.

All analogies are deficient, by nature. A continuum metaphor provides for construing two possible directions for the discourse—toward the two ends of the continuum—rather than depicting the possible shifts that actually take place among multiple interactional frames (cf. Tannen and Wallat 1987). Perhaps the emblematic designs in medieval woodcuts would serve better; these nonlinear designs show connections among a variety of symbols. In an emblem, movement would be possible to shift focus among coexisting frames. But the continuum metaphor does allow a representation, however limited, of variation in discourse genre—variation that is highly significant in my study of the ways doctors and patients negotiate to achieve their agendas.

Patients' Power-Claiming Talk

This book is about people using speech activities to claim power in the medical encounter. Speech activities and social identities are rich, complex resources for both patients and physicians, as they cooperatively construct talk (a joint effort) and claim power for themselves (an individual effort). The previous chapters painted very detailed pictures of this complex use of speech activities. These detailed pictures both advance discourse theory and clarify the nature of the medical encounter as it is constructed through discourse. In this section I briefly summarize these pictures of active patients.

Following is a list of examples, from throughout the book, of seven ways in which patients verbally claimed power—were active—in the medical encounters I studied. Usually, the physician cooperated with these attempts to claim power, and so the attempts succeeded. It is in this sense that we might say that physicians empower patients.[1]

Patients used linguistic resources to:

Control topic and choose speakers   Resources: topic-transition activities (chapter 3); questions (chapter 4)

In chapter 3, we saw patients making about 40% of the topic transitions. Usually, they did this after a sequence of reciprocal (power-sharing) activities rather than making sudden unilateral topic changes.

Patients also used questions to control topic. A question both sets the topic for its answer and chooses the answerer. In chapter 4, patients were documented asking 39% of the unambiguous questions in 40 encounters. Gender, diagnosis, and initial versus repeat encounter made a difference in number of questions asked.

Offer a candidate diagnosis   Resources: story structure, displaced authorship (chapters 6 and 7)

Patients offered a number of candidate diagnoses in the previous chapters. In many of these cases, the physician either accepted the candidate diagnosis outright or accepted it as a plausible hypothesis.

Chapter	Patient	Candidate diagnosis
2	Ms. Hazen	Cancer recurrence or surgery aftermath
5	Ms. Lane	Medication side effects
6	Ms. Wells	Anxiety attacks
7	Ms. Feblen	Hemachromatosis
7	Ms. Evans	Not a yeast infection
7	Mr. Mahon	Heart trouble

Ms. Hazen, Ms. Wells, and Ms. Feblen attributed the candidate diagnosis to someone else (other family members). In this way, they avoided a direct, me-to-you challenge of the physician's role of diagnosing.

Co-construct diagnoses   Resources: narrative and story structure (chapter 7)
As part of the diagnostic process described in chapter 7, Mrs. Feblen proposed both the Hemachromatosis and Toxic Fumes diagnostic narratives and helped construct and deconstruct the three narrative storyworlds under consideration.

Challenge diagnoses   Resources: narrative and story structure, inference (chapter 7)
In chapter 7, both Mr. Mahon and Ms. Evans used new evidence to suggest a rewrite of a physician's diagnosis narrative. In each case, the patient cited evidence and allowed the physician to infer the challenge.

Propose treatment   Resources: displaced authorship (chapter 2); "treatment questions" (chapters 4 and 5)
Ms. Hazen (chapter 2) proposed treatment in a deferent way by displacing onto her children the question whether she should be treated with a whirlpool bath: "My kids was wondering. . . ." Ms. Hazen was simultaneously displacing authorship and using a "treatment question."
Treatment questions (chapters 4 and 5) are one of the major ways patients propose treatment. By phrasing the suggestion as a question, the patient defers to the physician's right to propose treatment. In chapter 4, we saw Mr. Brade use a question to suggest a specific possible treatment (a "spray bottle").

Carry out potentially face-threatening acts   Resources: ambiguous rhetorical questions, ambiguity of voice (chapter 5)
True questions are inherently face threatening because they directly request an answer. One way of being deferent is to question without requiring an answer. Chapter 5 examines questions that are functionally ambiguous—marked as a rhetorical question which requires no answer but simultaneously interpretable as a true (face-threatening) question. Using this strategy, as well as ambiguity of voice, Ms. Lane questions her physician's competence and Mr. Frisell makes sexual references (both cited in chapter 5). Ms. Lane's strategy appeared to succeed in getting Dr. Mey's attention and cooperation, while Mr. Frisell's sexual rhetorical questions were laughed off by Dr. Finn.

Face-threatening activities may be either appropriate or inappropriate. From my perspective, Ms. Lane's claim to power was appropriate because Dr. Mey was not responding to her questions, but Mr. Frisell's claims were inappropriate. These unusually strong claims to power relate to the question of which claims to power should be supported. Dr. Mey was able to hear Ms. Lane's frustration, in her strong claim to power, and to start listening carefully. Dr. Finn chose a way of dealing with Mr. Frisell that was comfortable for her; someone else might have decided to discourage his sexual joking.

Frame the medical encounter as friendly and invoke favorable cultural schemas in defining the self   Resources used: story structure, culturally significant images (chapter 6)

In chapter 6, Mrs. Melan's oncology encounter began with a co-constructed story. Storytelling, apart from the content of the story, is a speech activity which can invoke a friendship frame as one of the multiple interactive frames of the encounter (K. Davis 1988; Tannen 1987). Besides setting a friendly tone, Ms. Melan's story helped define her self, portraying her as a valued member of a strong social network—three generations in one family, getting together to celebrate the beginnings of a new life.

Perhaps the most important ability patients have is their capacity to make sense of their illnesses. Doing this is an action—people have to work to arrive at acceptance of their new way of life. Patients have many ways of coming to terms with illness. One major way is to tell a story about this new life.

Chapter 6 shows Ms. Melan and Ms. Wells using stories to integrate their medical- and life-world experiences. Chapter 7 shows Ms. Feblen using narratives and stories to co-construct possible diagnostic worlds—one of which will become her reality.

Physicians' Talk: Changing Modes of Discourse

Where we have come from: Traditional medical talk

All research on medical encounters, including my own, has found instances of physician domination of talk. It is worthwhile to pause to consider why this is so.

In conversational talk, speakers share control over the floor and the topic. Traditionally, for several reasons, physicians often conclude that talk in a medical setting is not, and should not be, at all conversational.

First, physicians often have certain specific goals that they must accomplish during the talk. They have (justifiably) been required to memorize lists of questions to be asked during the encounter. Because the memorized list serves to structure the encounter, talking with a patient probably seems much like filling out a form. In fact, often the physician *is* filling out a written form while the talk goes on. The need to get specific information, to fill in the blanks in the mental and written forms, is very great. This may push physicians toward regarding their talk with patients as nonconversational.

Another force pushing physicians away from a conversational model of medical encounters is their compelling need to maintain emotional equilibrium in the face of illness and death. Being a physician places complex demands on a person: How to have a happy life of one's own, in the face of so much trouble in patients' lives? One solution physicians often reach is to keep the patient in a distant position, in the role of object to be studied. Conversational talk then may be seen as allowing an unwanted closeness and acknowledging a painful kinship.

There is also the difficulty, the uncertainty, in diagnosing and healing. Diagnosing often—much more often than we can comfortably acknowledge—involves guesswork, highly educated though the guesses may be. But this fact threatens physicians' identities. A physician is one who can diagnose and heal, one who knows the answer to the puzzles of illness. Another way of saying it is that much of a physician's identity and authority flows from Aesculapian medical knowledge (H. Brody; see chapter 2).

The problem is that medical knowledge is tentative and limited, and each individual's knowledge of medical lore is necessarily even more limited. What, then, will serve as the source of an authoritative identity if not absolute, assured knowledge? For some physicians, certain kinds of power-claiming talk constitute institutional authority.

Evidence for the preceding two reasons is found in Broncato's (1992) focus interview with four medical students about their use of jargon. The students agreed that their primary reasons for using medical jargon included their perceived need to maintain emotional distance from, and authority over, patients.

Another reason for avoiding conversational talk is physicians' need to conserve time. Physicians may not realize that social gestures and reciprocal talk take only seconds and pay off in patient independence.

And finally, there is the rigid system of domination and subordination that characterizes some kinds of medical education. Certainly, for physicians, long-standing authoritarian practices and models have characterized physicians' education in hospitals and residencies. Medical education and hospitals are extremely hierarchical social structures, and because student and resident physicians are at the bottom of the pecking order, they often live in what the *American Medical Association Newsletter* (July 22/29, 1983) described as a "lethal lifestyle."

This lethal lifestyle includes excessive and poorly organized work assignments. For instance, in a system mysterious to outsiders, residents are assigned to 36 continuous hours on duty instead of being given alternating shorter shifts. As well as ensuring that fateful decisions will be made by sleep-deprived brains, this system embodies contempt for the residents themselves. Also, ways of teaching medical students and residents often include the use of humiliation to drive home a point. Again, the lesson is one in treating others with contempt.

Young physicians may come to accept domination and contempt as the way less knowledgeable people are treated in medicine. If apprentice physicians do accept contempt as the appropriate way of viewing those who are less knowledgeable, they will have difficulty regarding their less knowledgeable patients as conversational partners, much less as partners in a therapeutic alliance.

Where we are going: Cooperative medical discourse

The most fundamental requirement in conversation is to acknowledge, and show respect for, the other person's self. The physicians I studied did this.

SOCIAL GESTURES   One important way this happened was not described in previous chapters, but it deserves mention. All these physicians—except Dr. Miller, the only authoritarian physician I studied—made the basic gestures of conversation: greetings, introductions, handshakes, smiles, good-byes. (Even Dr. Miller used some of these.) These are all ways of acknowledging another person's self and showing respect for the person.

Introductions, smiles, good-byes, and the rest were appropriate precisely because conversation was an integral part of discourse in the medical encounters I studied.

SPEECH ACTIVITIES   In previous chapters, I described three major speech activities that were important in the encounters I studied: topic control, questions, and stories. In carrying out each of these, physicians demonstrated that they were cooperative: that they were listening and that they respected the right of the patient to be heard and responded to.

Topic maintenance   Resources: repetition, anaphora, inference (chapters 3, 6, and 7)

Dr. Finn, in chapter 6, used anaphora ("where'd you find *that*?") to maintain Ms. Melan's topic (her cold, her granddaughter's christening). Dr. Myhill (chapter 7) maintained Ms. Feblen's topic (toxic fumes) in co-constructing a diagnosis.

Reciprocal topic transitions   Resources: formulations, exchanged affirmations, arrangements (chapter 3)

Physicians produced about 60% of the topic transitions described in chapter 3, which means that they cooperated in their patients' 40% of the transitions. Physicians used more reciprocal transitions than unilateral ones, by a 2.5-to-1 ratio.

"Reciprocal" means that both physician and patient had a hand in closing down the topic. Some major ways of achieving reciprocity in the topic change were exchanged affirmations, formulations, and arrangements.

Of these, formulations seem to me especially important. A formulation is a rephrasing, summary, or assessment of what was just said. If you can rephrase and summarize the message ("formulate" it), you undoubtedly heard it. If your rephrasing is inaccurate, the other speaker can correct it.

Nonreciprocal topic transitions   Resources: minimal links, links, sudden topic changes (chapter 3)

Noncooperative—unilateral—closings also were used by physicians, and at a far higher ratio to reciprocal activities than patients used them (patients: 1 to 13.5; physicians: 1 to 2.5). In fact, the three unilateral ways of changing topic were used chiefly by physicians.

In history taking and other lists of questions, unilateral topic change is often appropriate. But that does not explain the high physicians' counts, because we did not include history taking, etc., in our counts.

It could be argued that physicians must use unilateral topic closings to accomplish their medical goals. That argument founders, however, when we examine data on gender of physicians. Female physicians functioned quite well while using unilateral closings only one fifth of the time, whereas male physicians used them almost half the time (1.4 reciprocal to 1 unilateral). This suggests that the overall frequency of unilateral topic transitions could be reduced substantially.

Questioning   Resources: cooperating with questioning, recognizing indirect questions (chapter 4); recognizing multiple-purpose questions (chapter 5)

Physicians can cooperate with patients' attempts to question. As with topic transitions, patients controlled about 40% of the 838 true, unambiguous questions asked in the 40 encounters studied in chapter 4. For this to happen, physicians must have been, in general, open to questioning.

With true questions—again, as with topic control—in my data it made a difference whether the physician was male or female. When the physician was a woman, about 50% of the questions were asked by patients. When the physician was a man, about 26% of the questions were asked by patients.

Future research might focus on what happens after a patient asks a question in relation to the number of subsequent questions. What physician behaviors serve to encourage more questioning? But this will be difficult to examine other than anecdotally because of the huge number of ways answers can be woven into the complex fabric of the encounter.

I have one suggestion: When physicians find themselves talking at length, they should stop along the way—not at the end of the disquisition—and find ways to involve patients. Questions are not always the best way to do this because they exert restrictions on topic. Physicians can use nonverbal signals, such as a pause combined with an inquiring gaze directed at the patient. They can also invite the participation they would like; for example, "I'm interested in your ideas about this possibility."

Another important way to encourage participation is to suppress any amusement at errors. I recorded a meeting between an oncologist and several breast cancer patients; one patient asked a question in which she repeatedly mentioned her "nymph nodes." The oncologist accepted this effort by the patient, refraining from publicly correcting the phrase and answering the question with no sign of amusement or superiority.

Physicians can learn to recognize indirect and multiple-purpose questions. Chapter 4 describes questions that look, structurally, like a statement rather than a question. But they are statements by one speaker about something only the other speaker knows (A statements about a B event). When patients make such statements ("The tests must have come back."), they count as questions, because the physician knows the answer. Likewise, patients use statements prefaced with "I was wondering" or "I didn't know if." These are indirect questions.

Even more indirect are ambiguous questions, such as those described in chapter 5. Patients routinely use "functional" ambiguity: They ask questions which might be taken either as true questions or as suggestions.

If in doubt about a patient's intention to question or to suggest treatment, a physician can ask about those intentions: "Is there something about (the topic) you'd like to discuss?" "Are you thinking that (the treatment) might be a next step?"

Stories   Resources: narrative and story structure; Labovian, habitual, and hypothetical narratives (chapters 6 and 7)

Patients must continually rewrite their life stories, incorporating illness. The process of doing this is a means of accepting a new reality, but it is more than that. During this process the person actually creates some aspects of this new reality, as well. For instance, each cancer patient comes to terms with having cancer. This is the immutable part of their common experience. But patients differ in the way they conceptualize cancer and its role, what it means to them.   While telling a story, a patient makes concrete his or her concept of a new reality, one in which illness plays a role. For the patient, the story is the reality.

So to interrupt a story is to interrupt a healing process. This does not mean that physicians must become passive audiences for every reminiscence of every patient. But, like Dr. Finn and Dr. Munn in chapter 6, physicians can recognize important stories, coooperate with the telling, and learn a great deal about patients' specific needs in the process.

Patients' Resources and Physicians' Responsibilities

Stories are one resource patients have for healing themselves. They have other resources, as well. In many cases, a patient has an entire array of personal, social, and community resources for becoming whole again.

Physicians and other providers can help patients articulate their strengths and resources. Providers themselves, of course, are resources. It is important for providers to discuss their roles in the overall array in such a way that their concern, commitment, and availability are clear. There is a delicate line between helping patients recognize their resources and directing patients elsewhere in order to reduce demands on the provider.

Medical settings are prime locations for displays of information on community resources. It is especially important that patient groups or match-ups with patient survivors be available when the illness is chronic or life threatening. Providers can start such groups, but the groups should be controlled by patients.

Providers should acknowledge the contribution patients can make personally. The obvious contributions include learning about the illness (public and medical libraries, telephone hot lines) and supporting the body's defenses (diet, exercise, relaxation). But patients also should be told that whatever nurtures the spirit also nurtures the body. This will have different meanings for different people. It could apply to social activities, religion, artwork, music, hobbies, writing a journal, travel, reading—the list is endless.

Providers also can ask how the patient coped with other difficult times in the past, and whether it will be possible to use those resources at present. But it is also important to find new ways of coping, such as splitting tasks into smaller units.

Patients should be encouraged to listen to themselves and take their wishes seriously: "If you hear yourself telling people you wish you could see your brother in another state—stop. Pay attention to what you are saying. Could you go there? Could he come here? Could you talk on the phone for an hour every other week (cheaper than airfares!)?" When patients learn to see and meet their own needs, their physical health can only benefit and their dependence on providers is reduced.

A talk about resources should end with the remark that the patient, providers, and support people will continue to work together to find ways of dealing with the illness. Patients need to know that they will have support in the future.

Somehow, in our health system, we have developed a belief in physicians' all-encompassing responsibility to bring patients back to full health. Accompanying that idea is a belief that patients have little to offer in improving their health. But patients I studied were actively trying to participate in their own health care, and most of the physicians I studied were supporting and cooperating with these efforts rather than diminishing or dominating patients.

I end this book with examples of patients who worked to heal themselves, both by making sense of their experiences and by showing others how they felt. They did this through artwork and writing about their illnesses. Their work is part of an exhibit called "The Art of Healing: Works by People Touched by Cancer," organized by Gay Walker, of the Chrysalis Community Cancer Help Program in Kalamazoo, Michigan. Each work of art is an artistic and personal achievement.

The photograph on this book's cover is titled *Sunbeams*. Photographer David Lubbers's [2] three experiences with critical illness—his mother's cancer and his two episodes of cerebral bleeding—moved him in profound ways. He took the cover photograph in Yosemite Valley, California. His statement:

> When I saw this scene, I knew it was a magic moment. The sun represents the future. The fog and mist are illnesses. The trees are obstacles that you have to get past to reach the future. The fog and mist allow the sunbeams to be visible.
>
> The future may not be what you had hoped for, but it is the only option. We can either be pessimistic and stay in our misery, thinking about the past, or we can use what remains and go forward. This photograph is inspirational and dramatizes the healing rays of the sun.
>
> Sadness is close to beauty and wisdom. We gain a measure of wisdom from the illness.

Figure 8–1, *I feel the same*, is a crayon drawing by Mark Kemp (age 8). Mark's statement is on the drawing: "I feel the same with cancer." Mark survived cancer and a recurrence. For me, Mark's picture and statement capture a familiar experience: the need to be recognized as fundamentally the same person that I was before cancer. Again we see patients (Mark and me) constructing the self. Mark pictures himself as active and capable, playing basketball as before. I also have resisted being seen as diminished by illness. In my life, stereotyping and fear (both my own

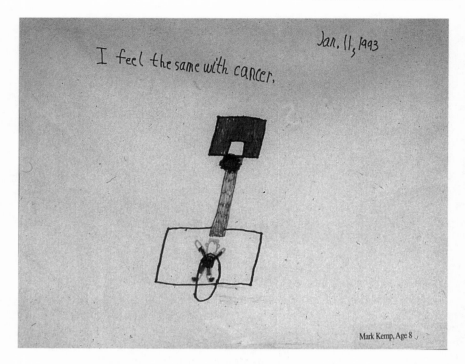

I feel the same with cancer.

Jan. 11, 1993

Mark Kemp, Age 8

Figure 8–1   I Feel the Same—Mark Kemp

and others') have been almost as great a problem as the illness itself. Much of my time in the first few years after diagnosis was spent trying to resist these socially taught attitudes.

Figure 8–2, *Tender Release*, is a lithograph by Susan Teague. This is her statement:

> In 1995 my eleven-year-old son, Chad, was diagnosed with end stages of cancer. The uncertainty of his future—his life, his death—crowded my thoughts with innumerable fears and doubts. *Tender Release* is an expression of the moment of acceptance, letting go and putting into God's hands my loved one.
>
> The open hand with tears shed not only expresses the letting go, but also the openness to help and share with others the experience. The unwound cloth symbolizes the healing process. The bandages no longer need to protect the wound.
>
> The healing has come with tender release.

Susan Teague found the creative, emotional, and spiritual resources she needed to heal herself. Art was one of those resources. A provider might suggest that Susan turn to art and that she write about her work, but no provider could have taken Susan's hand, guided it in a drawing, and told her its significance.

In the artwork on the cover and in figures 8–1 and 8–2, we see patients healing outside the medical encounter. This artwork shows the ability to integrate old

Figure 8–2   Tender Release—Susan Teague

and new lives. Patients say who they are and what they have learned from life's hardest lessons.

In these patients' work, we can see the will to be whole, even after great loss. Curing the body may be contributed to in various degrees by physician or patient; sometimes physicians alone bring about a cure, sometimes the patient's involvement is crucial. Healing the self is even more complex; here the patient always plays a crucial role. There are those who believe that the body cannot easily heal without healing of the self. If that is true, then the patient's role in getting well is even more important than we have thought.

I do not wish to diminish the critical roles of providers as healers. Doctors and nurses can do enormous good or enormous damage by what they say, and there are many other books (virtually all the other books regarding provider–patient talk) that focus on what should and should not be said by providers to help bring about healing. But I think that medical education in the United States often implies that only providers are healers. Doctors and nurses who accept this idea take on an unnecessary burden.

Patients, too, have enormous contributions to make to their own well-being. The three works of art reproduced here distill patients' thoughts and feelings in a way we can quickly grasp. H. Brody, discussing stories about illness, suggests that "suffering is produced, and alleviated, primarily by the meaning that one attaches to one's experience" (1987:5). In these patients' artwork and artists' statements, we can see their actions—how they attached meaning to their illnesses, how they healed their damaged selves.

It is more difficult to see the significance of patients' speech activities in emerging talk. That is what I described in this book. I tried to attend fully to patients' efforts to control their medical experiences by appropriately claiming power over emerging discourse. Claiming power is one attempt to heal, to participate in attaching meaning to the illness. I described the modulation of this power-claiming process (for example, ways in which claims to power vary with diagnosis and gender). I argued that medical encounters subsume both ritualized and conversational modes, and I suggested that the conversational mode—in which patients have greater parity than in ritualized talk—should receive more research attention.

Our models of the medical encounter must acknowledge its partially conversational nature in order to legitimize the role of physicians' intuitions. I am suggesting that physicians' orientation toward accomplishing medical goals is fully compatible with their intuitions about courteous, respectful talk. I am not suggesting that physicians abandon medical goals in favor of warm chats to no purpose. Physicians must be effective in their jobs, and that means gathering information efficiently and conserving time spent with patients. However, in my data, respectful, conversational talk such as that of doctors Finn and Myhill seemed more efficient in accomplishing medical goals than the wordy, authoritarian talk of Dr. Miller.

Early in this book, I analyzed power and the many ways it can be claimed. In this chapter, I critiqued theories about the medical encounter. These dissections of power and the encounter allow us to recognize that a physician can retain one kind of power (e.g., structural power) while sharing another (control over the emerging discourse).

The physicians I studied often cooperated with patients' claims to power. Physicians can cooperate without compromising their own selves. Patients' appropriate efforts to take control of illness translate directly into better treatment and reduced demands on overburdened physicians.

These patients and doctors stand as examples of active partners in therapeutic relationships that are constructed, moment to moment, in details of discourse in medical encounters.

Transcribing Conventions

One of the important features of a transcript is that it should not have too much information. A transcript that is too detailed is difficult to follow and assess. A more useful transcript is a more selective one. . . . But selectivity should not be random and implicit. . . . The transcript should reflect the particular interests, the hypotheses to be examined—of the researcher. —Ochs 1979:44

All transcription systems are ultimately inadequate, in part due to the extreme complexity of oral language. If we really did put down on paper everything we heard, the transcript would be so cluttered as to be unreadable. In part, however, transcript inadequacy is due to the inadequacy of our theories (e.g., continuing problems with defining "turn").

Because of these significant problems, we are forced to choose transcription conventions that describe only part of oral language. Most transcribers try to capture as much relevant information as possible while preserving readability. Readability depends in part on the audience and its background in discourse study. In this case, there was a dual audience (linguists and nonlinguists).

I chose transcription conventions that would be easily read by nonspecialists but would also capture some significant aspects of intonation, timing, and other features of the language as it was spoken. In choosing conventions, I drew on M. Goodwin (1990), Tannen (1989a, 1989b, 1989c), and many articles in Edwards and Lampert (1993).

These transcriptions were first done in rough form and then redone in a detailed format. Because language is perceived with slight differences from person to person, each transcript in this book was reviewed in its detailed form by at least two transcribers.

The issue of respelling to represent pronunciation is problematic. Respelling in transcription is ubiquitous in discourse study. I discussed this significant theoretical and methodological issue at the end of chapter 1.

Timing and Intonation

Punctuation symbols at the end of an utterance do not have their usual meaning. They shown intonation, not pragmatic or grammatical status. It is especially important to note that question marks do not identify utterances that function as questions but rather those that end with rising intonation.

Intonation conventions include the following:

. indicates sentence final falling contour

, indicates clause-final intonation ("more to come")

? indicates rising contour

A number of articles in Edwards and Lampert (1993) suggest that each line, beginning at the left margin of transcription, should capture an *intonation unit*. This seems to me desirable because it helps the reader reconstruct the sound of talk. However, some speakers pause so frequently as they speak that, if each pause were to be considered a boundary of an intonation unit, the transcript would lose readability to a significant degree. In those cases, I used a syntactic unit, the clause, as the organizing concept.

If a phrase or clause was bounded by a pause, or by clause-final intonation (. or ,), it was given the status of an intonation unit. If, on the other hand, a clause contained several brief pauses, I did not regard each of these as bounding a new intonation unit and did not begin again at the left margin of transcription.

Other syntactic considerations, and discourse functions as well, also affected the decision to use a separate line. Intonation, syntax, and pragmatics are organized in concert by the speaker, so usually our decisions were easy to make because the speaker placed pauses and intonation markers at syntactic and pragmatic junctions.

If the intonation unit was too long to fit on one line, its continuation was shown by indenting the part left over, as illustrated in the following excerpt. Excerpt 1 illustrates transcription by intonation unit. The intonation unit on line 160 is bounded by a pause; the two intonation units on line 161–162 and 163 are each bounded by clause-final intonation.

(1)

160	Dr. Munn:	I was *talk*ing to the *dau*:ghter .
161		after the patient went out to check
162		back,
163		*Y'*know to get another *appoint*ment,

{WL3, 2–160}

In most cases, I did not try to show timing of the beginning of a new turn in relation to the previous utterance. Instead, when a speaker ended his or her talk with sentence-final intonation, or a pause, and another speaker then takes a turn, I transcribed the new turn beginning at the left margin of transcription (two spaces after the speaker's name). In excerpt 2, Ms. Hazen ends line 34 with the falling intonation characteristically used at the end of a sentence. In line 35, Dr. Miller's talk then is transcribed beginning at the left margin.

(2)

34 Ms. Hazen: How does *that* look today.
35 Dr. Miller: Ah, white count is *3.7,*

Sometimes, however, a second speaker places a brief utterance such as "M-hm" or "Uh-huh" in a pause while the first speaker is still holding the floor—for example, the first speaker may pause in the midst of a sentence, and the second speaker murmurs, "M-hm." When there is no attempt to take over the floor, a *backchannel* occurs.

When a backchannel occurred during someone else's turn, or when a second speaker finished a first speaker's sentence, we placed the second speaker's word or phrase in relation to the first speaker's words so that it iconically represented the timing of the utterances. In excerpt 3, Dr. Miller uses a rise–fall clause-final intonation at the end of line 34, symbolized in our transcription by a comma. Ms. Hazen's utterance in line 35 begins immediately after Dr. Miller's ends, and Dr. Miller's utterance in line 36 is a continuance of his turn begun in line 34.

(3)

34 Dr. Miller: Ah, white count is *3.7,*
35 Ms. Hazen: Uh huh
36 Dr. Miller: which is a
37   *LITTLE* low,

{RH1, 1–34}

Readers should note that these decisions about the initiation and boundaries of turns are not simple because there are many theoretical difficulties with defining turns.

Overlaps are enclosed in square brackets which are aligned at the onset of the overlap. These brackets appear in both speakers' utterances. In lines 24 and 25 below, "Well" overlaps "work." When overlaps occur in immediately successive utterances such that there could be confusion about which talk overlaps which, the sets of square brackets are alternated with double square brackets, as in lines 26 through 29:

(4)

24 Ms. Hazen: Gettin' back to [work]?
25 Dr. Miller: [Well] I'm wonderin if .
26   [yeah]
27 Ms. Hazen: [yeah]
28 Dr. Miller: [[yeah]]

29   Ms. Hazen: [[Being]] off work for a week I got off .
30   my routine of . . LIFTING and . . .
31   Dr. Miller: I don't *know*.

                                                            {RH1, 1–25}

Usually there were no more than three people in the examining room at a time, and no more than two were overlapping at once. However, in the Wells–Munn excerpt in chapter 6, four people were present, and three overlapped at once. All three overlapping utterances were placed in single square brackets.

Pauses are also part of timing. Two ways of showing pauses appear in excerpt 5. Pauses of three seconds or less are indicated with periods in lines 2–6 and 8; each period represents one-half to one second. Longer pauses are shown by numbers of seconds enclosed in parentheses, as in line 7. The pause of four seconds is placed on a separate line, flush left, in order to avoid attributing it to either speaker.

(5)

1   Ms. Hazen: It ACHES right in here it just RUBBIN' it
2   hurts .
3   an' that . when I . it just, y'know,
4   PULLS 'n .
5   LAST night I could just feel it .
6   tightening right up . in my *chest*
7   (4 sec)
8   Dr. Miller: Did you do anything exceptionally .
9   heavy?

                                                            {RH1, 1–1}

I have chosen not to use the "latching" or equals sign (=). This symbol is widely used to indicate close placement of a second speaker's utterance at the end of the utterance by a first speaker. In my data, perhaps because of the time constraints on doctors and patients, there was a great deal of close placement. I tried using latching signs, but the timing they represent never became an issue in my analysis, and their abundance interfered with readability.

Loudness and Pitch

As in excerpt 6, loudness (increased volume) is represented by capital letters, and raised pitch is represented by italics. These can be combined, producing italic capitals when the word is both loud and has raised pitch. But it must be acknowledged that separating loudness and pitch is difficult, and these distinctions were demanding.

Softness (i.e., notable change in volume downward) is signaled by angled brackets, pointing inward, enclosing the quiet words. I chose this representation rather than the more commonly used superscript ° for three reasons:

First, the ° bears no iconic relationship to contrast between two states (a louder state and a quieter one, in this case). The angled symbols, however, are easy to associate with change/contrast because of their wider-to-narrower shape, which iconically depicts change from more to less or vice versa. This shape is used in mathematics as the mathematical symbol for "less than" and "greater than," an association that supports readers' understanding of the symbols as they are used here.

Second, the ° is problematic because it is strongly associated with degrees Fahrenheit, an association I often find distracting as I read published transcripts using °.

Finally, ° is not directional; the shape of the symbol does not provide an iconic indication of whether the softness is beginning or ending (although an indication is provided by the contiguity of the ° and the word that follows or precedes it). However, angled brackets have a right and left version, such that they can literally point to the portion of talk involved.

In the following example, Ms. Lane says "No" softly, in comparison with the higher volume of Dr. Mey's remark:

(6)

```
121   Dr. Mey:   And you . have you ATTEMPTED suicide .
122                  in the last MONTH or so?
123   Ms. Lane:  >No<
```
{LAF1, 3–121}

Other Conventions

Question marks within single parentheses indicate inaudible utterances. Single parentheses surround uncertain transcriptions; double parentheses surround explanatory notes by the transcriber:

(7)

```
22   Mr. Cox:   I've got to go up to a CORRECtional
23                  institution Wednesdays now,
24   Dr. Finn:  ((laughter))
25   Mr. Cox:   next Wednesday.
26              I said,
27              "MAYbe they WON'T let me out."
28              [((chuckle))]
29   Fiancee:   [((laughter))]
```
{CR3, 1–22}

It is important to indicate a speaker's laughter. However, I have not followed the common practice of attempting to describe the exact sound the speaker made because that practice seems to me to place distracting demands on the reader. My reading of transcript has often come to a stop while I tried unsuccessfully to hear "hengh-engh," or some similar attempt to reproduce the way laughter sounds.

In this book laughter is indicated both by explanatory notes within double parentheses, as in excerpt 7, and also with the @ sign, as in excerpt 8. If the laughter was placed before or after an utterance, double parentheses were used. If it seemed important to show the precise onset of laughter or the fact that a brief laugh sound was integrated into the utterance, so as to express the speaker's point of view, the @ sign was used.

In excerpt 8, Dr. Miller made a brief laugh sound (@) just before the spoken word "Annie." I interpret Dr. Miller's choice as marking the upcoming information as laughable (to him).

(8)

27	Dr. Miller:	And *HE* had a . tattoo up on his *shoul*der,
28		that said "Annie"?
29	Mr. Dunham:	Yeah?
30	Dr. Miller:	and then he di*VORCED* Annie.
31	Mr. Dunham:	((snickers))
32	Dr. Miller:	Okay?
33		And he HAD to get rid of "*ANN*ie".
34	((both laugh))	
35	Dr. Miller:	because *SANDRA* didn't *LIKE* @"Annie"
36		being up there.

{DW1, 3–27}

When a speaker cannot be identified, the utterance is attributed to "X:"

(9)

114	Dr. Munn:	That's the [TRUTH] .
115	Ms. Wells:	[*THANK*] you!
116	Dr. Munn:	Yeah.
117		*IT* IS.
118	X Wells:	(???)

{WL3, 2–58}

NOTES

INTRODUCTION

1. The term is sometimes used in a more limited sense—Levinson (1983) restricts its meaning to speech–act theory, which is only one type of discourse analysis.

CHAPTER 1

1. As I use the term, "discourse analysis" refers to the study of naturally occurring sequences of utterances which form speech activities within speech events. Tannen (1989b) and M. Goodwin (1990) are examples, studying dinner-table conversation and adolescent street talk, respectively.

2. I use the term in this way because anthropologists, who are usually identified with ethnography, do accept a wide range of data as evidence.

3. From these remarks, it will be clear that I do not use the definition for "discourse analysis" found in Levinson (1983), where this approach is identified with speech-act theory.

4. There is controversy over the best terminology to use in regard to gender. Sociologists consider the terms "woman" and "man" to be socially constituted categories while "male" and "female" refer to physical sexual characteristics. This point is apparently made in an attempt to stress the socially constructed nature of gender.

In practice, separating gender and sex in ethnographic study is difficult. Physical sexual characteristics and observed choices about appearance are what we have to go on. It should be noted that sexual preference is not at issue because sexual preference is different from gender identity.

The prescriptive grammarian would suggest that "male" and "female" are adjectives, and "man" and "woman" are nouns. Therefore, we should not talk of "four males and three females." It probably has not yet occurred to prescriptive grammarians to object to the recent practice of using "man" and "woman" as adjectives: "woman physician," "man physician." Another linguistic focus could be on the appearance in contemporary speech and texts of the plurals of these terms to agree in number with the following noun: "women physicians," "men physicians." This is a unique example of revival of Old English syntax in contemporary English usage.

I see no reason to make an issue of the choice of adjectives. The fact that gender is socially constructed seems to me to be noncontroversial among this academic audience. As for distinguishing gender from sex, that too seems to be unnecessary in this study. Participants appeared to have sexual physical characteristics that were in accord with the gender identities they signaled through appearance and behavior.

For all these reasons, I follow the prescriptive path in using "female" and "male" as adjectives and "man" and "woman" as nouns.

CHAPTER 2

1. As Howard Brody has pointed out (personal communication), Ms. Hazen must be entertaining two diagnoses. She says that the closeness of the lump to her neck is frightening and makes clear that she is afraid it is a cancer recurrence. At the same time, she suggests treatment with a whirlpool bath for her pain. Clearly, whirlpool treatment would not address a cancer recurrence, so Ms. Hazen must be entertaining the idea that the pain might be something else, related to her surgery.

CHAPTER 3

1. However, Maltz and Borker's suggestion apparently is based on unpublished research.

2. Their article draws heavily on Schegloff and Sacks (1984). Schegloff and Sacks are the originators of theoretical conversation analysis, in which turn-by-turn organization is the primary (often the only) type of "sequential" organization.

3. Words, phrases, and clauses can be deleted by redundancy rules even though they are in the underlying meaning of the sentence.

4. This word count is given in order to allow specification of the size of the database and to make possible judgments of comparability within categories (e.g., amount of data on male vs. female physicians, or within specific interviews) and with other studies. A word count is an accurate way of establishing the quantity of data, in comparison with numbers of transcribed pages, which will vary with the transcription system.

5. All raters throughout this project were graduate students who had taken a graduate-level course in discourse analysis.

6. This ambiguity is related to the controversial question as to whether discourse markers have semantic content (cf. Schiffrin 1987). Though my analysis focuses on discourse function rather than semantic content, I believe that these particular markers do retain some semantic content. It is this semantic ambiguity that leads to the confusion in discourse interpretation of backchannels remarked on by Maltz and Borker (1982).

CHAPTER 4

1. Fishman (1983) even sees frequent questioning as an indicator of the relatively powerless position of the speaker. She studied three couples, finding that the women asked many more questions than did the men, apparently as a way of maintaining interaction. In her study men's silence was seen as an exercise of power. The use of questions in Fishman's

study, in a domestic context, does not compare directly with the use of questions in an institutional context. In the domestic context talk may have as a central purpose the creation of intimacy. Even in the domestic context, questions can be an attempt to control the discourse, as both speakers negotiate—one using questions, one using silence.

2. The publication date for this study is variously given as 1979 and 1984. As I read the publication data in Psathas's book—the book in which the Frankel article first appeared (see citation for Frankel [1979])—1979 is the correct date.

3. It is not clear whether Biesecker and Biesecker's definition excluded requests for confirmation, action, and permission, which overlap with requests for information in many instances.

4. This difference involved our definitions of a subcategory of tag questions.

5. On several points in this section, ten Have (1991) and I independently reached similar conclusions. The fact that we were studying data from differing countries and languages makes this especially interesting.

6. My interview with Mr. Brade, conducted in his home, included questions about his occupation. He worked in a shop where small motors were repaired. He referred directly to income problems in his talk with Dr. Miller, and his home reflected economic difficulties. Mr. Brade's grammar was that of someone without advanced education. For these reasons, I am confident that he would be considered to be in a low socioeconomic group.

In recognition of the fact that low prestige often is accorded to those who lack money, I would like to say a bit more about Mr. Brade. Mr. Brade's socioeconomic group was irrelevant to his courage, his intelligence, his generosity with his time in spite of his difficulties, and the obvious love between his family and him. If character, not socioeconomic level, determined prestige, Mr. Brade would be in the highest prestige group.

7. Maya Angelou's autobiographical *I Know Why the Caged Bird Sings* (1969) describes differences between whites and blacks in questioning; Angelou says that blacks avoid direct personal questions.

CHAPTER 5

1. The other two encounters included one at a ready-care center (Ms. Jubb and Dr. Moltner) and one in which the physician was being consulted for a second opinion (Ms. Ivey and Dr. Miller).

2. For simplicity, I use this definition, which does not distinguish between ambiguity and polysemy.

3. Schegloff has suggested that "Why don't you" is a member of a class of constructions which can be named "injunction mitigators" (1984:32).

4. See chapter 2 for a discussion of structural power.

5. In analyzing rhetorical questions, I draw on all three of the encounters between Mr. Frisell and Dr. Finn. However, I return to chapter 2 for quantitative data on true questions. There only the first two encounters were considered.

6. Line numbers were started anew on each page of these transcripts, so they do not reflect the location of the excerpt in the overall transcript. Practice varied on this point during the two research projects; some transcripts are numbered consecutively throughout.

CHAPTER 6

1. In Western cultures, stories are often chronologically ordered. But Riessman (1991, 1993) argues that they can describe habitual events that are not ordered chronologically in relation to one another.

2. Stories can also bridge cultural gaps. They do this when the participants are able to come to a shared understanding of the point of the story, through discussion.

3. When I asked for details, he was unable to provide them.

4. Because the following excerpts from ML1 are contiguous with this first excerpt and one another, no other attribution lines for this story are given.

5. I cannot explain the dismissive remarks made by the family members. In many ways, when I was talking with them and also during the three encounters I recorded, they were concerned and supportive toward Ms. Wells. Perhaps her panic frightened them, and their fear was expressed as anger.

6. Again, subsequent excerpts do not have an attribution line, as all were contiguous.

CHAPTER 7

1. Tellers sometimes omit overt evaluation, relying on hearers to infer the significance of events. When this happens, the lines between descriptions, reports, and stories are blurred. Whether we call the narrative a story or a report then depends in part on hearers' background knowledge and other sources of their ability to make inferences as to events' significance to the teller. This explains why Riessman (1993) struggles with a definition of story which rests on overt structural features; Riessman quotes one long stretch of discourse which does not meet structural criteria, maintaining that this discourse should be regarded as a story. Riessman is able to make inferences that establish the reported events' cultural and social significance, and so the discourse is a story for her.

2. This subtlety is appropriate to the setting, topic, and roles at hand. Friends having a night out might evaluate their stories in much more dramatic ways.

3. This attribution line is the only one for the excerpts from Ms. Feblen's encounter. Likewise, at the end of the chapter, only one attribution line is given for excerpts from each encounter.

4. It is worth noting that even then, the diagnostic process may involve more than one person, since diagnosis and treatment are often negotiated among several caregivers.

CHAPTER 8

1. Because medical encounters happen on caregivers' turf, and for the many reasons discussed in chapter 2, caregivers usually are conceded the right to accept or reject patients' attempts to claim power. An exception is Ms. Lane's response to Dr. Mey's refusal to consider changes in her "new meds." Ms. Lane challenged Dr. Mey's refusal, insisting that the side effects were not easing up, and then implying lack of knowledge on Dr. Mey's part. Thus she refused to concede to him the right to reject her claim to power.

2. These artists' names are not pseudonyms.

BIBLIOGRAPHY

Ainsworth-Vaughn, Nancy. 1992a. Questions with dual functions: The "Treatment" question in medical encounters. *Medical Encounter* 9(1):5–6.

———. 1992b. Topic transitions in physician–patient interviews: Power, gender, and discourse change. *Language in Society* 21:409–26.

———. 1994a. "Is that a rhetorical question?" Ambiguity and power in medical discourse. *Journal of Linguistic Anthropology* 4(2):194–214.

———. 1994b. Negotiating genre and power: Questions in medical discourse. In *Text and talk in professional contexts*, ed. Britt-Louise Gunnarsson, Per Linell, and Bengt Nordstrom, 149–66. Uppsala, Sweden: Association Suédoise de Linguistique Appliquée.

Angelou, Maya. 1969. *I know why the caged bird sings*. New York: Random House.

Arnold, Robert M., Lachlan Forrow, and L. Randol Barker. 1995. Medical ethics and doctor/patient communication. In *The medical interview: Clinical care, education, and research*, ed. Mack Lipkin, Samuel Putnam, and Aaron Lazare, 345–67. New York: Springer-Verlag.

Arnold, Robert M., Steven C. Martin, and Ruth M. Parker. 1988. Taking care of patients— does it matter whether the physician is a woman? *Western Journal of Medicine* 149: 729–33.

Auer, Peter, and Aldo di Luzio, eds. 1992. *The contextualization of language*. Philadelphia: John Benjamins.

Bain, J. G. 1976. Doctor–patient communication in general practice consultations. *Medical Education* 10:125–31.

Bauman, Richard. 1986. *Story, performance, and event: Contextual studies of oral narrative*. Cambridge studies in oral and literate culture. Cambridge: Cambridge University Press.

Bauman, Richard, and Joel Sherzer, eds. 1989. *Explorations in the ethnography of speaking.* Cambridge: Cambridge University Press.

Beckman, Howard B., and Richard M. Frankel. 1984. The effect of physician behavior on the collection of data. *Annals of Internal Medicine* 101:692–96.

Bennett, Adrian. 1982. Strategies and counterstrategies in the use of yes–no questions in discourse. In *Language and social identity*, ed. John Gumperz, 95–107. Cambridge, England: Cambridge University Press.

Benson, Herbert. 1975. *The relaxation response.* New York: William Morrow.

———. 1996. *Timeless healing: The power and biology of belief.* New York: Scribner.

Berger, C. R., and T. Luckmann. 1966. *The social construction of reality: A treatise in the sociology of knowledge.* Garden City, N.Y.: Doubleday.

Biesecker, Analee E., and Thomas D. Biesecker. 1990. Patient information-seeking behaviors when communicating with doctors. *Medical Care* 28(1):19–28.

Bonanno, Michelina. 1982. Women's language in the medical interview. In *Linguistics and the professions*, ed. Robert J. DePietro, 27–38. Norwood, N.J.: Ablex.

Boreham, P., and D. Gibson. 1978. The informative process in private medical consultations: A preliminary investigation. *Social Science and Medicine* 12:409–16.

Brody, Howard. 1987. *Stories of sickness.* New Haven, Conn.: Yale University Press.

———. 1992. *The healer's power.* New Haven, Conn.: Yale University Press.

Brody, Jill. 1991. Indirection in the negotiation of self in everyday Tojolab'al women's conversation. *Journal of Linguistic Anthropology* 1 (June):78–96.

Broncato, Peter. 1992. Doctor's jargon. Unpublished paper. State University of New York, Buffalo.

Brown, Gillian, and George Yule. 1983. *Discourse analysis.* Cambridge Textbooks in Linguistics. Cambridge: Cambridge University Press.

Burbules, Nicholas C. 1986. A theory of power in education. *Educational Theory* 36 (Spring): 95–114.

Byrne, P. S., and B. E. L. Long. 1976. *Doctors talking to patients.* London: HMSO.

Cameron, Deborah, Elizabeth Frazer, Penelope Harvey, M. B. H. Rampton, and Kay Richardson. 1992. *Researching language: Issues of power and method.* London: Routledge.

Charon, Rita. 1989. Doctor–patient/Reader–writer: Learning to find the text. *Soundings* 72:137–52.

Cheepen, Christine. 1988. *The predictability of informal conversation.* London: Pinter Publishers.

Cicourel, Aaron V. 1982. Language and belief in a medical setting. In *Georgetown University Round Table on Languages and Linguistics 1982*, ed. Heidi Byrnes, 48–78. Washington, D.C.: Georgetown University Press.

———. 1987. The interpenetration of communicative contexts: Examples from medical encounters. *Social Psychology Quarterly* 50(2):217–26.

Clayman, Steven E. 1992. Footing in the achievement of neutrality: The case of news-interview discourse. In *Talk at work: Interaction in institutional settings*, ed. Paul Drew and John Heritage, 163–98. Cambridge: Cambridge University Press.

Coupland, Justine, Jeffrey D. Robinson, and Nikolas Coupland. 1994. Frame negotiation in doctor–elderly patient consultations. *Discourse and Society* 5(1):89–124.

Crow, Bryan K. 1983. Topic shifts in couples' conversations. In *Conversational coherence: Form, structure, and strategy*, ed. Robert T. Craig and Karen Tracy, 136–56. Sage Series in Interpersonal Communication. Beverly Hills, Cal.: Sage Publications.

Davis, Kathy. 1988. *Power under the microscope.* Dordrecht, Holland: Foris Publications.

Davis, Milton S. 1971. Variation in patients' compliance with doctors' orders: Medical practice and doctor–patient interaction. *Psychiatry in Medicine* 2:31–54.

Dillon, James T. 1982. The multidisciplinary study of questioning. *Journal of Educational Psychology* 74(2):147–65.

———. 1986. Questioning. In *A handbook of communication skills*, ed. Owen Hargie, 95–127. New York: New York University Press.

———. 1990. *The practice of questioning.* New York: Routledge.

Dye, Nancy E., and M. Robin DiMatteo. 1995. Enhancing cooperation with the medical regimen. In *The medical interview: Clincial care, education, and research*, ed. Mack Lipkin, Samuel M. Putnam, and Aaron Lazare, 134–44. New York: Springer-Verlag.

Edwards, Jane A., and Martin D. Lampert. 1993. *Talking data: Transcription and coding in discourse research.* Hillsdale, N.J.: Erlbaum.

Eisenberg, Ann R. 1986. Teasing: Verbal play in two Mexicano homes. In *Language socialization across cultures*, ed. Bambi Schieffelin and Elinor Ochs, 182–98. New York: Cambridge University Press.

Epps, Roselyn Payne. 1991. Commencement address. Michigan State University College of Human Medicine. East Lansing, Mich.

Erickson, Frederick, and Jeffrey Schultz. 1977. When is a context? Some issues and methods in the analysis of social competence. *Quarterly Newsletter of the Institute for Comparative Human Development* 1 (February):1–10.

Fairclough, Norman. 1989. *Language and power.* London: Longman.

Ferrara, Kathleen Warden. 1994. *Therapeutic ways with words.* Oxford Studies in Sociolinguistics. New York: Oxford University Press.

Fisher, Sue. 1986. *In the patient's best interest: Women and the politics of medical decisions.* New Brunswick, N.J.: Rutgers University Press.

Fisher, Sue, and Stephen B. Groce. 1990. Accounting practices in medical interviews. *Language in Society* 19:225–50.

Fisher, Sue, and Alexandra Todd, eds. 1993. *The social organization of doctor–patient communication.* 2d ed. Norwood, N.J.: Ablex.

Fishman, Pamela M. 1983. Interaction: The work women do. In *Language, gender, and society*, ed. Barrie Thorne, Cheris Kramarae, and Nancy Henley, 89–102. Cambridge, Mass.: Newbury House.

Frank, Arthur W. 1995. *The wounded storyteller: Body, illness, and ethics.* Chicago: University of Chicago Press.

Frankel, Richard. 1979. Talking in interviews: A dispreference for patient-initiated questions in physician-patient encounters. In *Everyday language: Studies in ethnomethodology*, ed. George Psathas, 231–62. New York: Irvington.

Giddens, Anthony. 1976. *New rules of sociological method: A positive critique of interpretive sociologies.* London: Hutchinson.

———. 1984. *The constitution of society.* Cambridge: Polity Press.

Goodwin, Charles, and Marjorie H. Goodwin. 1987. Concurrent operations on talk: Notes on the interactive organization of assessments. *IPRA Papers in Pragmatics* 1(1):1–54.

Goodwin, Marjorie H. 1990. *He said she said: Talk as social organization among black children.* Bloomington: Indiana University Press.

———. 1993. Tactical use of stories: Participation frameworks within boys' and girls' disputes. In *Gender and conversational interaction*, ed. Deborah Tannen, 110–42. New York: Oxford University Press.

Goody, Esther N. 1978. Towards a theory of questions. In *Questions and politeness*, ed. Esther N. Goody, 17–43. New York: Cambridge University Press.

Graddol, David, and Joan Swann. 1989. *Gender voices.* Cambridge, Mass.: Blackwell.

Grimshaw, Allen D. 1987. Disambiguating discourse: Members' skill and analysts' problem. *Social Psychology Quarterly* 50(2):186–204.

———, ed. 1990. *Conflict talk: Sociolinguistic investigations of arguments in conversations.* Cambridge: Cambridge University Press.

Gumperz, John. 1982. *Discourse strategies.* Cambridge: Cambridge University Press.

Gumperz, John J., and Dell Hymes. 1964. The ethnography of communication. Special Issue. *American Anthropologist.* Menasha, Wis.: American Anthropological Association.

———. 1972. *Directions in sociolinguistics: The ethnography of communication.* New York: Holt, Rinehart and Winston.

Heath, Christian. 1992. Diagnosis in the general-practice consultation. In *Talk at work,* ed. Paul Drew and John Heritage, 235–67. Cambridge, England: Cambridge University Press.

Heath, Shirley Brice. 1983. *Ways with words.* Cambridge, England: Cambridge University Press.

Hein, Norbert, and Ruth Wodak. 1987. Medical interviews in internal medicine: Some results of an empirical investigation. *Text* 7(1):37–65.

Helman, Cecil G. 1984. The role of context in primary care. *Journal of the Royal College of General Practitioners* 34:547–550.

Henzl, Vera M. 1990. Linguistic means of social distancing in physician-patient communication. In *Doctor-patient interaction,* ed. Walburga von Raffler-Engel, 77–91. Philadelphia: John Benjamins.

Heritage, John, and J. Maxwell Atkinson. 1984. Introduction. In *Structures of social action: Studies in conversation analysis,* ed. J. Maxwell Atkinson and John Heritage, 1–15. Cambridge: Cambridge University Press.

Honneth, Axel. 1991. *Critique of power: Reflective stages in a critical social theory.* Cambridge, Mass.: MIT Press.

Houtkoop-Steenstra, Hanneke. 1995. The interactive construction of answers in research interviews. Presented at the annual meeting of the American Association for Applied Linguistics, Long Beach, Cal.

Hunter, Kathryn M. 1991. *Doctors' stories: The narrative structure of medical knowledge.* Princeton, N.J.: Princeton University Press.

Hymes, Dell. 1972. Models of the interaction of language and society. In *Directions in sociolinguistics: Ethnography of communication,* ed. John J. Gumperz and Dell Hymes, 35–71. New York: Holt, Rinehart & Winston.

Ilie, Cornelia. 1994. What else can I tell you? A pragmatic study of English rhetorical questions as discursive and argumentative acts. Unpublished Ph.D. dissertation, Uppsala University. Uppsala, Sweden.

Jacoby, Sally, and Elinor Ochs. 1995. *Co-construction.* Mahwah, N.J.: Lawrence Erlbaum.

James, Deborah, and Sandra Clarke. 1993. Women, men, and interruptions: A critical review. In *Gender and conversational interaction,* ed. Deborah Tannen, 231–80. New York: Oxford University Press.

James, Deborah, and Janice Drakich. 1993. Understanding gender differences in amount of talk: A critical review of research. In *Gender and conversational interaction,* ed. Deborah Tannen, 281–312. New York: Oxford University Press.

Jefferson, Gail, and J. R. E. Lee. 1981. The rejection of advice: Managing the problematic convergence of a "troubles-telling" and a "service-encounter." *Journal of Pragmatics* 5:399–422.

Johnston, Jennifer. 1995. Discourse analysis. Unpublished paper. Michigan State University.

Johnstone, Barbara. 1993. Community and contest: Midwestern men and women creating their worlds in conversational storytelling. In *Gender and conversational interaction,* ed. Deborah Tannen, 62–80. New York: Oxford University Press.

Josselson, Ruthellen, and Amia Lieblich. 1993. *The narrative study of lives*. Newbury Park, Cal.: Sage.

Kaplan, Craig. 1995. Hypothesis testing. In *The medical interview: Clinical care, education, and research*, ed. Mack Lipkin Jr., Samuel M. Putnam, and Aaron Lazare, 20–31. New York: Springer-Verlag.

Kaplan, S. H., S. S. Greenfield, and J. E. Ware. 1989. Assessing effects of physician–patient interaction on outcomes of chronic disease. *Medical Care* 27(3):s110–27.

Katz, Jay. 1984. *The silent world of doctor and patient*. New York: Free Press.

Kirshenblatt-Gimblett, Barbara. 1989. The concept and varieties of narrative performance in East European Jewish culture. In *Explorations in the ethnography of speaking*, ed. Richard Bauman and Joel Sherzer, 283–310. Cambridge: Cambridge University Press.

Kleinman, Arthur. 1988. *The illness narratives: Suffering, healing and the human condition*. New York: Basic Books.

Kochman, Thomas. 1981. *Black and white styles in conflict*. Chicago: University of Chicago Press.

Korsch, Barbara M., and Vida F. Negrete. 1972. Doctor–patient communication. *Scientific American* 227(2):66–74.

Labov, William. 1972a. *Language in the inner city: Studies in the black english vernacular*. Philadelphia: University of Pennsylvania Press.

———. 1972b. The transformation of experience in narrative syntax. In *Language in the inner city*, by William Labov, 354–96. Philadelphia: University of Pennsylvania Press.

Lakoff, Robin. 1990. *Talking power: The politics of language in our lives*. Basic Books.

Lazare, Aaron, Samuel M. Putnam, and Mack Lipkin Jr. 1995. Three functions of the medical interview. In *The medical interview: Clinical care, education, and research*, ed. Mack Lipkin, Jr., Samuel M. Putnam, and Aaron Lazare, 3–19. New York: Springer-Verlag.

Levinson, Stephen C. 1983. *Pragmatics*. Cambridge: Cambridge University Press.

Lincoln, Y., and E. Guba. 1985. *Naturalistic inquiry*. Beverly Hills, Calif.: Sage Publications.

Linn, Lawrence S., Dennis W. Cope, and Barbara Leake. 1984. The effect of gender and training of residents on satisfaction ratings by patients. *Journal of Medical Education* 59:964–66.

Lipkin, Mack, Jr., Samuel M. Putnam, and Aaron Lazare, eds. 1995. *The medical interview: Clinical care, education, and research*. New York: Springer-Verlag.

Lock, Margaret, and Deborah Gordon, eds. 1988. *Biomedicine examined*. London: Kluwer Academic Publishers.

Maltz, Daniel N., and Ruth A. Borker. 1982. A cultural approach to male–female miscommunication. In *Language and social identity*, ed. John J. Gumperz, 196–216. Cambridge: Cambridge University Press.

Marshall, Catherine, and Gretchen B. Rossman. 1989. *Designing qualitative research*. Newbury Park, Cal.: Sage Publications.

Maynard, Douglas W. 1980. Placement of topic changes in conversation. *Semiotica* 30(3/4):263–90.

———. 1991. Interaction and asymmetry in clinical discourse. *American Journal of Sociology* 97 (September 1991):448–95.

———. 1995. On receiving a diagnosis of diabetes and giving up maple syrup. *Medical Encounter* 11(3):15–18.

Mehan, Hugh. 1979. *Learning lessons*. Cambridge, Mass.: Harvard University Press.

Miller, Peggy. 1986. Teasing as language socialization and verbal play in a white working-class community. In *Language socialization across cultures*, ed. Bambi Schieffelin and Elinor Ochs, 199–212. New York: Cambridge University Press.

Mishler, Elliot. 1984. *The discourse of medicine.* Norwood, N.J.: Ablex.

Mishler, Elliot G., Jack A. Clark, Joseph Ingelfinger, and Michael P. Simon. 1989. The language of attentive patient care: A comparison of two medical interviews. *Journal of General Internal Medicine* 4 (July/August):325–35.

Mitchell-Kernan, Claudia. 1972. On the status of Black English for native speakers: An assessment of attitudes and values. In *Functions of language in the classroom*, ed. Courtney Cazden, Vera P. John, and Dell Hymes, 195–210. New York: Teacher's College Press.

Moerman, Michael. 1988. *Talking culture: Ethnography and conversation analysis.* Philadelphia: University of Pennsylvania Press.

Murray, Stephen O. 1985. Toward a model of members' methods for recognizing interruptions. *Language in Society* 14:31–40.

Myerscough, Philip R. 1989. *Talking with patients: A basic clinical skill.* Oxford: Oxford University Press.

Ochs, Elinor. 1979. Transcription as theory. In *Developmental pragmatics*, ed. Elinor Ochs and Bambi Shieffelin, 43–72. New York: Academic Press.

Philips, Susan U. 1987. The social organization of questions and answers in courtroom discourse. In *Power through discourse*, ed. Leah Kedar, 83–112. Norwood, N.J.: Ablex.

Pizzini, Franca. 1991. Communication hierarchies in humor: Gender differences in the obstetrical gynaecological setting. *Discourse and Society* 2(4):477–88.

Polanyi, Livia. 1979. So what's the point? *Semiotica* 25(3/4):207–41.

———. 1985. *Telling the American story: A structural and cultural analysis of conversational storytelling.* Norwood, N.J.: Ablex.

Riessman, Catherine Kohler. 1991. Beyond reductionism: Narrative genres in divorce accounts. *Journal of Narrative and Life History* 1(1):41–68.

———. 1993. *Narrative analysis.* Qualitative research methods series. Newbury Park, Cal.: Sage Publications.

Roter, D. L. 1977. Patient participation in the patient–provider interaction: The effects of patient question asking on the quality of interaction, satisfaction, and compliance. *Health Education Monographs* 5:281–315.

———. 1984. Patient question asking in physician–patient interaction. *Health Psychology* 3:395–409.

Roter, Debra L., Judith A. Hall, and Nancy R. Katz. 1988. Patient–physician communication: A descriptive summary of the literature. *Patient Education and Counseling* 12(2):99–119.

Sacks, Harvey. 1984. Notes on methodology. In *Structures of social action: Studies in conversation analysis*, ed. J. Maxwell Atkinson and John Heritage, 21–27. Cambridge: Cambridge University Press.

Sacks, Harvey, Emanuel Schegloff, and Gail Jefferson. 1974. A simplest systematics for the analysis of turn-taking in conversation. *Language* 50:696–735.

Sandelowski, Margarete. 1991. Telling stories: Narrative approaches in qualitative research. *Image: Journal of Nursing Scholarship* 23 (Fall):161–66.

Schegloff, Emanuel A. 1984. On some questions and ambiguities in conversation. In *Structures of social action: Studies in conversation analysis*, ed. J. Maxwell Atkinson and John Heritage, 28–52. Cambridge: Cambridge University Press.

———. 1991a. Conversation analysis and socially shared cognition. In *Perspectives on socially shared cognition*, ed. Lauren B. Resnick, John M. Levine, and Stephanie D. Teasley, 150–71. Washington, D.C.: American Psychological Association.

———. 1991b. Reflections on talk and social structure. In *Talk and social structure*, ed. Deirdre Boden and Don Zimmerman, 44–70. Berkeley: University of California Press.

Schegloff, Emanuel A., and Harvey Sacks. 1984. Opening up closings. In *Language in use: Readings in sociolinguistics*, ed. John Baugh and Joel Sherzer, 69–99. Englewood Cliffs, N.J.: Prentice Hall.

Schieffelin, Bambi B. 1986. Teasing and shaming in Kaluli children's interactions. In *Language socialization across cultures*, ed. Bambi B. Schieffelin and Elinor Ochs, 165–81. New York: Cambridge University Press.

Schiffrin, Deborah. 1984. How a story says what it means and does. *Text* 4(4):313–46.

———. 1987. *Discourse markers*. Studies in interactional sociolinguistics, vol. 5. Cambridge: Cambridge University Press.

Scotton, Carol Myers. 1983. The negotiation of identities in conversation: A theory of markedness and code choice. *International Journal of the Sociology of Languages* 44:115–36.

Shotter, John. 1993. *Conversational realities: Constructing life through language*. Inquiries in Social Construction Series. London: Sage Publications.

Shuy, Roger. 1983. Three types of interference to an effective exchange of information in the medical interview. In *Social organization of doctor-patient communication*, ed. Sue Fisher and Alexandra D. Todd, 189–202. Washington, D.C.: Center for Applied Linguistics.

Silverman, David. 1987. *Communication and medical practice*. London: Sage Publications.

Smith, R. C., and R. Hoppe. 1991. The patient's story: Integrating a patient-centered approach to interviewing. *Annals of Internal Medicine* 115:470–77.

Smitherman, Geneva. 1986. *Talkin and testifyin*. Detroit: Wayne State University Press.

Snow, Loudell F. 1993. *Walkin' over medicine*. Boulder, CO: Westview Press.

Sontag, Susan. 1977. *Illness as metaphor*. New York: Farrar, Straus and Giroux.

Starr, Paul. 1982. *The social transformation of American medicine*. New York: Basic Books.

Stenström, Anna-Brita. 1984. *Questions and responses in English conversation*. Lund Studies in English. Malmö, Sweden: Liber Förlag.

Strauss, Anselm, and Juliet Corbin. 1990. *Basics of qualitative research*. Newbury Park, Calif.: Sage Publications.

Tannen, Deborah. 1987. Remarks on discourse and power. In *Power through discourse*, ed. Leah Kedar, 3–10. Norwood, N.J.: Ablex.

———. 1989a. "Oh talking voice that is so sweet": Constructing dialogue. In *Talking voices: Repetition, dialogue, and imagery in conversational discourse*, by Deborah Tannen, 98–133. Cambridge: Cambridge University Press.

———. 1989b. Repetition in conversation: Towards a poetics of talk. In *Talking voices: Repetition, dialogue, and imagery in conversational discourse*, by Deborah Tannen, 36–97. Cambridge: Cambridge University Press.

———. 1989c. *Talking voices: Repetition, dialogue, and imagery in conversational discourse*. Cambridge, England: Cambridge University Press.

———. 1990. *You just don't understand: Women and men in conversation*. New York: William Morrow.

———. 1993a. *Framing in discourse*. New York: Oxford University Press.

———, ed. 1993b. *Gender and conversational interaction*. New York: Oxford University Press.

———. 1993c. The relativity of linguistic strategies: Rethinking power and solidarity in gender and dominance. In *Gender and conversational interaction*, ed. Deborah Tannen, 165–88. Oxford Studies in Sociolinguistics. New York: Oxford University Press.

———. 1994. *Gender and discourse*. Oxford University Press.

———. 1995. *Talking from 9 to 5*. New York: Morrow.

Tannen, Deborah, and Cynthia Wallat. 1983. Doctor/mother/child communication: Linguistic analysis of a pediatric interaction. In *The social organization of doctor–patient communication*, ed. Sue Fisher and Alexandra Todd, 203–20. Washington, D.C.: Center for Applied Linguistics.

———. 1987. Interactive frames and knowledge schemas in interaction: Examples from a medical examination interview. *Social Psychology Quarterly* 50(2):205–16.

Taylor, Kathryn M. 1988. Physicians and the disclosure of undesirable information. In *Biomedicine examined*, ed. Margaret Lock and Deborah Gordon, 377–414. London: Kluwer Academic Publishers.

ten Have, Paul. 1989. The consultation as genre. In *Text and talk as social practice*, ed. Brian Torode, 115–35. Dordrecht, Holland: Foris Publications.

———. 1991. Talk and institution: A reconsideration of the "asymmetry" of doctor–patient interaction. In *Talk and social structure: Studies in ethnomethodology and conversation analysis*, ed. Deirdre Boden and Don H. Zimmerman, 138–63. Berkeley: University of California Press.

Thorne, Barrie. 1993. *Gender play: Girls and boys at school*. New Brunswick, N.J.: Rutgers University Press.

Todd, Alexandra Dundas. 1989. *Intimate adversaries: Cultural conflict between doctors and women patients*. Philadelphia: University of Pennsylvania Press.

Tsui, Amy B. M. 1989. Beyond the adjacency pair. *Language in Society* 18:545–64.

Tuckett, David, Mary Boulton, Coral Olson, and Anthony Williams. 1985. *Meetings between experts: An approach to sharing ideas in medical consultations*. London: Tavistock Publications.

Waitzkin, Howard. 1985. Information giving in medical care. *Journal of Health and Social Behavior* 26(2):81–101.

———. 1991. *The politics of medical encounters: How patients and doctors deal with social problems*. New Haven, Conn.: Yale University Press.

Waitzkin, Howard, and T. Britt. 1989. Changing the structure of medical discourse: Implications of cross-cultural comparisons. *Journal of Health and Social Behavior* 30:436–39.

Walker, Anne Graffam. 1987. Linguistic manipulation, power, and the legal setting. In *Power through discourse*, ed. Leah Kedar, 57–82. Norwood, N.J.: Ablex.

Walters, Keith. 1984. It's like playing password: Questions and questioning at school. *Texas Linguistic Forum* 24:157–88.

Weber, Elizabeth. 1993. *Varieties of questions in English conversation*. Philadelphia: John Benjamins.

Weijts, Wies. 1993a. *Patient participation in gynaecological consultations: Studying interactional patterns*. Maastricht, The Netherlands: Uniprint Universitaire Drukkerij.

———. 1993b. Seeking information. In *Patient participation in gynaecological encounters: Studying interactional patterns*, by Wies Weijts, 39–64. Maastricht, The Netherlands: Uniprint Universitaire Drukkerij.

Weijts, Wies, Guy Widdershoven, Gerko Kok, and Pauline Tomlow. 1992. Patients' information-seeking actions and physicians' responses in gynecological consultations. Unpublished paper, University of Limburg, Netherlands.

West, Candace. 1984a. Questions and answers between doctors and patients. In *Routine complications: Troubles with talk between doctors and patients*, by Candace West, 71–96. Bloomington: Indiana University Press.

———. 1984b. *Routine complications: Troubles with talk between doctors and patients*. Bloomington: Indiana University Press.

———. 1984c. Turn-taking in doctor–patient dialogues. In *Routine complications: Troubles with talk between doctors and patients*, by Candace West, 51–70. Bloomington: Indiana University Press.

————. 1990. Not just doctor's orders: Directive–response sequences in patients' visits to women and men physicians. *Discourse and Society* 1(1):85–112.

————. 1993. Reconceptualizing gender in physician–patient relationships. *Social Science and Medicine* 36(1):57–66.

West, Candace, and Angela Garcia. 1988. Conversational shift work: A study of topical transitions between women and men. *Social Problems* 35 (December):551–73.

Widdowson, Henry. 1979. *Explorations in applied linguistics.* London: Oxford University Press.

Wilson, John. 1989. *On the boundaries of conversation.* Oxford: Pergamon Press.

Young, Katharine. 1989. Narrative embodiments: Enclaves of the self in the realm of medicine. In *Texts of identity,* ed. John Shotter and Kenneth Gergen, 152–65. Newbury Park, Calif.: Sage.

Zola, I. K. 1963. Problems of communication, diagnosis, and patient care: The interplay of patient, physician, and clinic organization. *Journal of Medical Education* 38:829–38.

INDEX

active patient, 73
adjacency pair, 77–78, 82
affirmative terms, 65–66, 69
agency, 23, 42
ambiguity, 84, 92, 97, 123–24, 186
  definition of, 106
  degree of, 89, 104–8
  of discourse function, 8, 17, 47, 67, 105–6, 120
  to manage face-threatening acts, 111–21
  of participant structure, 166
  in rhetorical questions, 10–11, 103–8, 111–21, 181
  of voice, 106, 108, 121–23, 181
  See also indirection
appropriateness, limits of, 118, 182
Arnold, R. M., et al., 56
arrangements, 66–67, 184
asymmetry, 6–7, 34, 50–51, 61, 65, 121, 126
  gendered, 73–74
  and questions, 76–77, 98–99
  reduced by co-construction, 125–46, 157, 169–71
  related to frames, 98
  structural vs. negotiable, 170, 179, 190

backchannels, 48, 65, 126, 193
Beckman, H. M., and Frankel, R. M., 57
Biesecker, A. E., and Biesecker, T. D., 79, 95
Boreham, P., and Gibson, D., 94
Brody, H., 43, 189
Brody, J., 49, 121, 124
Brown, G., and Yule, G., 58
Burbules, N. C., 41–42

candidate diagnosis, 139, 141, 150, 152, 180–81
Cicourel, A. V., 23–24, 149

clinic settings, 6, 78, 97–98
co-construction, 10–11, 125–28, 145–46, 154–71, 177, 184
  degrees of, 127
  discourse strategies for, 139, 141–46
coding in language study, 7–8, 21, 57
coherence, 59–61, 72
cohesion, 22, 59–62, 64–65, 68–70, 72
conversation. *See* genre, conversational
conversation analysis, 4, 21–23, 25, 60, 82
Coupland, J., et al., 126

Davis, K., 128–29
decision-making, 33, 47, 138, 170
deference, 11, 44, 98, 103, 181
  contrasted with passivity, 47
  definition of, 47
  discourse strategies for, 47–50, 84, 107, 161
  by physicians, 84, 100
  See also ambiguity; mitigation
definitions, problem of, 9, 77–78, 80, 82
discourse analysis, 8, 21–25
discourse change, 74
dominance, 11, 50–51, 72–73, 99–100, 182–83

empowering, 55–56, 125, 144–46, 180
ethics, 11, 51, 125, 127, 146, 148
  of generalizing qualitative findings, 72
  in obtaining consent, 30
  and quantitative studies, 99–100
  of relationships between researcher and participants, 20
ethnicity, 35, 56, 77–78, 93
ethnography, 3–4, 35, 90
  definition of, 17, 19, 21–23
  of discourse, 21–23, 25, 65, 71, 106